IMAGES
of America

McDONOUGH COUNTY HISTORIC SITES

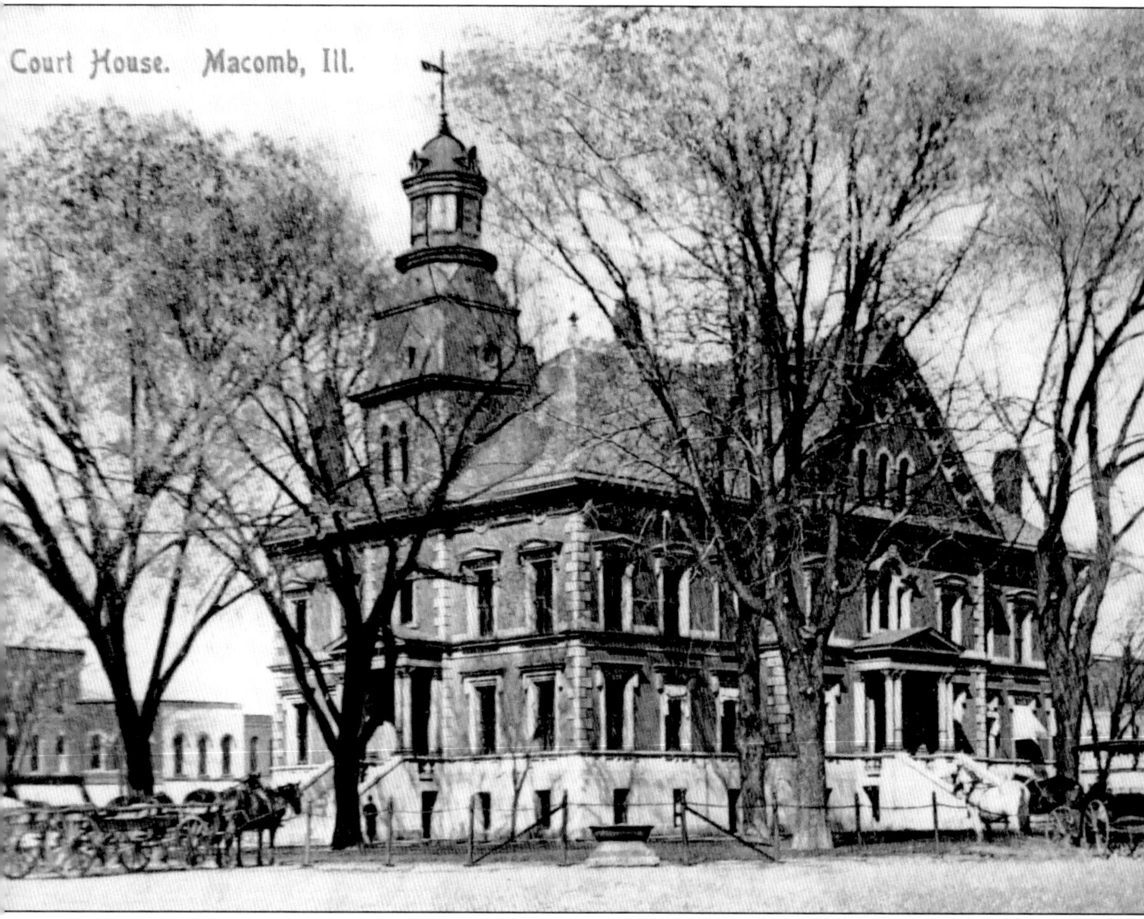
Court House. Macomb, Ill.

IMAGES
of America

McDONOUGH COUNTY HISTORIC SITES

John E. Hallwas

ARCADIA
PUBLISHING

ISBN 978-0-7385-2044-5

Published by Arcadia Publishing
Charleston, South Carolina

Printed in the United States of America

Library of Congress Catalog Card Number: 2002112246

For all general information contact Arcadia Publishing at:
Telephone 843-853-2070
Fax 843-853-0044
E-mail sales@arcadiapublishing.com
For customer service and orders:
Toll-Free 1-888-313-2665

Visit us on the Internet at www.arcadiapublishing.com

Contents

Acknowledgments

McDonough County Historic Sites benefited enormously from the assistance of a dozen authorities on local history who shared their expertise on various parts of the county: Martin and Pauline Calvert (Blandinsville), Wanda Hammond (Adair), Martha Hotchkiss (Macomb), Kathy Nichols (Macomb), Donald O'Harra (Colchester), Lee Ren (Good Hope and Sciota), Alan Walker (Industry and the southern townships), Wayne White (Tennessee and Argyle Park), Marla Vizdal (Macomb), Dorothy Williams (Bushnell), and Donna Young (Bardolph). Information on specific sites came from Sheila Boden, Chick Flack, Libby Grimm, Lynn Gustafson, Marge Harris, Viletta Hillery, Delores Keith, Lawrence and Judy Kerr, Carol Nelson, Gerald Prunty, Gerald and Madolyn Redman, Howard H. Smith, Mary Jane Sticklen, Cecil White, and Esther Willey.

Special thanks are due to archivist Kathy Nichols, who managed the photographic content of the book and provided information and editorial commentary; visual production specialist Diana Stephens, who supervised the photograph reproduction and cropping; cartographer Scott Miner, who produced the maps; and archivists Bill Cook and Marla Vizdal, who sought needed information and commented on drafts of the manuscript.

The vast majority of the historical photographs are courtesy of Archives and Special Collections at Western Illinois University Library. The Bushnell Historical Society provided several images, as did Alan Walker. Photographs also came from Frank and Elsie Archer, Rob Harrison, Millie Hunt, Lawrence and Judy Kerr, Earl Lindsey, Duane Smith, and Martha Standard.

McDonough County Historic Sites is also indebted to a number of previous publications, including the 1878 and 1885 histories of the county, and these more recent historical studies: *The History of McDonough County, Illinois* (1992) by Ruth Chenoweth and Sara Wisslead; *McDonough County, Illinois, Cemetery Location Maps and Index* (1987) by Libby Grimm; *McDonough County Heritage* (1984) and *Macomb: A Pictorial History* (1990) by John E. Hallwas; *Emmet Township Pioneers* (1986) by Marge Harris; *Rural Cemeteries of McDonough County, Illinois* (18 Vols, c. 1970) by Duane Lester; *Churches of McDonough County, Illinois* (1996) by Vivian S. Peter and Martha B. Hotchkiss; and *McDonough County Gazetteer* (draft copy, 2002) by Gordana Rezab.

The photographic reproduction for this book was paid for by the Haines Family Fund, created by Vilma Kinney, whose support of regional publications at Western Illinois University is deeply appreciated.

Introduction

McDonough County, Illinois, is an unspectacular corner of America, but like so many locations in the Midwest, it is an interesting place to live or visit if you know something about its heritage. This book intends to help readers know their way around the historical landscape. It includes photographs of historic structures that are no longer standing as well as ones that remain, and it also depicts some of the older cemeteries.

McDonough County was established in 1826, just 50 years after the Declaration of Independence, and in the years since, it has progressed through four historical phases. The frontier period was marked by small settlements and remote villages, by difficult transportation and widespread hardship. Small churches and rural schools were the characteristic institutions, and log homes slowly gave way to frame houses. Few buildings from that era have survived to the present day.

During what might be called the "Railroad Era" of the 1850s and 1860s, the Northern Cross (later Chicago, Burlington and Quincy) Railroad and the Toledo, Peoria and Warsaw Railroad caused a few existing villages to grow and fostered several new ones. Those railroads ended the frontier era and launched a period of small-town development and increasing agricultural production that lasted for several decades. Life was culturally limited but richly satisfying for most McDonough County residents, who identified intensely with their communities and rural neighborhoods.

A third phase began with the coming of automobiles and hard roads in the second and third decades of the 20th century. Those developments ended rural isolation but damaged the economic condition of most McDonough County towns. The Great Depression accelerated that decline, which then continued through the century. Meanwhile, Macomb, the county seat, continued to grow as the business center of the county and as a higher education center for the region, while the mass media (magazines, movies, radio, and television) brought a standardized American culture to villages and farms.

In recent years, a fourth phase has begun, as once-thriving towns have become bedroom communities for Macomb, now the main business and shopping center for the county and its surrounding areas. Meanwhile, other McDonough County communities have become service centers, with gas stations, restaurants, banks, and post offices, or, if smaller, simply rural neighborhoods. The county seat is also becoming a cultural center for the western Illinois region, as a result of Western Illinois University activities, the WIU Library and its archives, the Western Illinois Museum, and other cultural institutions. Some people are now moving into the McDonough County countryside, not to farm, but to enjoy living in a pleasant, uncrowded setting. Others are restoring older homes that reflect the county's heritage. Those trends will surely continue.

As the years progress toward the end of McDonough County's second century, there is an increasing need to appreciate facets of the local past, for they give the county a distinctive quality and make it a meaningful place to live. The remaining historic structures need to be cherished, maintained, and passed along to future generations. The culture they came from is now gone, but it was the source of what we have today. McDonough County has lost much of its architectural heritage, but it has some remarkably well-maintained sites, such as the Hammond farmstead near Adair, the Hicks (now Kerr) home in Blandinsville, the Ball Brothers Carriage

Repository in Bushnell, and the courthouse in Macomb. In coming years, we will probably lose the old hotel at Vishnu Springs, the Keith Store in Tennessee, the old Methodist Church in Colchester, and the town hall in Bardolph—to name just a few threatened structures.

Even cemeteries can decay and lose their historical value. The Old Macomb Cemetery on Wigwam Hollow Road is a case in point. Caretakers have allowed headstones to fall without being reset and have moved markers from their original positions. As a result, the historical and aesthetic experience once offered by that pioneer burying ground has been diminished. Likewise, the Atkinson Cemetery, now on the grounds of Argyle Park, is completely overgrown and untended—yet it contains the forgotten grave of a soldier who fought to create America during the Revolutionary War, as well as the now-damaged headstone of a former slave, the first black man known to have settled in McDonough County. This is a disgrace to the park and to the people of the county.

At a time when the American social fabric seems to be fraying, the past is a common memory that binds people together and instills appreciation for values that matter and for the roots of our culture. It is more essential to the well being of America than most people realize.

There is much that might be done. The McDonough County Board should develop an inventory of historic sites and work with communities, organizations, and individuals to preserve some of the most valuable and threatened ones. All 115 McDonough County cemeteries should be identified with signs, such as "Stickle Cemetery (1839)", so the public will know where they are and when they originated. Historical commemorations should be developed—such as a Memorial Day weekend tour of historic cemeteries, a summer or fall tour of historic farmsteads, and a Christmas season tour of historic McDonough County churches. Residents who want our heritage to be remembered or the culture they grew up in to be appreciated should provide bequests to the McDonough County Historical Society and other agencies that are committed to these goals. People who have photographs and other historical materials should contact the Archives of the WIU Library, so those can be copied for, or deposited in, the McDonough County Collection.

With such efforts, the fascinating story of McDonough County will always be known to residents and visitors, local contributions to American culture will always be appreciated, and the satisfaction of living in the county will be increased substantially for future generations as well as our own.

One

Macomb
The County Seat

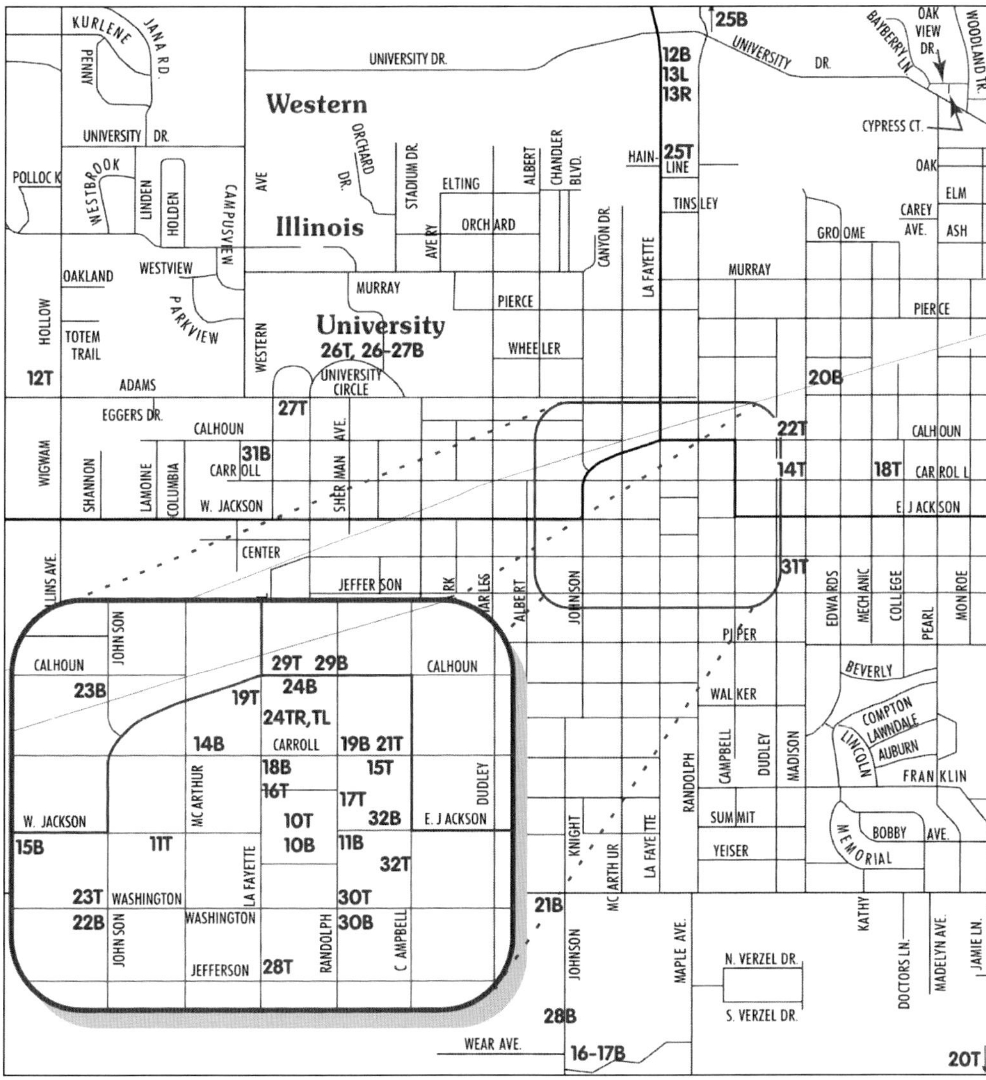

The maps that begin each chapter have numbers that correspond to the pages of this book, so it is easy to find the geographical location of any image that appears here. A "T" or "B" after a number signifies the top or bottom image on that page. In a few instances, an "L" or "R" after the number indicates the left or right photograph on a page, and a "TL" or "TR" indicates the top left or top right photograph on a page. Macomb is in the geographical center of McDonough County, which was established in 1826 in a region once known as the Illinois Military Tract.

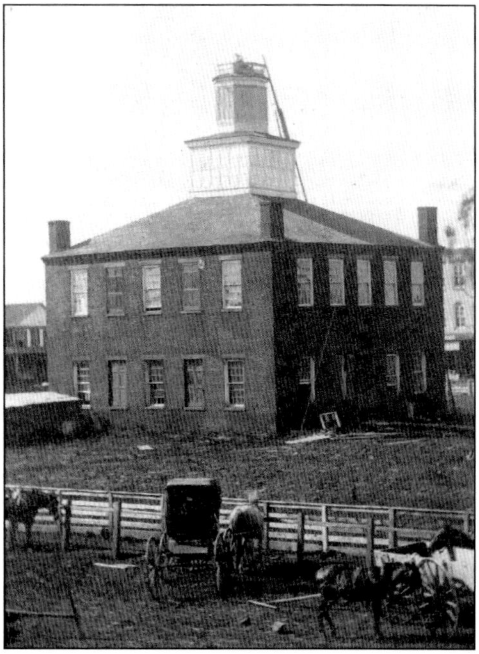

The first McDonough County Courthouse was built of logs in 1831, the year Macomb was laid out. It was followed by a more permanent brick structure, shown here, completed in 1835. The 11-room building was 46 feet square and cost $4,832. In a log cabin culture, it symbolized stability and progress. This 1860s photograph, located just a few years ago, shows a ladder on the backside of the roof. Workers were either repairing the massive cupola or starting to dismantle the building to make way for the post-Civil War courthouse.

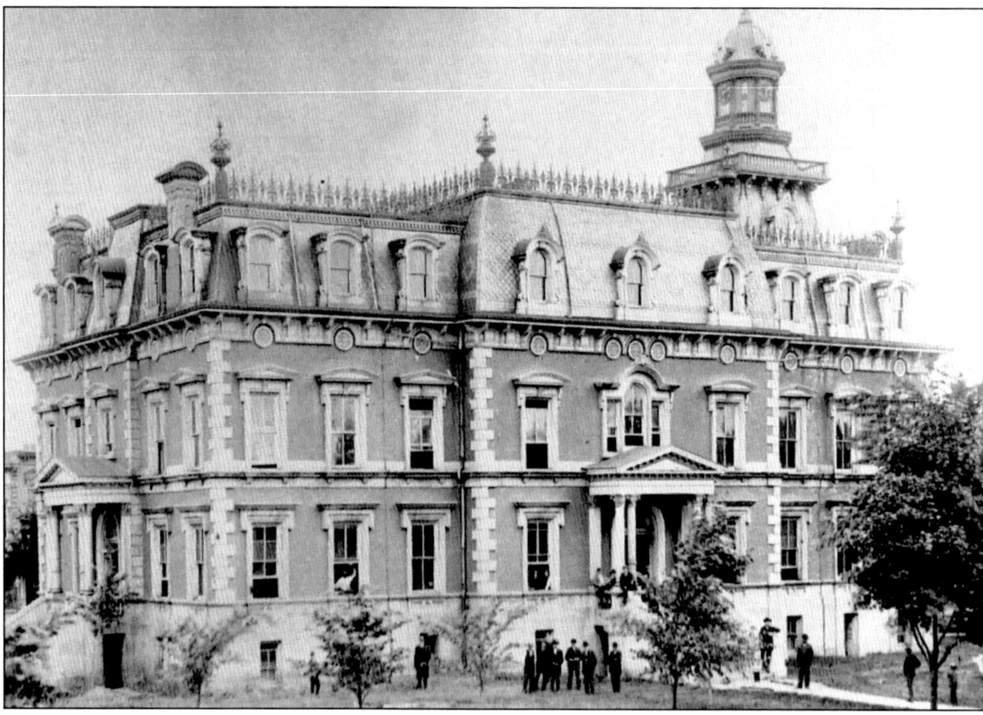

The current county courthouse, designed by architect Elijah E. Meyers of Springfield, was completed in 1872 at a cost of $155,000. As the photograph here shows, the magnificent building originally had a mansard roof with numerous windows, but that roof leaked, so it was soon replaced by a pitched one. The frontispiece to this book, from a turn-of-the-century postcard, shows the later, less elegant roof style, which the courthouse retains today. Restored a quarter-century ago (1976–1978), the courthouse is now on the National Register of Historic Places.

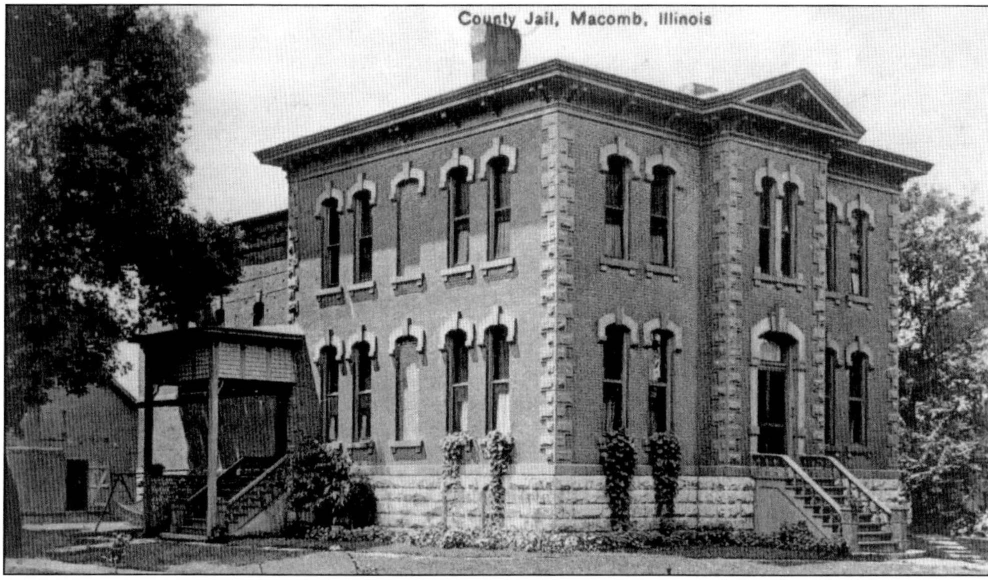

The first McDonough County Jail was built of logs in 1832, a few blocks west of the square. It was replaced by a brick one, constructed in 1856 at the southeast corner of Carroll and Lafayette Streets. That, in turn, was replaced in 1876 by a larger brick jail, shown here. Located at the southwest corner of Jackson and McArthur Streets, it was replaced on that site by the current jail, built in 1964. For many years, the county sheriff lived in this building.

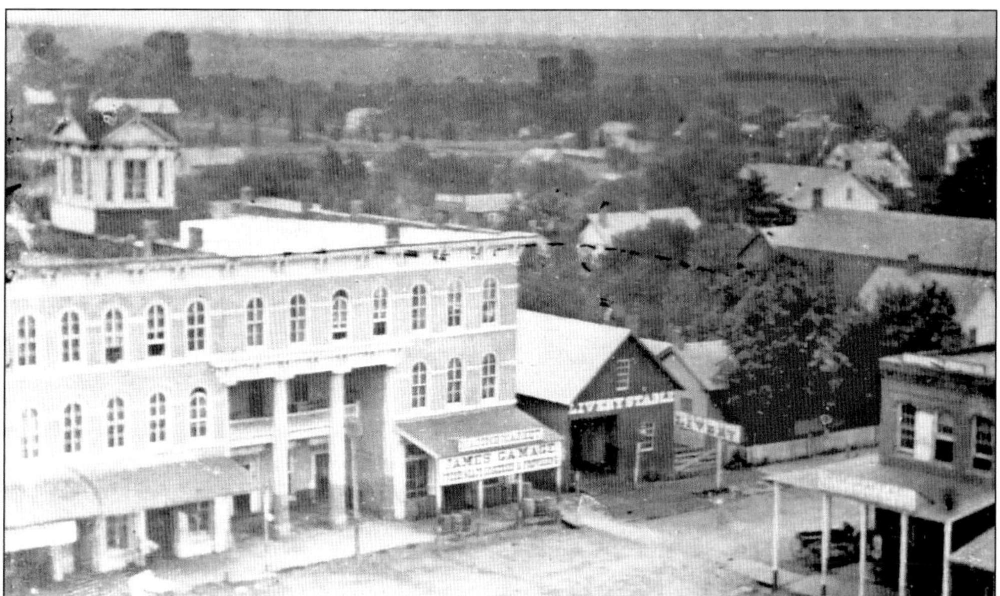

This photograph of the southeast corner of the square in 1873 shows the huge Randolph House Hotel and its livery stable. The magnificent hotel was built in 1857 by William H. Randolph, a grocer, sheriff, circuit clerk, and state legislator. Lincoln stayed there during his two visits to Macomb in 1858. His third-floor room was later regarded as a local historic site. The columned entrance was later eliminated, and in 1937, the north half of the building was torn down to make way for a Woolworth store.

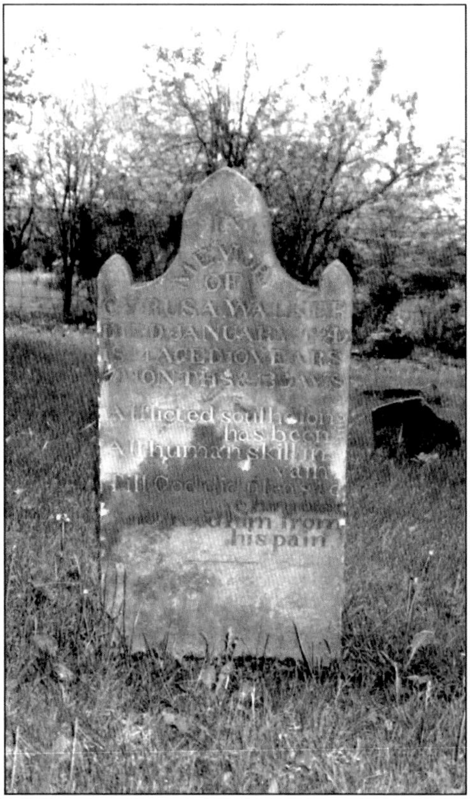

The Old Macomb Cemetery, located on Wigwam Hollow Road, was started in 1830 and became a public burying ground six years later. Many of the old slate markers, engraved by pioneer stone carver John Long, have poetic inscriptions. The old style headstone shown here, belonging to 10-year-old Cyrus A. Walker who died in 1844, tells of the boy's suffering: "Afflicted soul he long has been, / All human skill in vain, / Till God did please to give him ease / And freed him from his pain." Among the burials are veterans of the War of 1812 (two), the Black Hawk War (two), the Mexican War (one), and the Civil War (eleven).

In 1856, William H. Randolph laid out an 10-acre tract north of town for use as a public graveyard. Soon called Oakwood Cemetery, it eventually became the final resting place of many Macomb area residents. This photograph shows the headstones of (right to left) William and Sarah Allison and their son Harmon, who lived south of Macomb and were conductors in the Underground Railroad. Harmon's brother Andrew, also a conductor, is buried nearby.

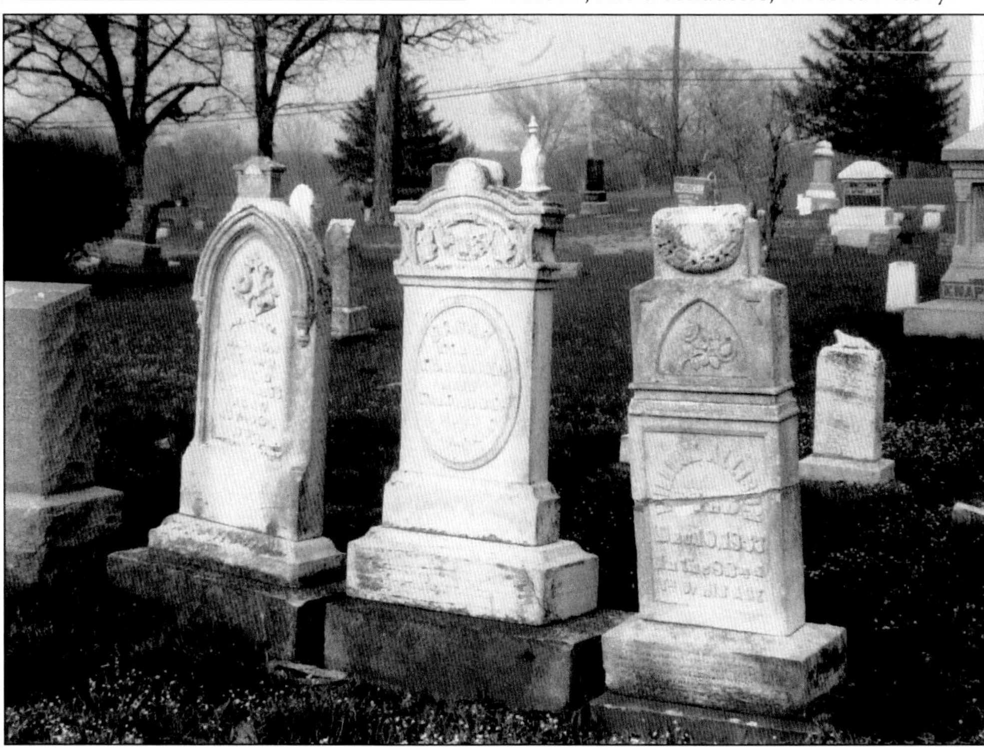

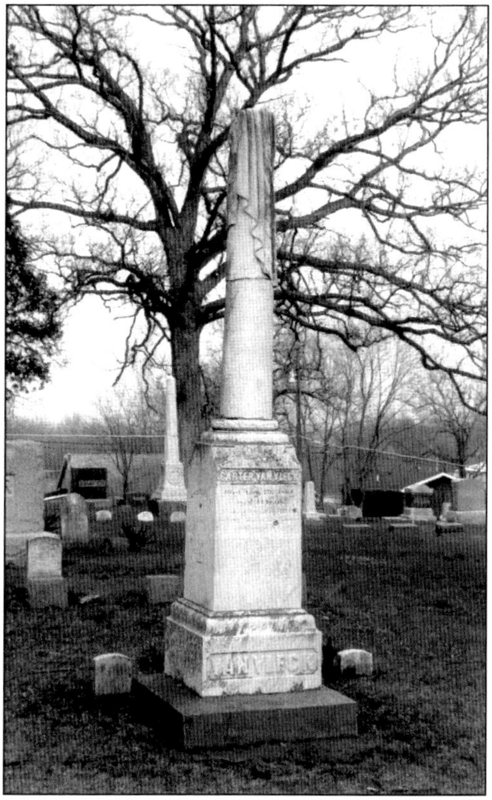

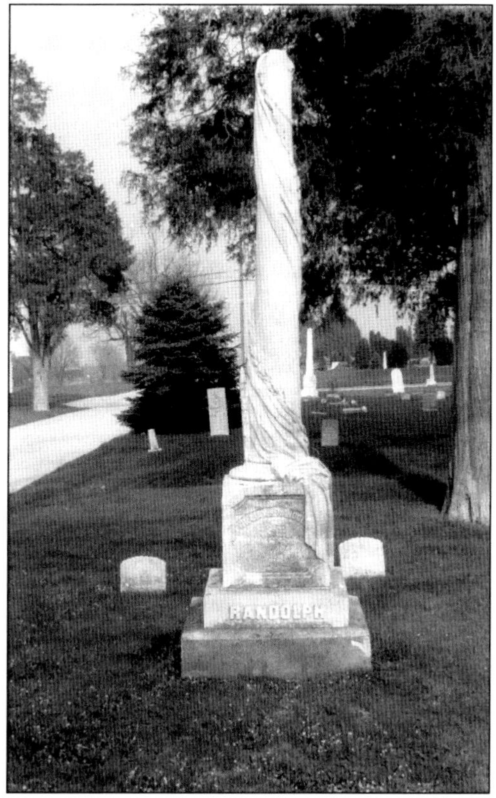

Among the Civil War veterans who are buried in Oakwood Cemetery is Carter Van Vleck, a Macomb lawyer who became colonel of the 78th Illinois Infantry Regiment. Killed near Atlanta in August 1864, he was hailed as a hero, and local residents contributed to the purchase of the tall obelisk marker shown at the left. Hotel owner and political leader William H. Randolph was also killed during the war. A Deputy Provost Marshal responsible for enforcing the Civil War draft, he was shot in Blandinsville by draft resistor John Bond on November 1, 1864, and died the next day. His death led to the controversial post-Civil War trials of John Bond, for murder, and his brothers, for conspiracy. No one was convicted, but this was the most famous murder case of the century in McDonough County.

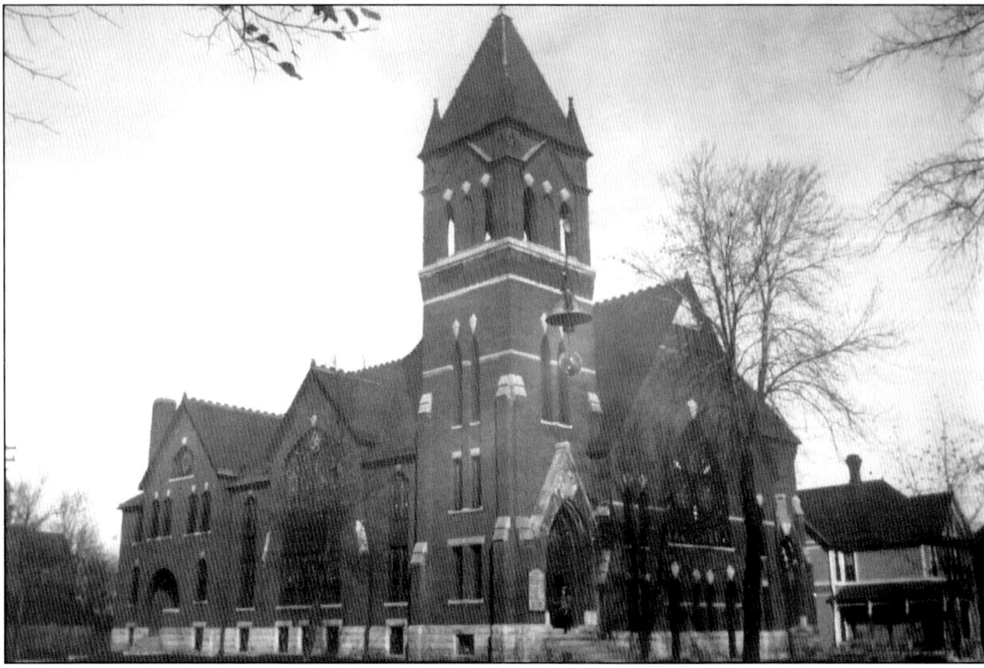

Macomb has a number of historic churches. The First Presbyterian Church, for example, was organized in 1832, and the congregation built churches in 1835 and 1852, near the site of the present one. This photograph shows the group's third building, which was dedicated in 1893. An educational wing was added in 1925. Located at the corner of Carroll and Dudley streets, this historic church building is still in use today.

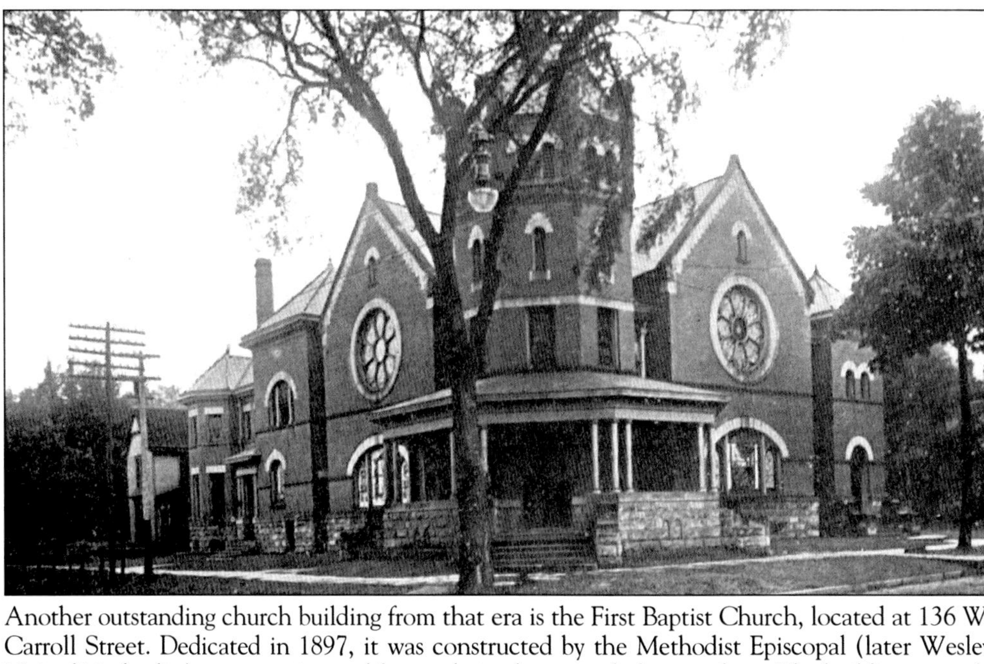

Another outstanding church building from that era is the First Baptist Church, located at 136 W. Carroll Street. Dedicated in 1897, it was constructed by the Methodist Episcopal (later Wesley United Methodist) congregation and featured circular stained-glass windows. The building was sold to the Calvary Baptist Church in 1963, and became the First Baptist Church in 1977.

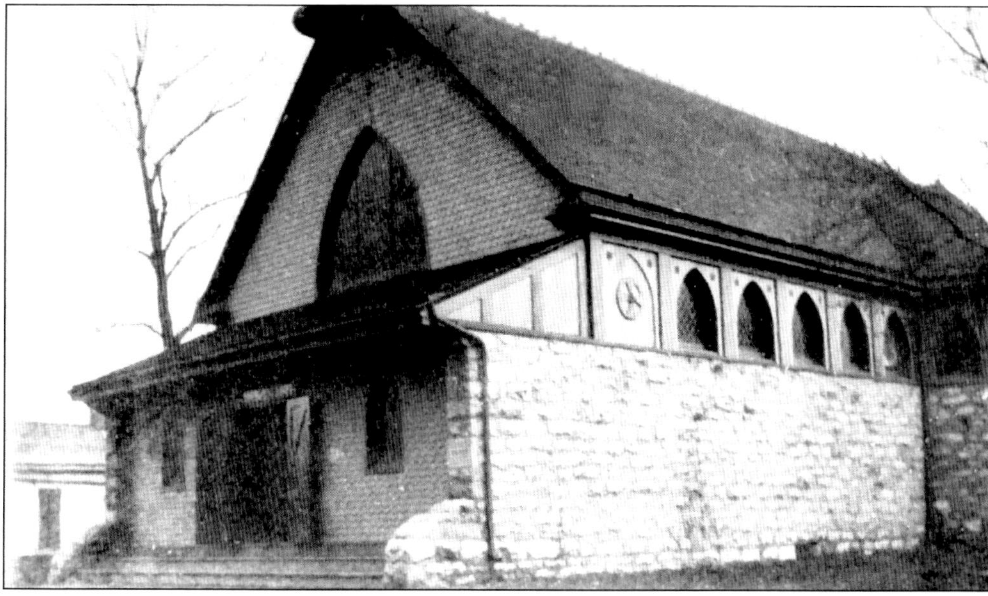

Another historic religious structure is St. George's Episcopal Church, built in 1895 at 231 E. Carroll Street. Romanesque in style, it was modeled after an Episcopal church in Boston. Fire gutted the interior of the church in 1957, but the congregation renovated the building and continued to worship there. An addition to the church is being constructed at the present time (2002).

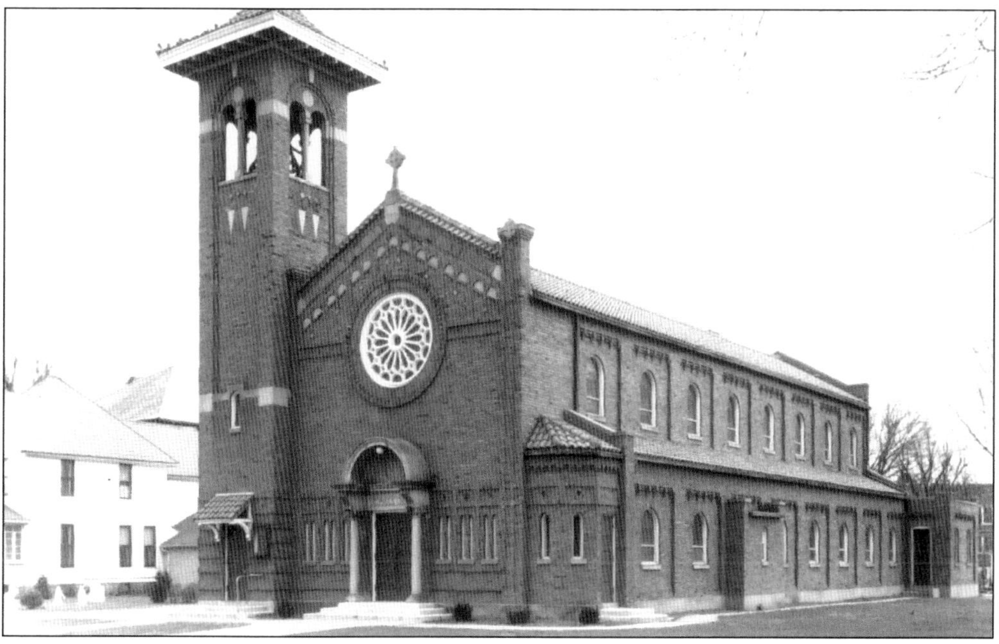

The first St. Paul's Catholic Church was a small frame building dedicated in 1867. It was succeeded on the same site, 309 W. Jackson Street, by the present large brick building, dedicated in 1926. The latter features a rose-shaped stained-glass window and a tall side belfry. A rectory and school were constructed on adjacent property in 1892 and 1902. Those structures have, in turn, been replaced by more modern buildings. This 1953 photograph shows the 1892 rectory at the left.

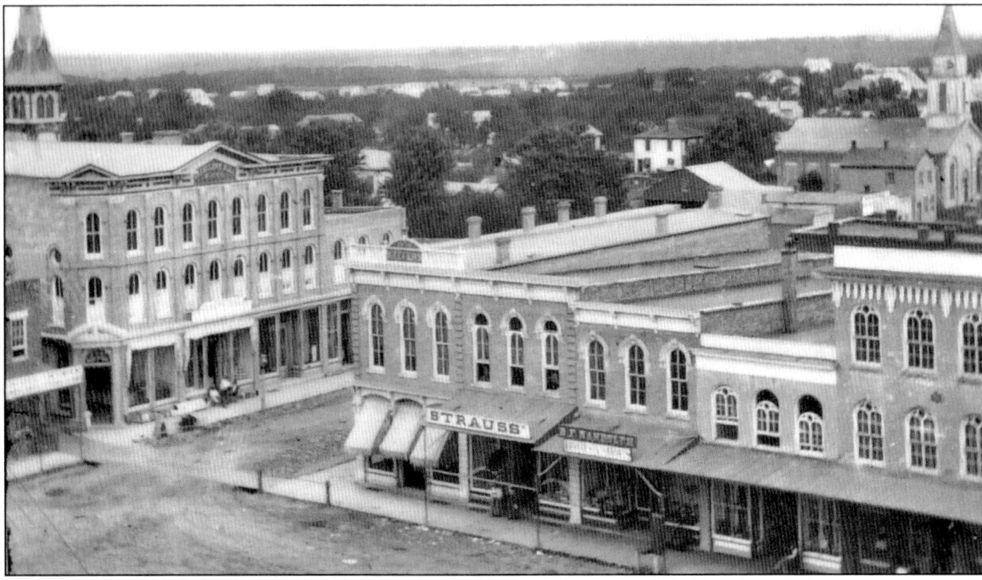

This 1873 photograph shows the northwest corner of the square. The large building at the left is the Chandler Block, or "Chandler's Hall," built in 1872 by McDonough County's wealthiest businessman, C.V. Chandler. The upper stories contained a magnificent opera house that seated 800 people. Across the street are the Keefer drug store, the Strauss clothing store, the Randolph boot and shoe store, and the Venable brothers dry goods store. The First Baptist Church spire is at the left; the Methodist Church is at the right in the background.

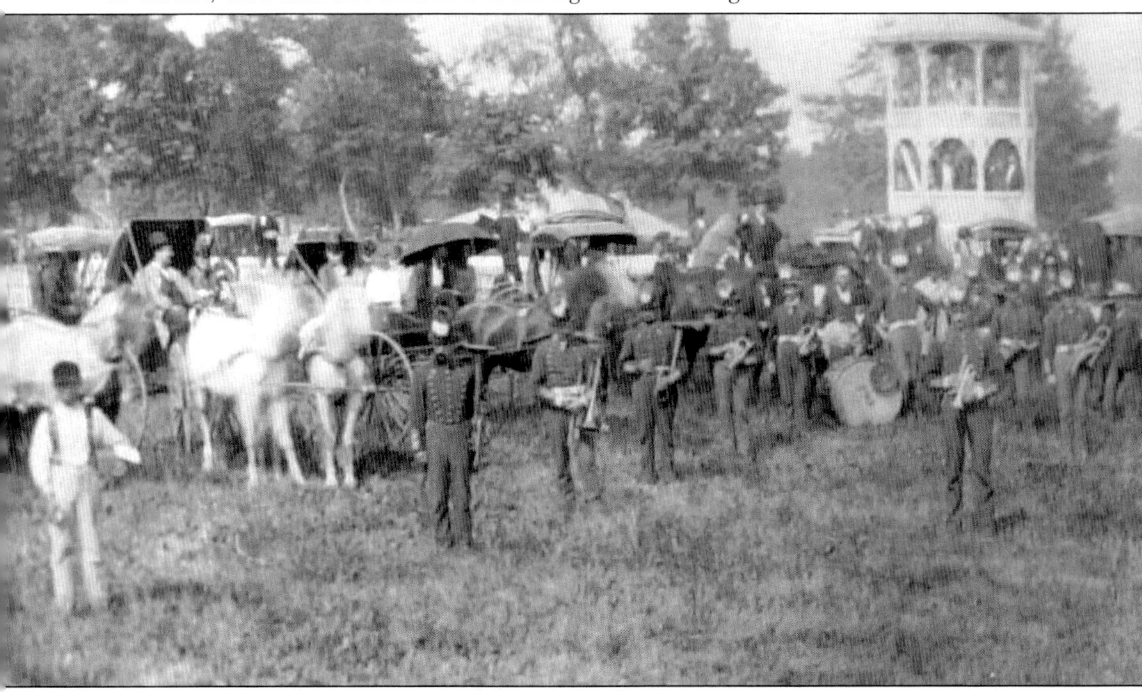

The McDonough County fairgrounds, which opened in 1867, encompassed 21 acres and included a half-mile racetrack. The grandstand, shown in this wide-angle photograph, could hold several hundred people, and in the later 19th century the trotting races drew capacity

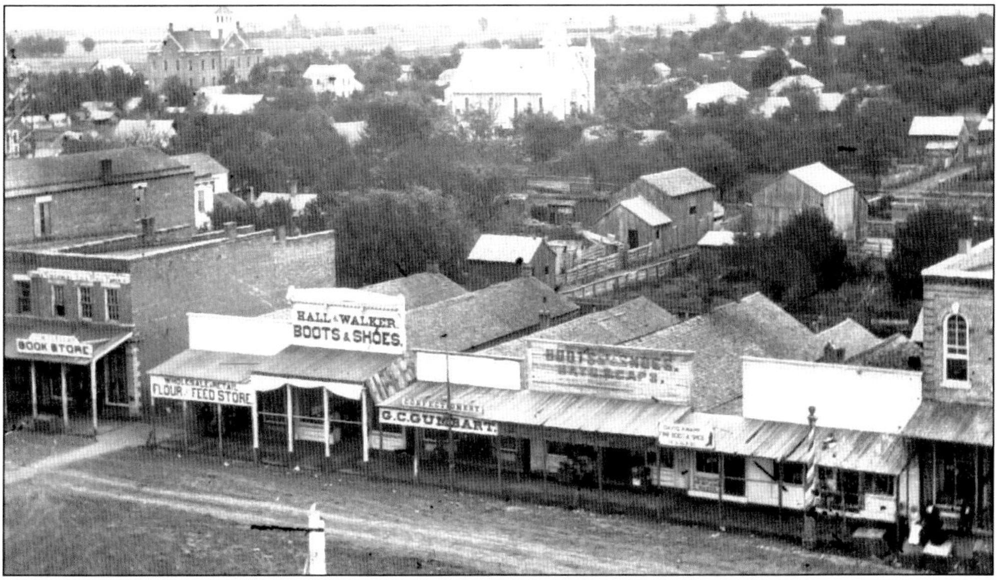

This 1873 photograph of the northeastern side of the square shows small frame buildings that had changed little since before the Civil War. From the left, the shops are Black's bookstore, Binnie's flour and feed store, Hall and Walker's boot and shoe store, Gumbart's "confectionary" (restaurant), Harding and Randolph's shoe and hat store, Knapp's tiny shoemaker shop, and Ball's barber shop. William Ball was the first black man to own a business in Macomb. In the background are the Presbyterian Church and, to the left, the Second Ward School.

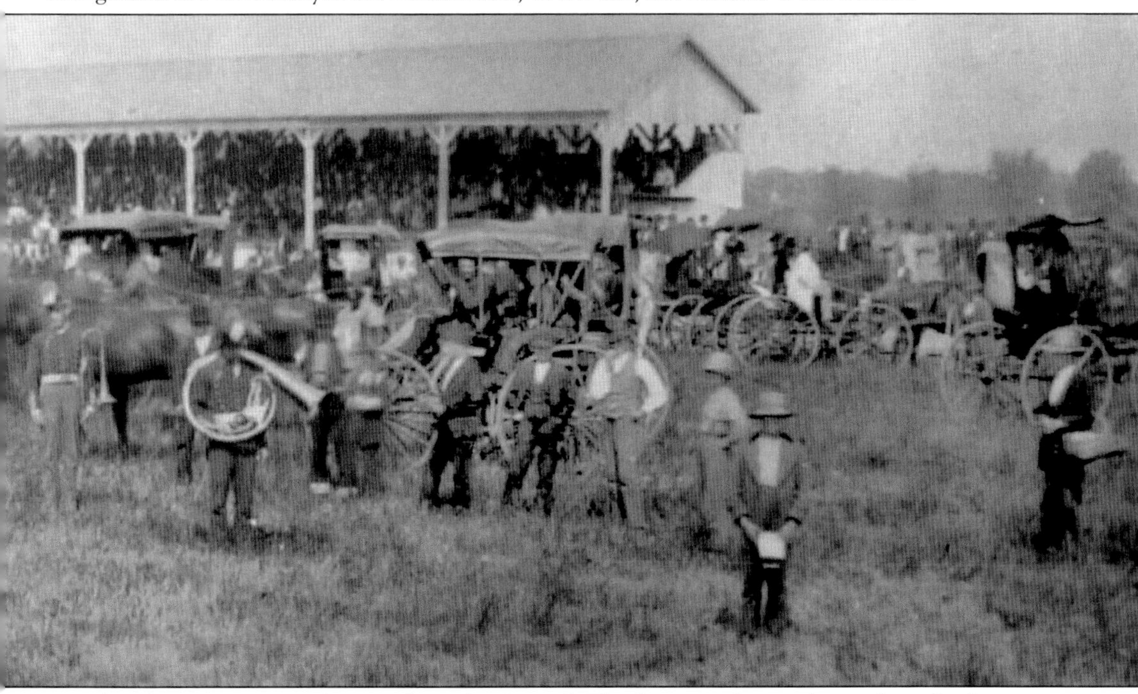

crowds. The two-story gazebo was the judges' stand. The fairgrounds were located south of town, where the present Macomb High School was later constructed. In the foreground are members of the Macomb Band.

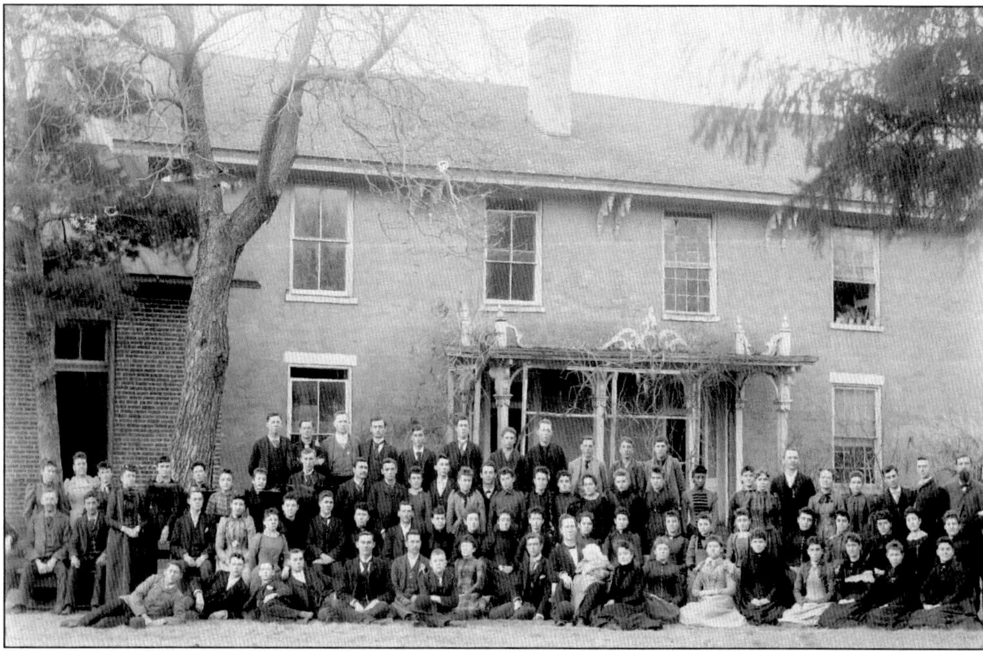

Chartered in 1836, McDonough College opened in 1837 in a new building at Carroll and College Streets. It lasted only a few years, then re-opened in 1849 and closed again in 1855. After the Civil War, it opened again and changed owners and names several times. When this photograph was taken, *c.* 1890, it was called Macomb Normal and Commercial College. It had a teacher training course, a commercial course, and a classical course.

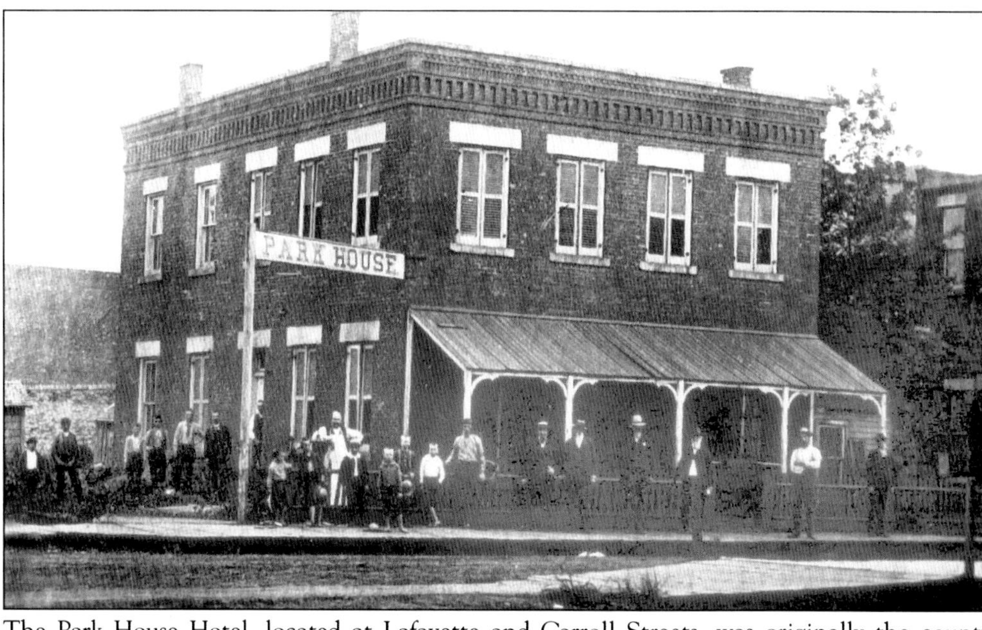

The Park House Hotel, located at Lafayette and Carroll Streets, was originally the county jail, built in 1856. It was not well constructed, so prisoners frequently escaped, including the notorious Ed Maxwell in 1875. The building became a hotel after the new jail was built in 1876, and it was razed in the late 1880s to make way for the second Chandler Block, built in 1889.

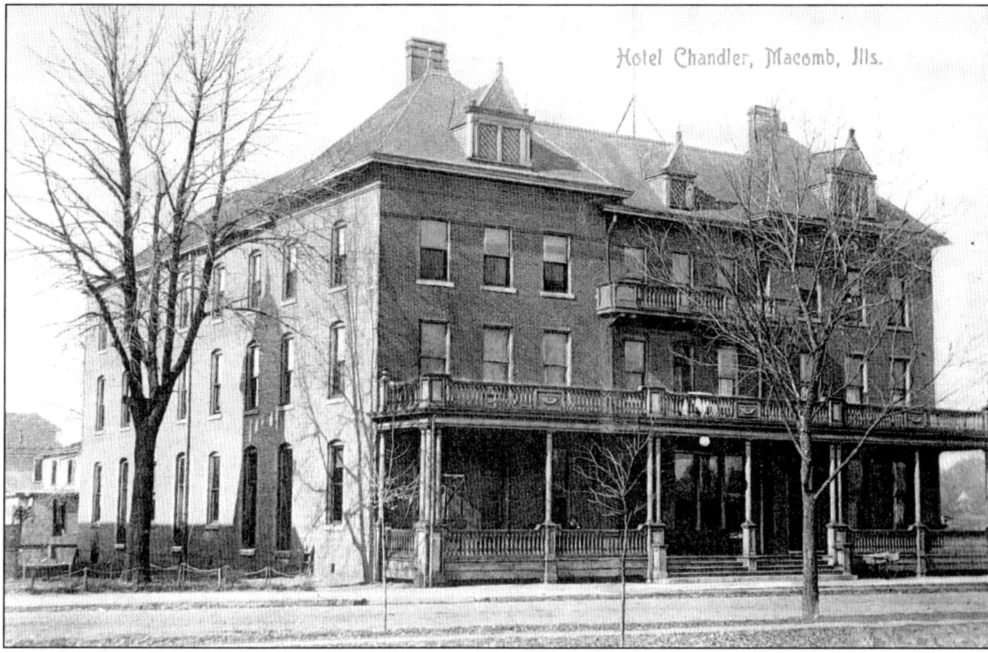

This photograph shows the Chandler Hotel, built by businessman C.V. Chandler in 1899, at the corner of Lafayette and Calhoun Streets. It was sold to J.M. Pace 10 years later. After an October 17, 1910 fire, the hotel was extensively remodeled, and when it opened early in 1911, it was renamed the Pace Hotel. The Change of Pace bar, started on the lower floor in 1973, became a popular hangout for WIU students. The building was razed in 1990.

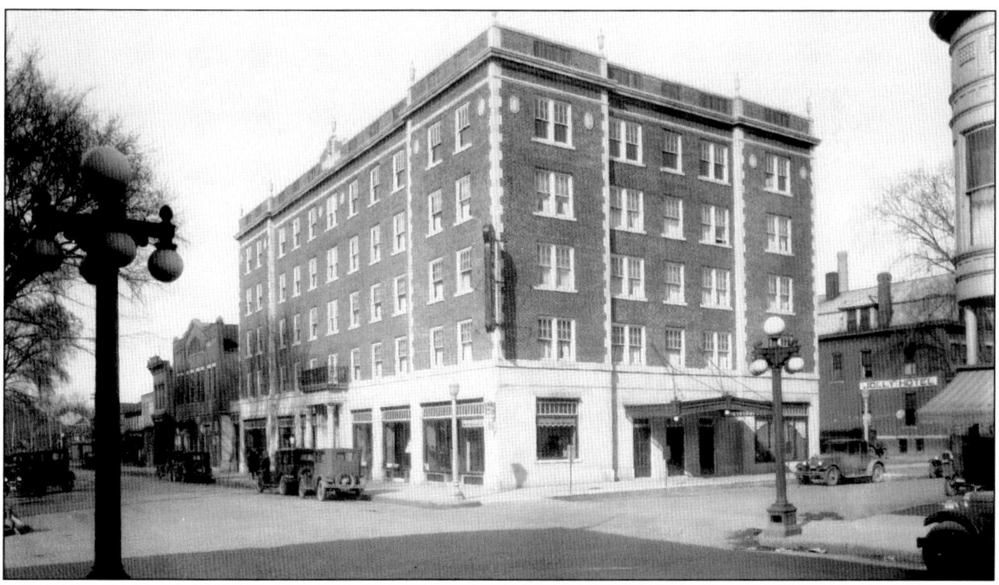

Built in 1926–1927 at Lafayette and Carroll Streets after a community investment campaign, the Lamoine Hotel had 86 rooms, plus an elegant dining room, a barber shop, a soda fountain, and other amenities on the first floor. For many years, the Rotary and Kiwanis clubs held their meetings in the dining room, which was also the location for many other gatherings. In 1999, the building was acquired by the *Macomb Journal*, which now has its offices on the main floor.

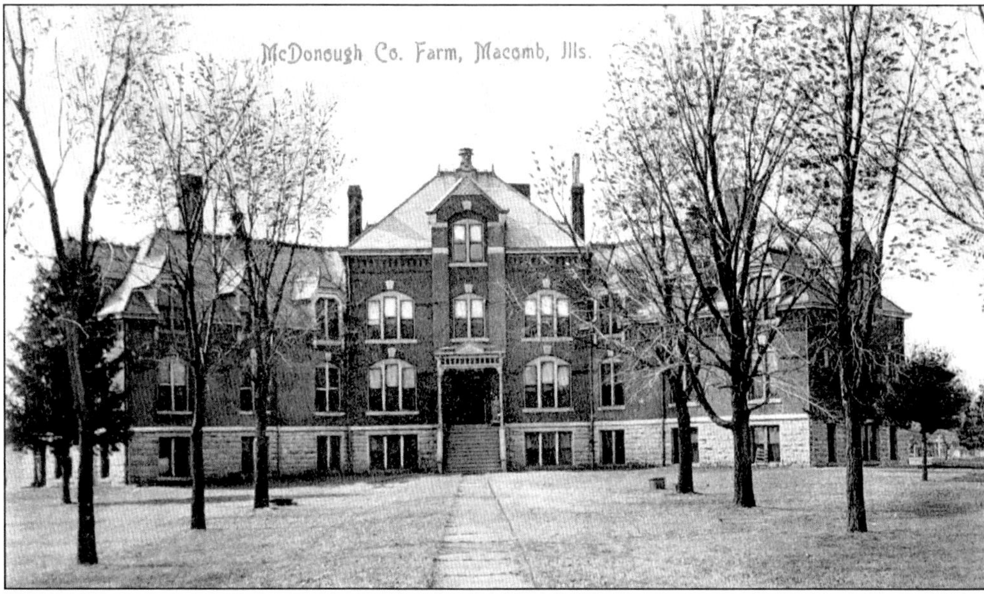

The McDonough County Almshouse, where chronically ill and homeless residents were cared for, was built in 1884 two miles southeast of the square, at the intersection of roads 750N and 1300E. The magnificent Queen Anne-style structure was 144 feet across the front and had 85 rooms, including 50 bedrooms and 2 dining halls. It was the last building constructed by William O. Thomas, the most important Macomb builder of the 19th century. In 1949, it became The Elms nursing home, and it was torn down about 10 years later.

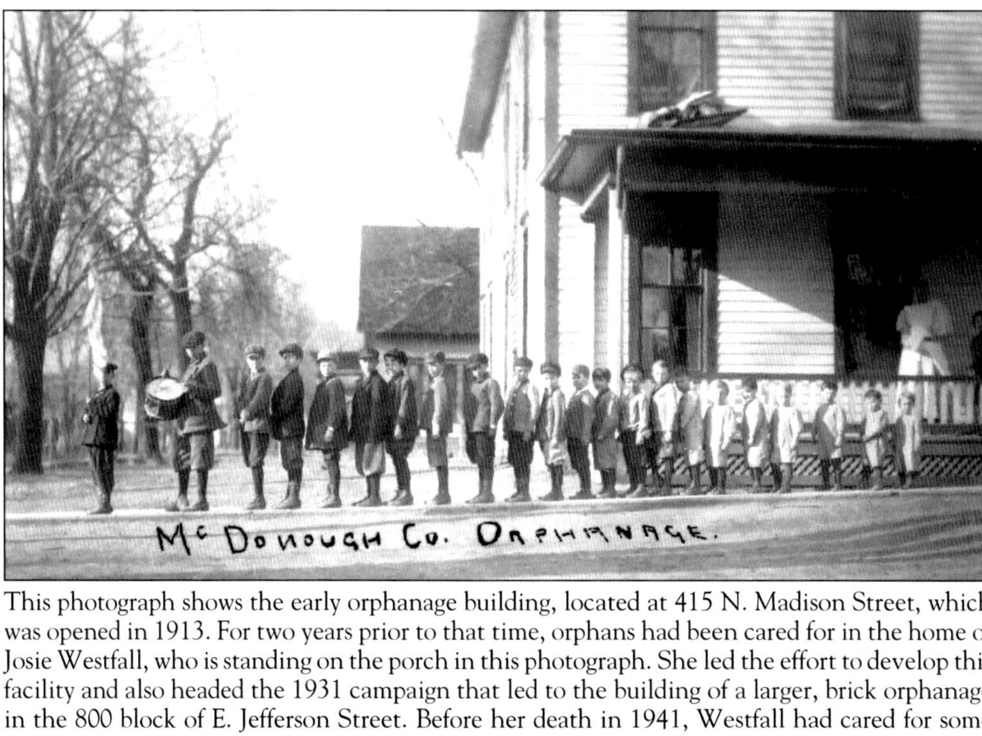

This photograph shows the early orphanage building, located at 415 N. Madison Street, which was opened in 1913. For two years prior to that time, orphans had been cared for in the home of Josie Westfall, who is standing on the porch in this photograph. She led the effort to develop this facility and also headed the 1931 campaign that led to the building of a larger, brick orphanage in the 800 block of E. Jefferson Street. Before her death in 1941, Westfall had cared for some 500 children.

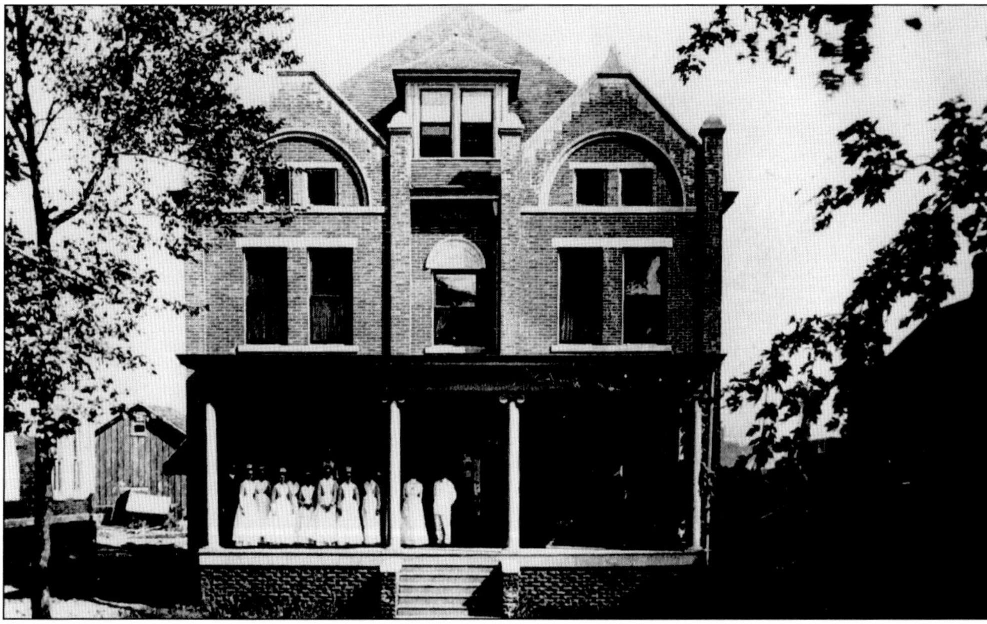

Marietta Phelps provided $8,200 for the building lot and construction of Macomb's first hospital, located at 218 E. Carroll Street. The 14-room facility was planned and supervised by Dr. S.C. Stremmel, who also provided $7,500 of his own funds. Phelps Hospital had only two ward rooms, one for women and one for men, until 1906, when a $10,000 addition included eight private rooms. Nurses were trained at Phelps for many years. The hospital closed in 1966 and was razed in 1974.

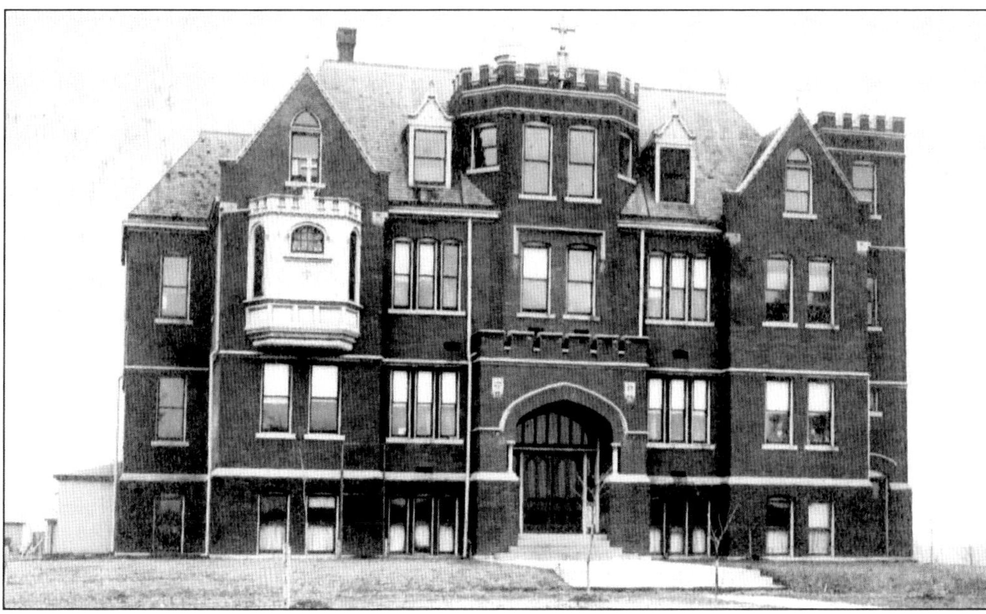

St. Francis Hospital, located at the end of S. Johnson Street, was founded by Dr. Joseph B. Bacon. He and his wife, Elizabeth, contributed $3,000, and he raised funds from others in the area. He also arranged for the Sisters of St. Francis to operate the facility. The original building, which cost $30,000, was completed in 1903, and wings were added in 1912 and 1927. The hospital operated until 1967 and was torn down six years later.

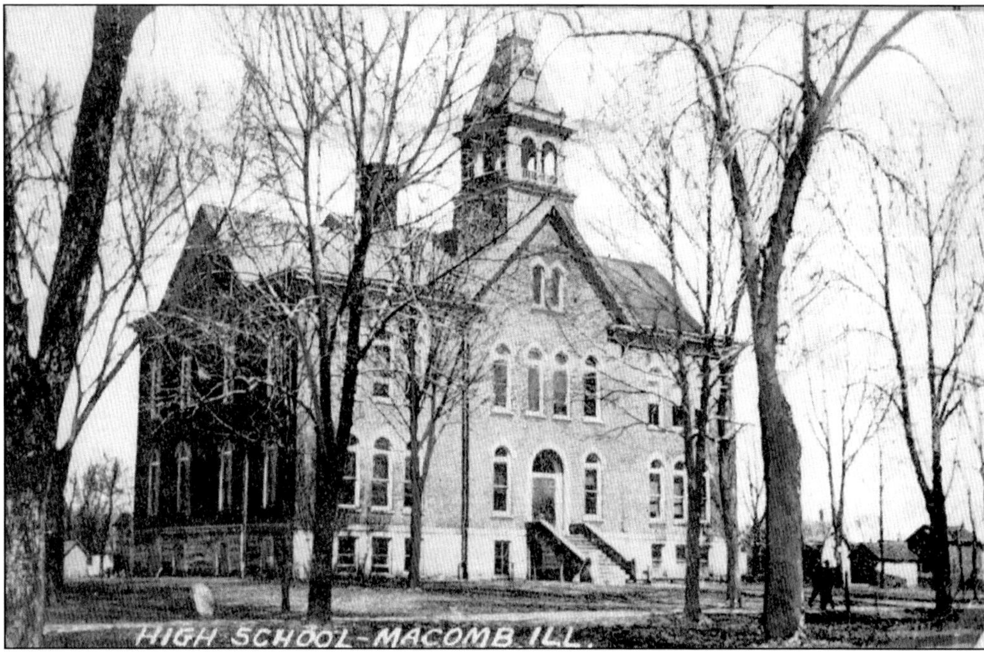

In 1866, Macomb's first high school was erected on E. Calhoun Street on the site now occupied by the YMCA. For many years there were only two teachers, and one was the principal, H.H. Smith. Destroyed by fire in 1886, the structure was replaced on the same site. Only the upper floor housed high school classes. The lower floor was the Second Ward School. In later years, the building was known as Lincoln School, until it closed in 1958.

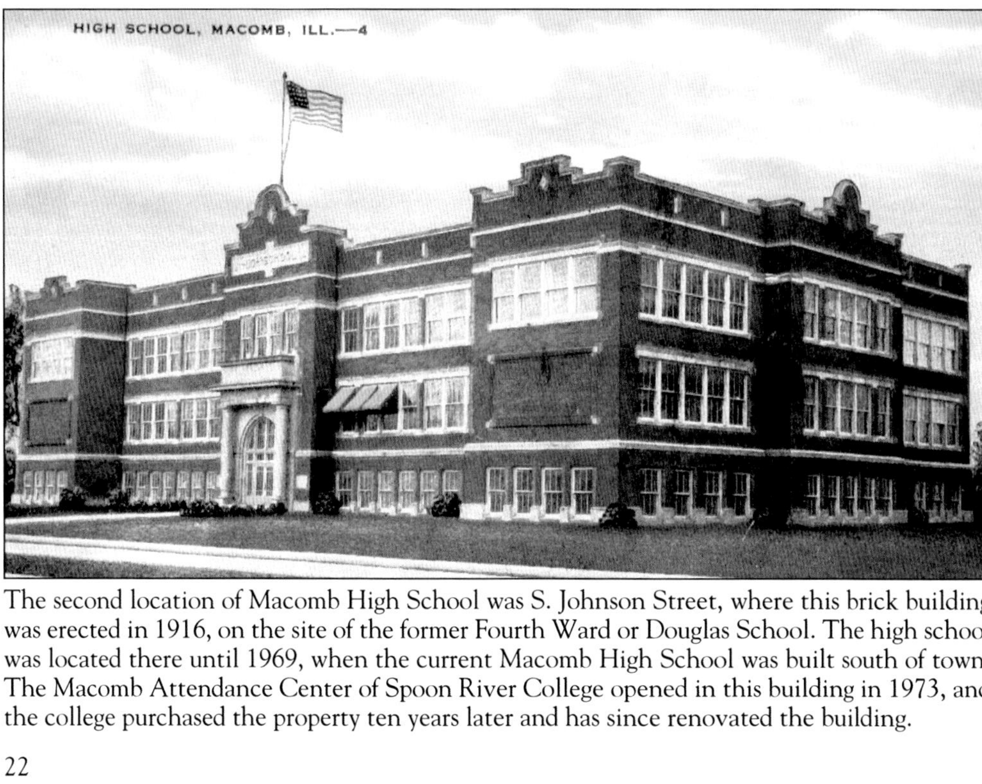

The second location of Macomb High School was S. Johnson Street, where this brick building was erected in 1916, on the site of the former Fourth Ward or Douglas School. The high school was located there until 1969, when the current Macomb High School was built south of town. The Macomb Attendance Center of Spoon River College opened in this building in 1973, and the college purchased the property ten years later and has since renovated the building.

Located on Johnson Street, near the Catholic Church, the first St. Paul's School was a red brick building with stone arches over the lower windows. Father F.G. Lentz led the campaign to raise funds, as it was an expensive structure for that era—$15,000. The building was razed in 1959 and was replaced by the present St. Paul's School, which faces Washington Street.

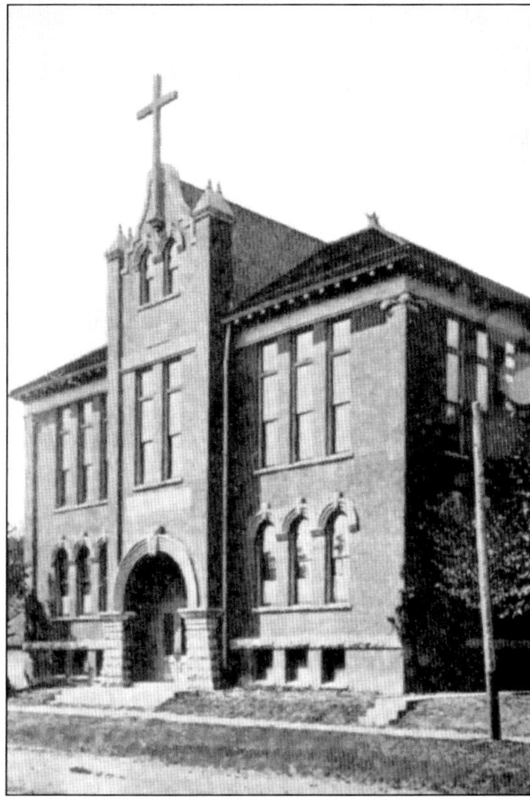

Built in 1877, Wiley School was once located east of Macomb. In 1971, it was donated to the community by Clarence Watson, the founder of Watson Seed Farms, to serve as a country school museum, and it was moved to town the following year. At the time this photograph was taken in 1990, it also housed the Macomb Area Convention and Visitors Bureau. Located on W. Calhoun Street, it is now occupied by Bridgeway and is known as the Wiley Occupational Resource Center. The country schoolroom is still available to visitors who call ahead.

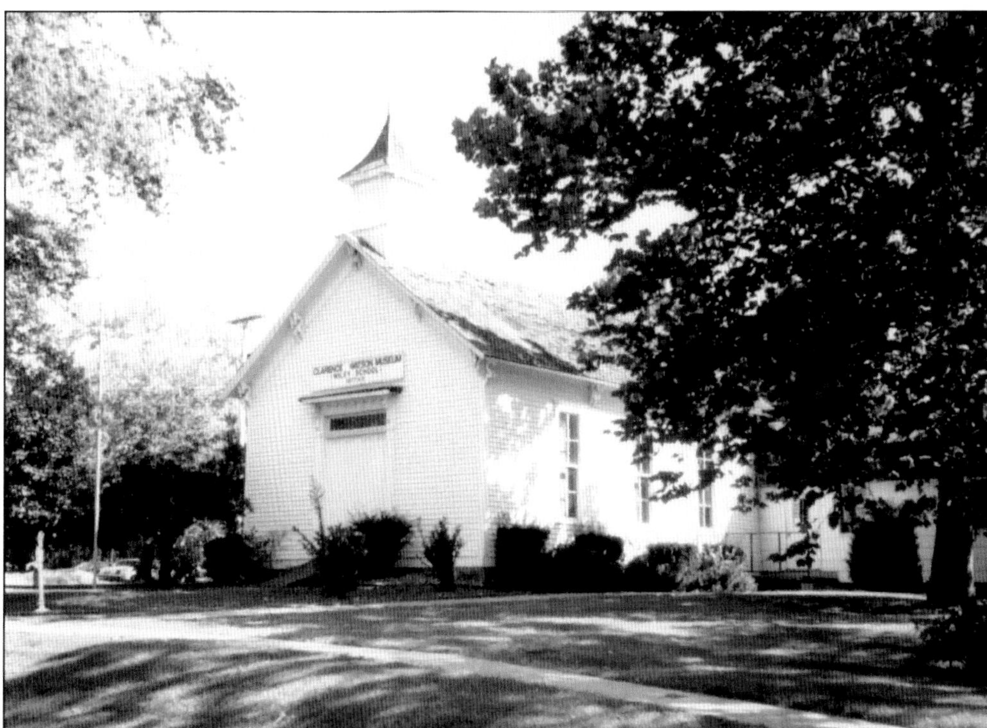

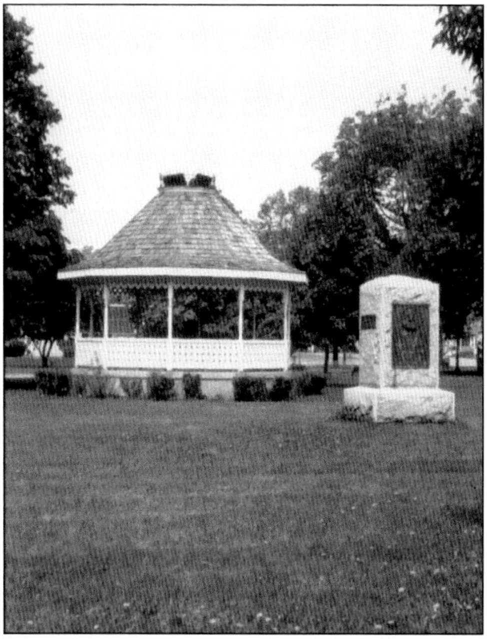 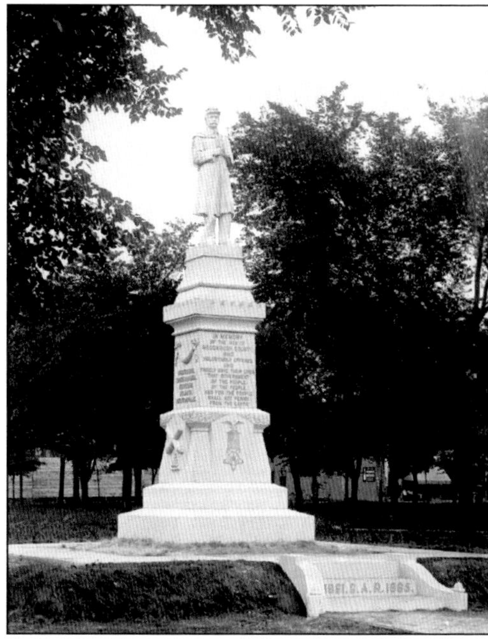

The Chandler Park gazebo was erected in 1982. Nearby is the monument to Commodore Thomas Macdonough and General Alexander Macomb, heroes of the War of 1812, for whom the county and town were named. Given to Macomb by banker Albert Eads, it was dedicated on September 11, 1914. The most well-known monument in Macomb is the 20-foot-high statue that portrays a Civil War soldier at rest. Given to the community by businessman C.V. Chandler, himself a Civil War veteran, it was dedicated on August 3, 1899, to honor county men who died in the war. The park also has a 1956 VFW monument to Macomb area soldiers who died in 20th century wars.

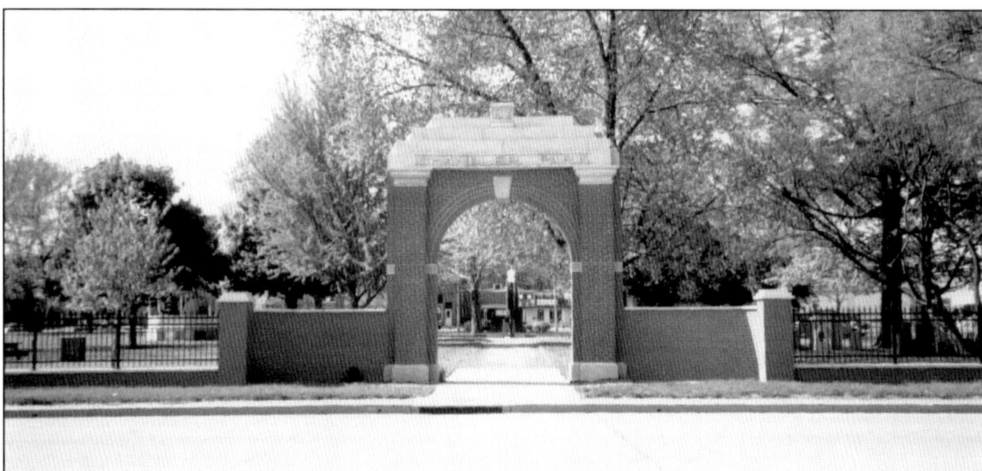

After C.V. Chandler had lost his fortune trying to boost the town and region with the Macomb and Western Illinois Railway early in the 20th century, he left the community. But in the late 1920s, Macomb residents gathered donations for a memorial to honor him and to thank him for his unselfish community leadership, including the donation of Chandler Park. The memorial arch shown here was dedicated on September 17, 1929. Chandler, then 87, was present at the ceremony. The fence attached to the arch was added in 1997.

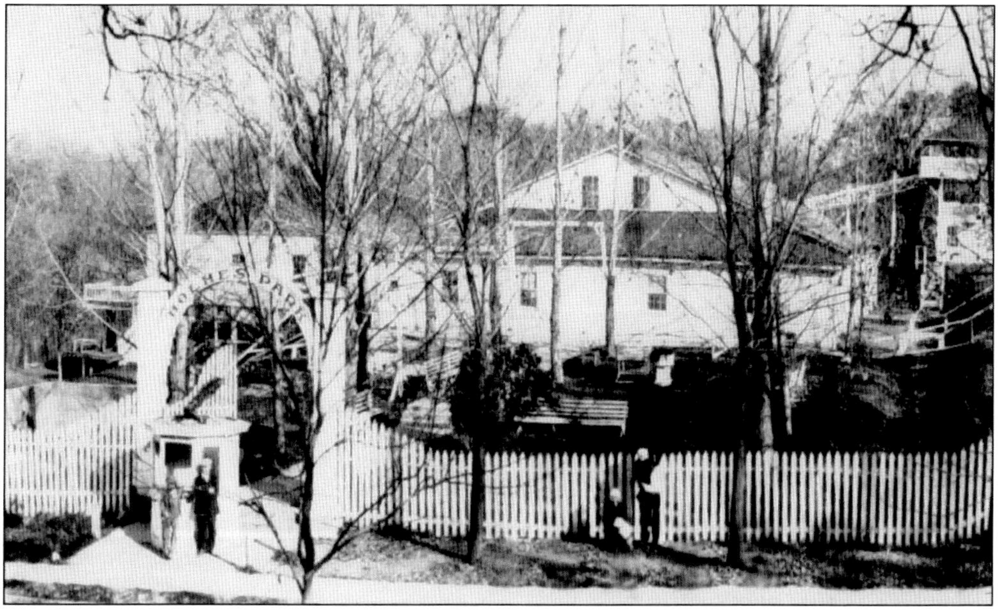

Located at 827 N. Lafayette Street, Holmes Park was developed by Frank Holmes in the early years of the 20th century. The park included a roller-skating rink, a man-made lake, a boat house, and a chute-the-chute ride. Starting in 1914, it also had a small zoo. The park changed hands twice before closing in the late 1920s. However, the roller-skating rink was used until it was destroyed by fire in 1965.

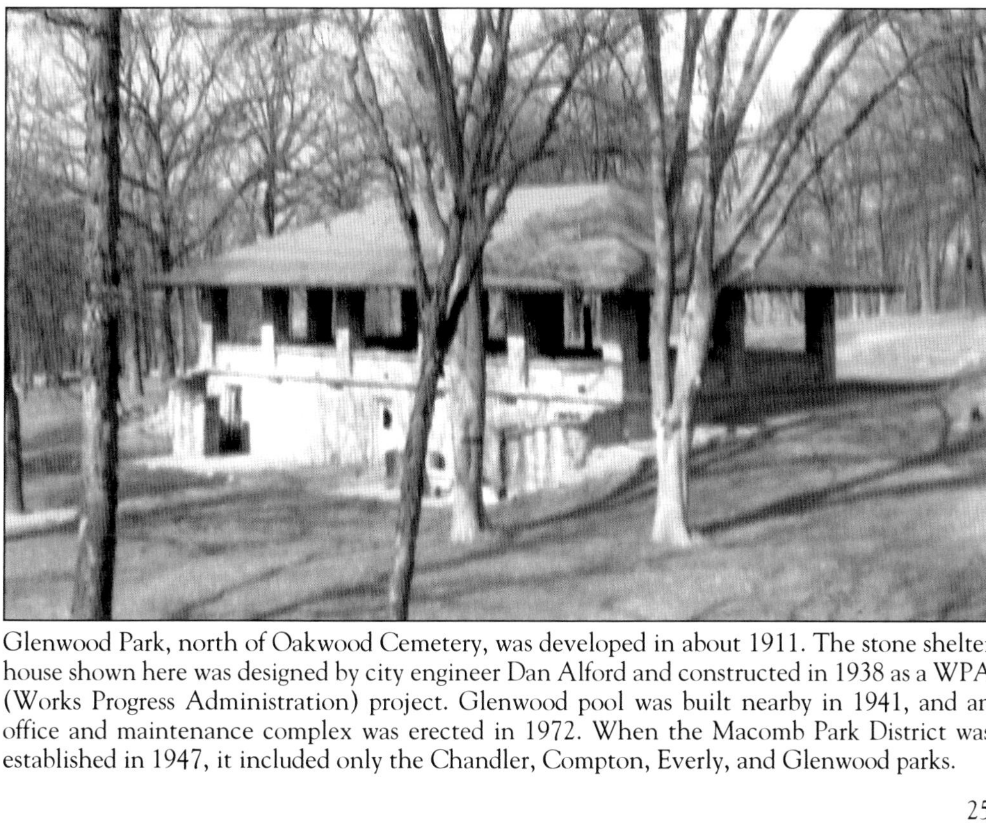

Glenwood Park, north of Oakwood Cemetery, was developed in about 1911. The stone shelter house shown here was designed by city engineer Dan Alford and constructed in 1938 as a WPA (Works Progress Administration) project. Glenwood pool was built nearby in 1941, and an office and maintenance complex was erected in 1972. When the Macomb Park District was established in 1947, it included only the Chandler, Compton, Everly, and Glenwood parks.

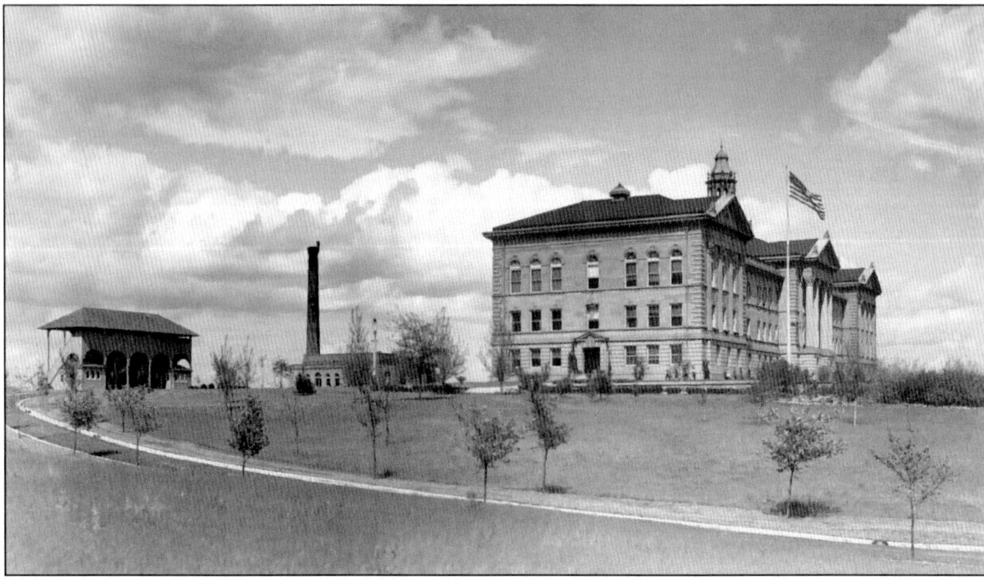

This photograph shows the main building of Western Illinois State Normal School in about 1906. Later called Sherman Hall, it was opened for classes on September 23, 1902, but since the mid-1960s it has housed only administrative offices. In recent years the huge stone building has been put on the National Register of Historic Places. Directly behind it is the powerhouse, which became the academy building in 1928, and is now the WIU Art Gallery. At the far left is the grandstand, built in 1905 beside the early football field.

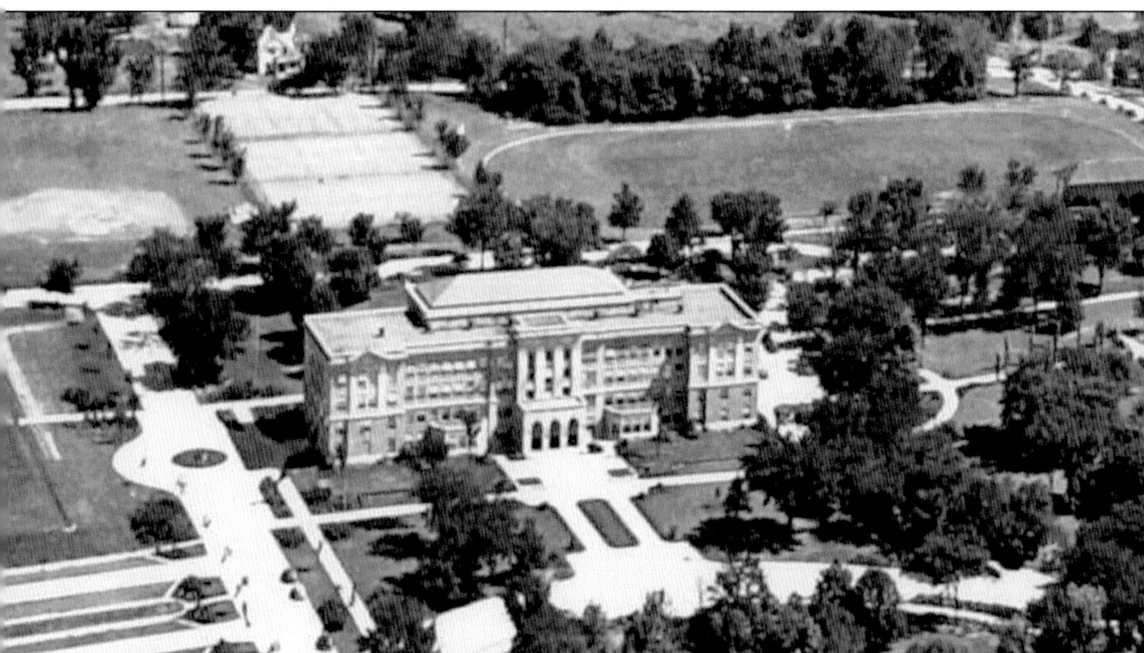

This photograph of Western, c. 1940, shows the training school (at left), now Simpkins Hall, which was dedicated in 1939. Monroe (later Grote) Hall, a women's dormitory, is on the right. It was built in 1913 and razed in 1991. Also behind the main building are the Arts Building

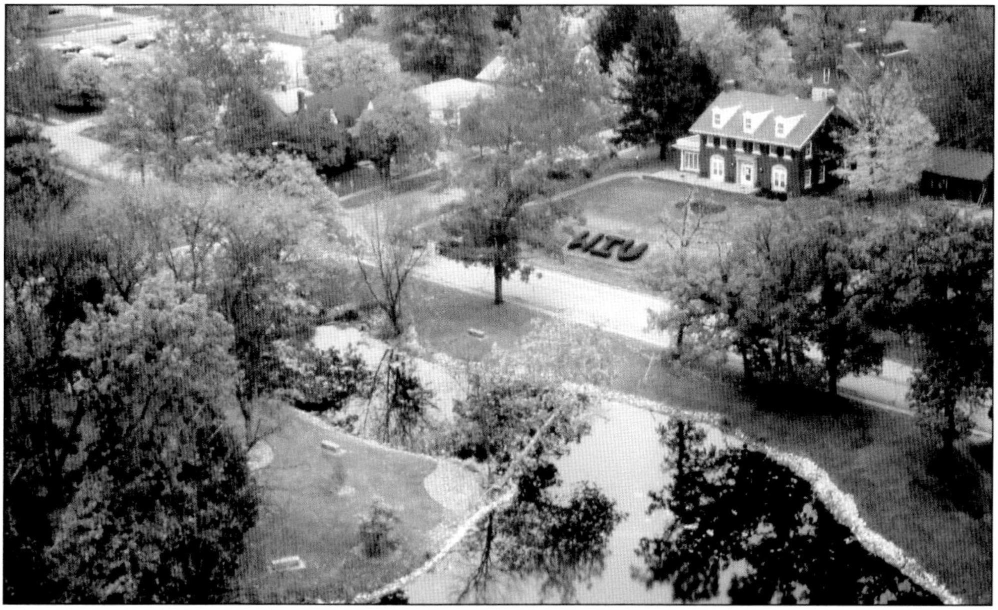

This photograph shows Lake Ruth and the Alumni House in the late 1990s. The lake was created in 1908 and 1909, and today it has lovely gardens on the north side. Built in 1924, the Alumni House was originally the home of Mr. and Mrs. H.P. Zahren, but the college bought it in 1940, and it became the Home Management House. The Alumni Programs Office has been located there since 1977, and hundreds of university gatherings have been held there in the past quarter century.

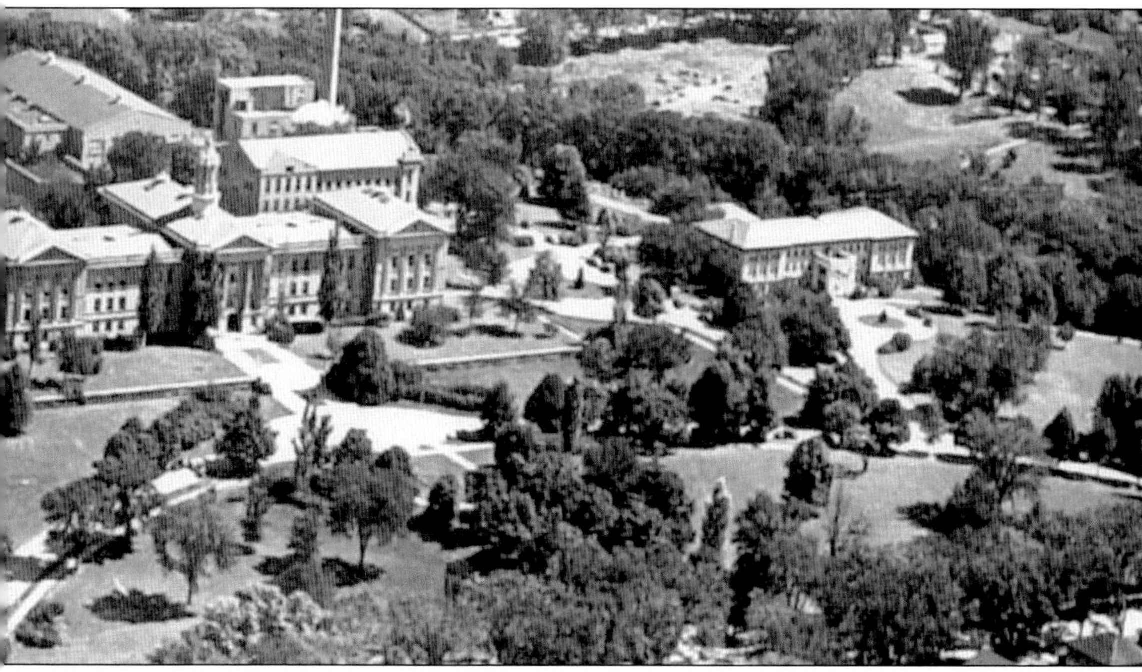

(now Garwood Hall), completed in 1918, and Morgan Gym, completed in 1928. The football field was still west of the gym, and beyond it were tennis courts and the baseball field. Morgan Gym (later Brophy Hall) was destroyed by fire on November 25, 1970.

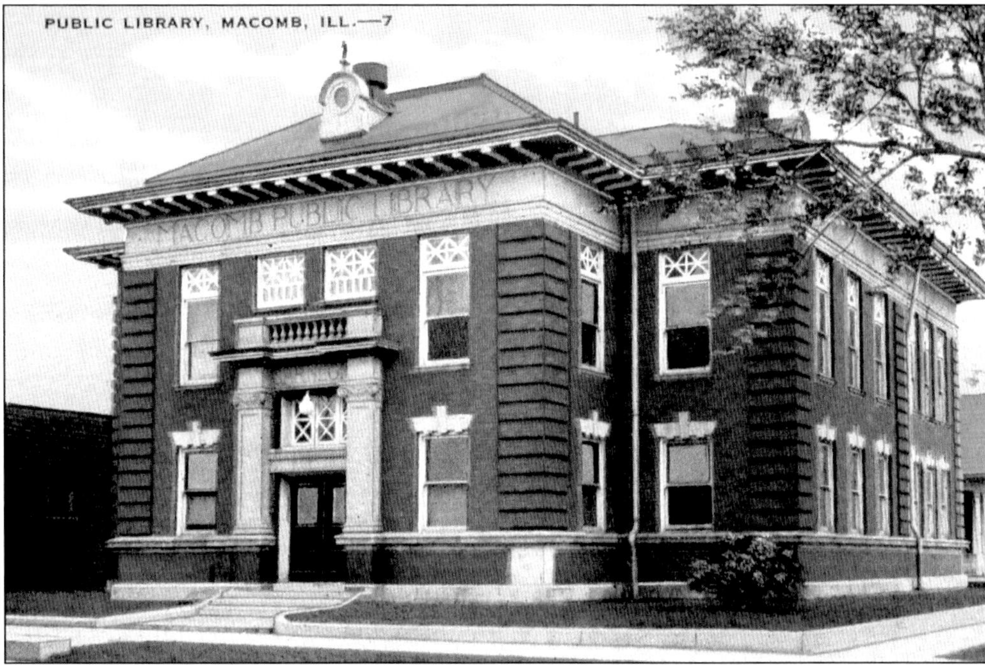

The Macomb Public Library was founded in 1881, and the current building was erected with funds supplied by industrialist Andrew Carnegie, who financed libraries for some 2,500 communities between 1886 and 1919. The handsome building opened in 1904 at Lafayette and Jefferson Streets. In the 1970s, the library acquired the nearby Holmes Building, which became the children's library in 1980 and was connected to the Carnegie structure by an addition.

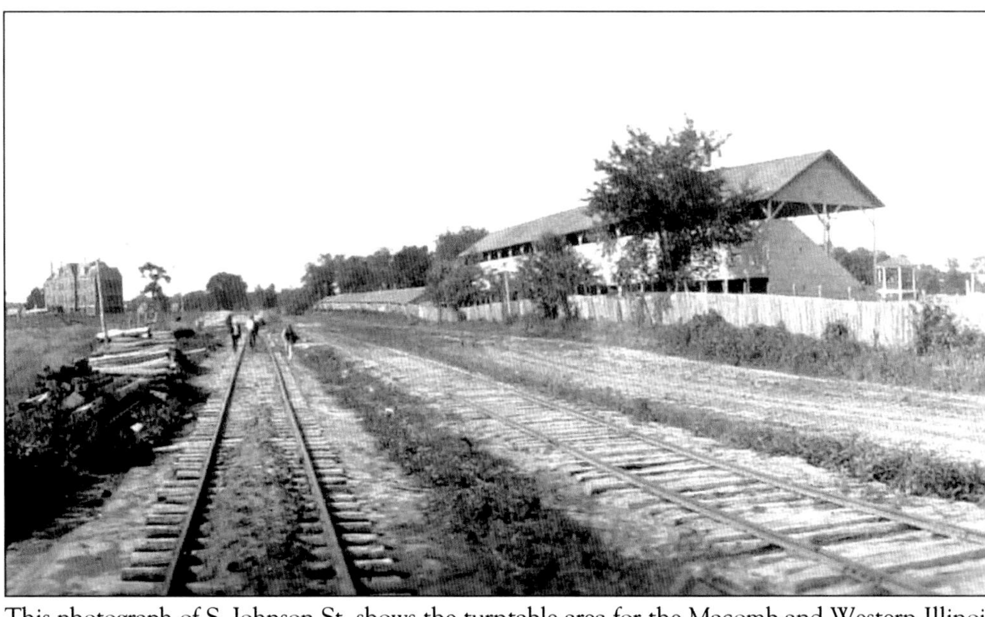

This photograph of S. Johnson St. shows the turntable area for the Macomb and Western Illinois Railway. The train made its first trip in January 1904, but went bankrupt in 1910. Between 1914 and 1932, it was revived as the Macomb, Industry and Littleton Railroad. At the right is the grandstand of the county fairgrounds, and in the distance at the left is St. Francis Hospital.

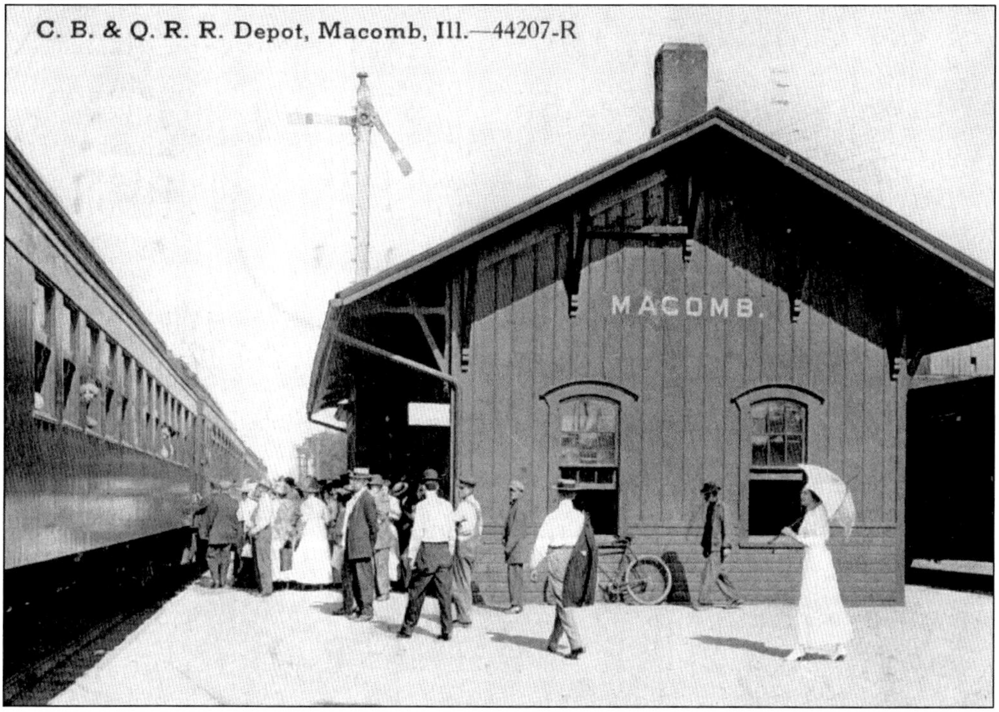

This turn-of-the-century postcard shows the Chicago, Burlington and Quincy depot, which was built in 1866 just a few feet east of the present depot. It was destroyed by fire in 1879, but was immediately rebuilt. Before the coming of automobiles and hard roads, the depot was the busiest location in Macomb. In the late 19th century, 20 trains stopped in Macomb every day.

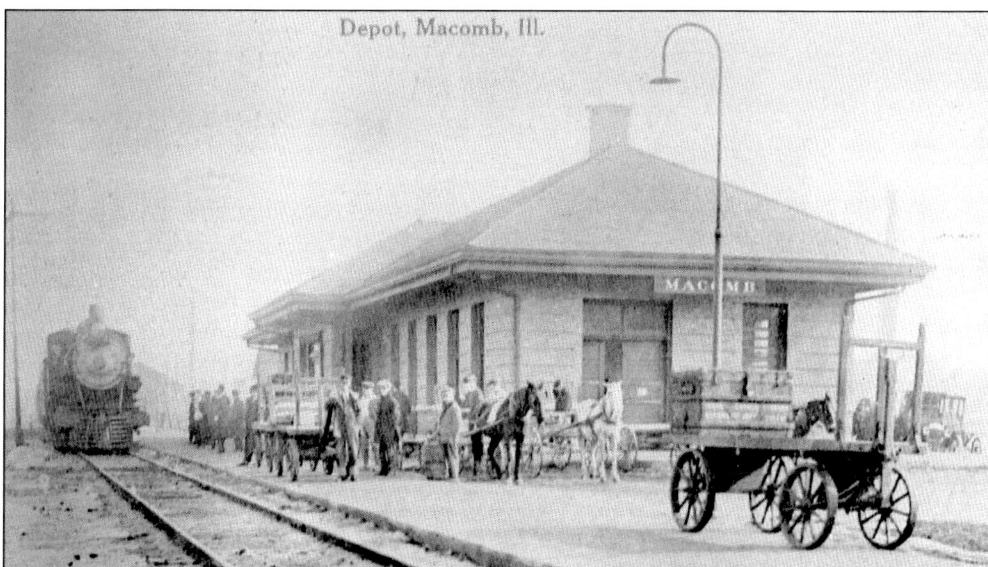

This postcard shows the present depot shortly after it was constructed in 1913. As the image reveals, horse-drawn dray wagons were still used to carry goods from the depot to stores in town, but they would soon be replaced by early trucks. The new brick structure featured separate waiting rooms for men and women. It was refurbished in 1976.

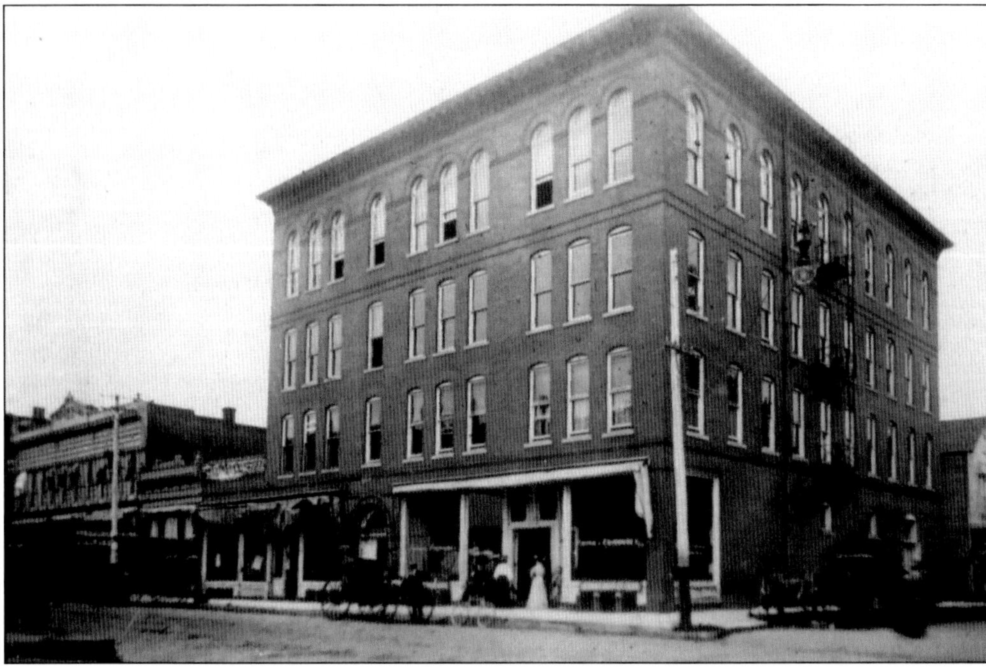

The first four-story block building in Macomb was constructed in 1898 just south of the square on Randolph Street by James Gamage, a local grocer. Most of the structure was devoted to office space, but from 1903 to 1905, the Central Preparatory School and Commercial College was located there, and from 1908 to 1919 the Macomb Conservatory of Music was housed there as well. In 1933, the building was purchased by the Masons, who met on the fourth floor, and since then it has been known as the Masonic Temple Building.

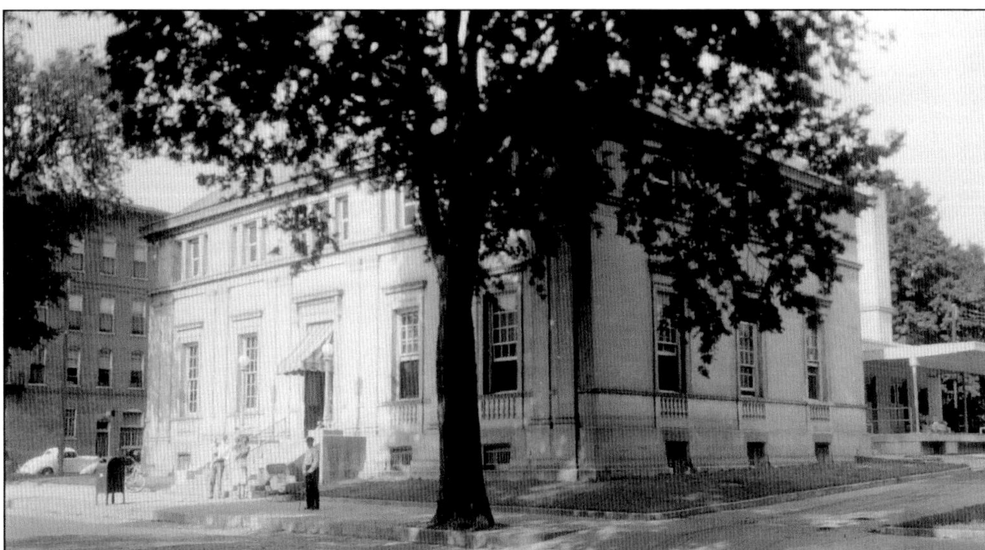

Just south of the Masonic Temple Building is the Macomb Post Office, which was erected during 1914 and 1915. A cornerstone ceremony was held on April 23, 1915, and the building opened on November 1. This photograph shows the limestone structure during the 1940s. It has had three additions, the most recent being the wing constructed in 1998.

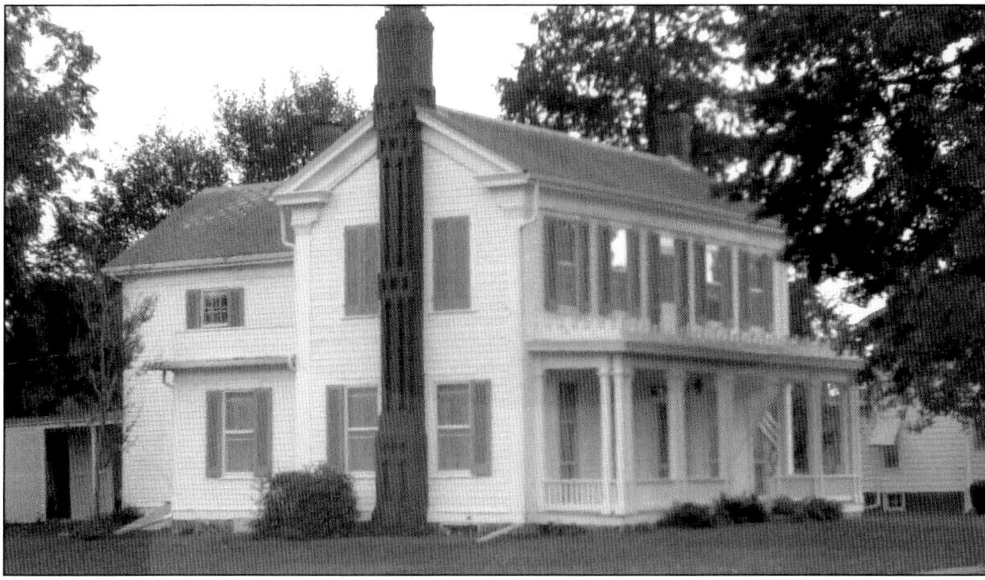

Macomb has a number of historic homes. One of the earliest is the white frame house at 423 E. Washington Street, which is now owned by Dr. and Mrs. Charles Weston. It was built in 1854–1855 by George W. Parkinson, and a wing was soon added by the second owner, Damon G. Tunnicliff, a noted lawyer and later, an Illinois Supreme Court judge. Local legend asserts that the home was a stop on the Underground Railroad, but so far there is no evidence that runaway slaves were ever hidden in the community.

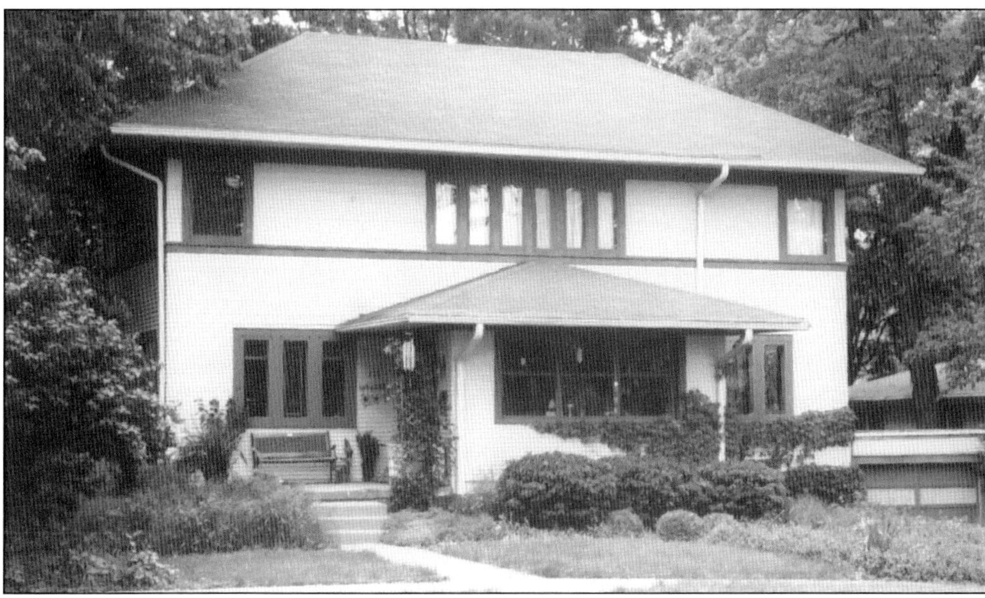

Built in 1918 by Western Illinois State Teachers College professor and athletic director Erskine Jay, this home at 216 N. Normal Street has an extensive yard that the second owner, Irving Garwood, planted as an Old English garden. The yard included an earthen stage, where Garwood's English students performed Shakespearean plays and British folk dances during the summer. By the early 1930s, the yard was known as "The Forest of Arden" and was a tourist attraction. The home is now owned by Dr. and Mrs. Donald Nelson.

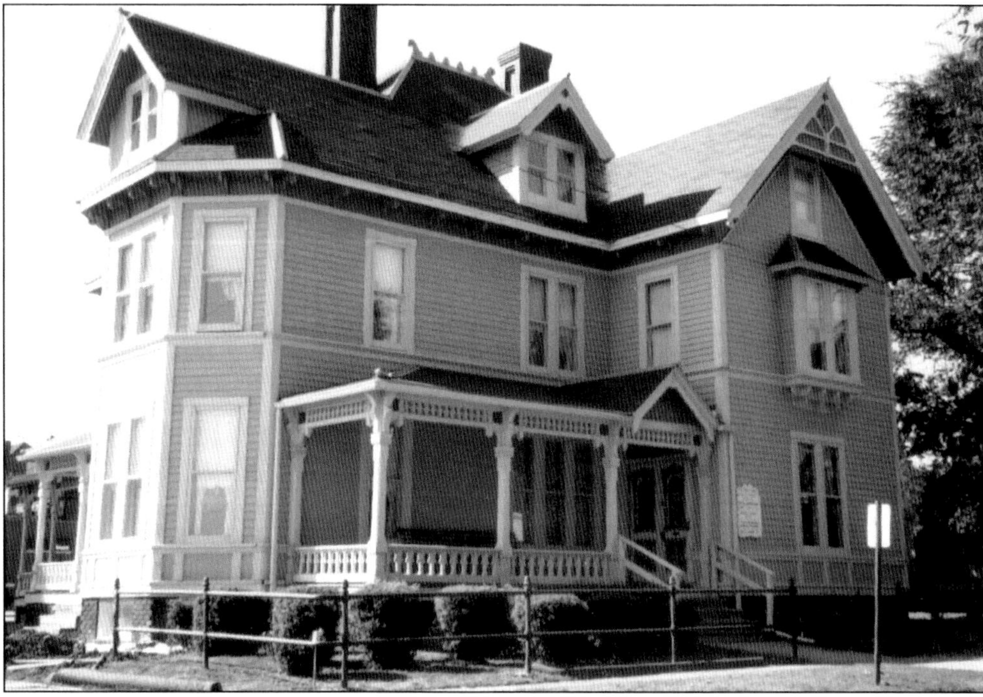

This photograph shows the Old Bailey House, a Victorian mansion located at 100 S. Campbell Street. Built in 1887 by W.S. Bailey, it was later the home of Harold Sullivan, a grocery store owner and, briefly in 1949, the Mayor of Macomb. In 1982, the McDonough County Historical Preservation Society was organized for the initial purpose of restoring the home, which was soon accomplished. The house has since served as a location for meetings and small gatherings.

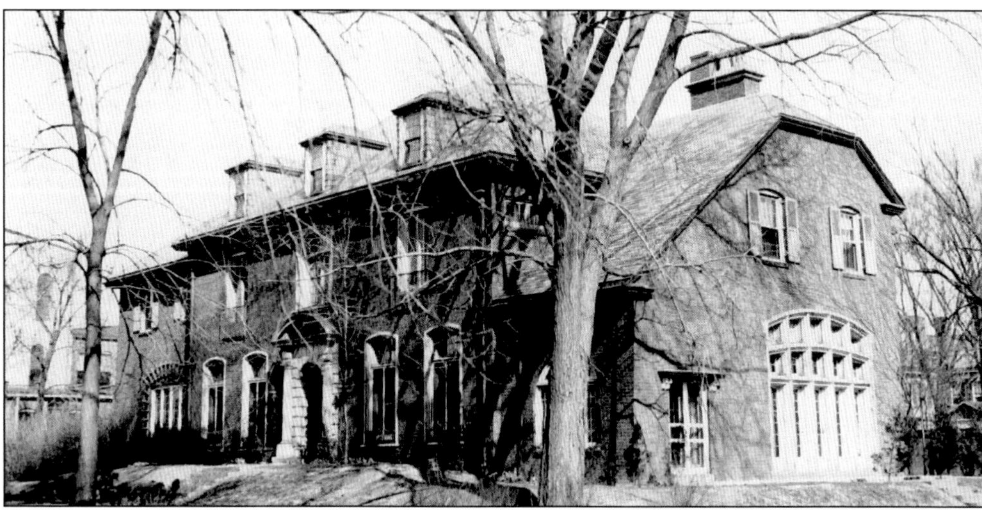

Built in 1919 just east of the square by Dr. and Mrs. Joseph Bacon, this home was probably the finest residence in Macomb and featured lovely gardens on the east side. After the Bacons died, the home became the Holland Clinic (1939–1943), then the Macomb USO (1943–1945), then a community building (1945–1949), and finally city hall (1949–present). Recently renovated and greatly expanded, it was rededicated on June 25, 2002. The building features dozens of oversized photographs of Macomb's heritage, as well as local art works.

Two

The Northwest Quarter of the County

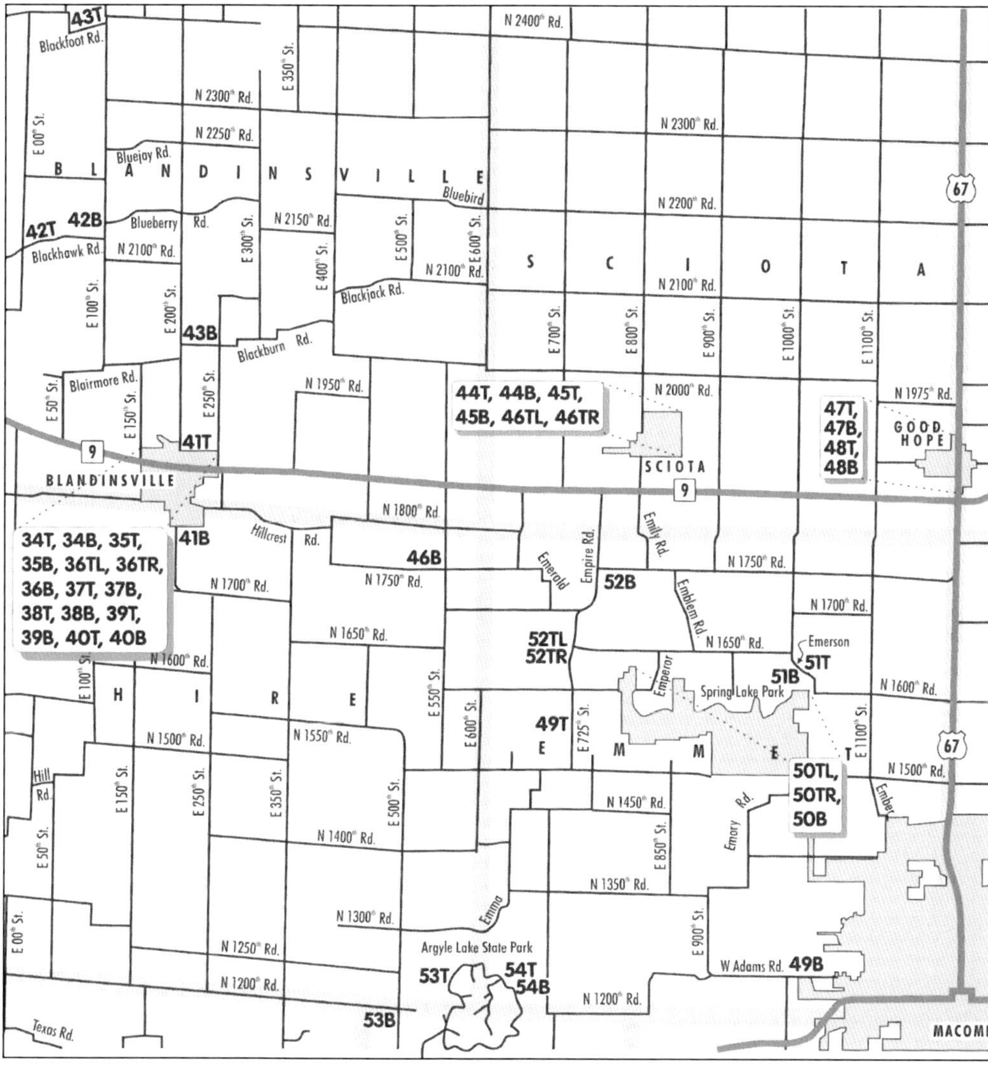

In the northwest quarter of McDonough County, the earliest community was Job's Settlement, established by William Job and others in 1826. That gathering of log cabins led to the platted town of Blandinsville. The only other communities came after the Civil War. Good Hope and Sciota were both laid out in 1867, when the Toledo, Peoria, and Warsaw (later Western) Railroad came through. All three towns became focused on shipping grain and livestock as farms multiplied, increased in size, and changed forever the prairie-and-timber landscape.

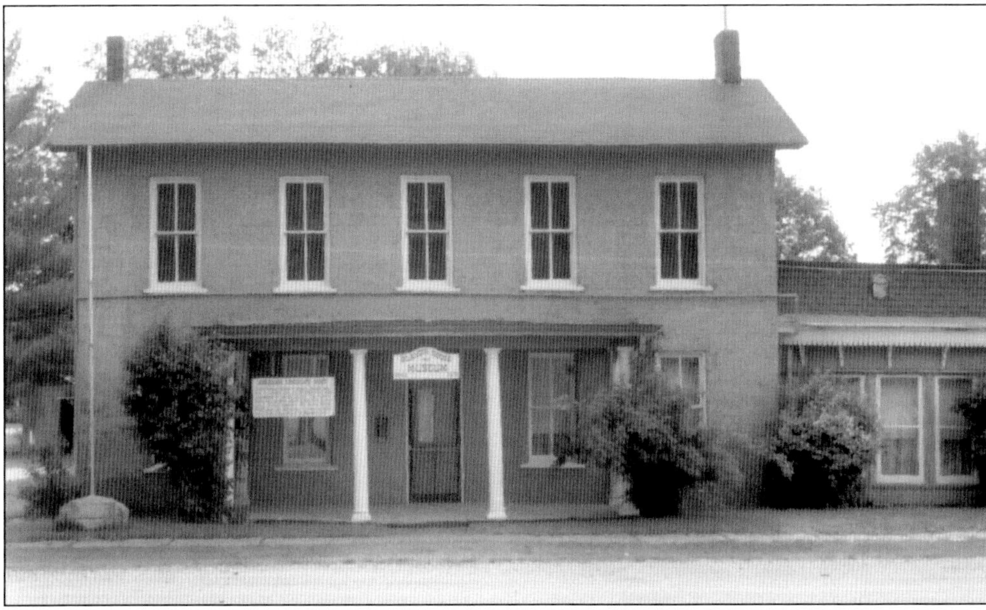

The town of Blandinsville was platted in 1842 by Joseph L. Blandin, a settler from Vermont who had come to Job's Settlement five years earlier. His brick home, built in the 1840s, stands on W. Chestnut Street, east of the city park. It was built with bricks that Blandin himself manufactured north of the railroad tracks. Since 1970, it has been the Blandin House Museum, which has photographs and other historical materials on display.

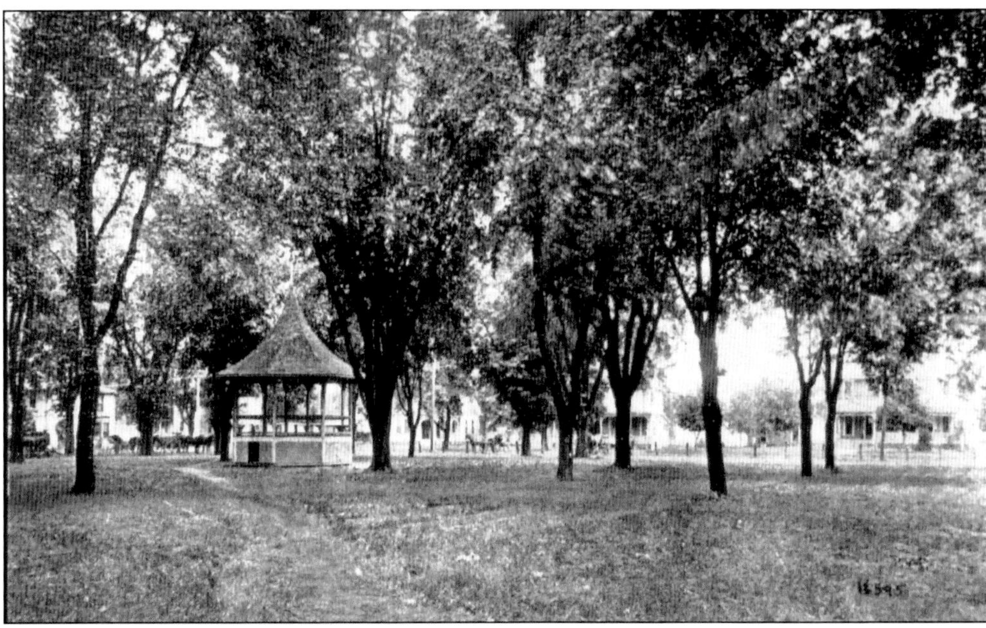

This postcard from the early 20th century shows the Blandinsville City Park. Once intended to be the town square, it was deeded to the community in 1902 by Winfield Scott Davis. During the early 20th century, the Blandinsville Band held concerts there. For the past century, the park has also been the location for the Blandinsville Farmers Picnic, which has been held every summer for 115 years.

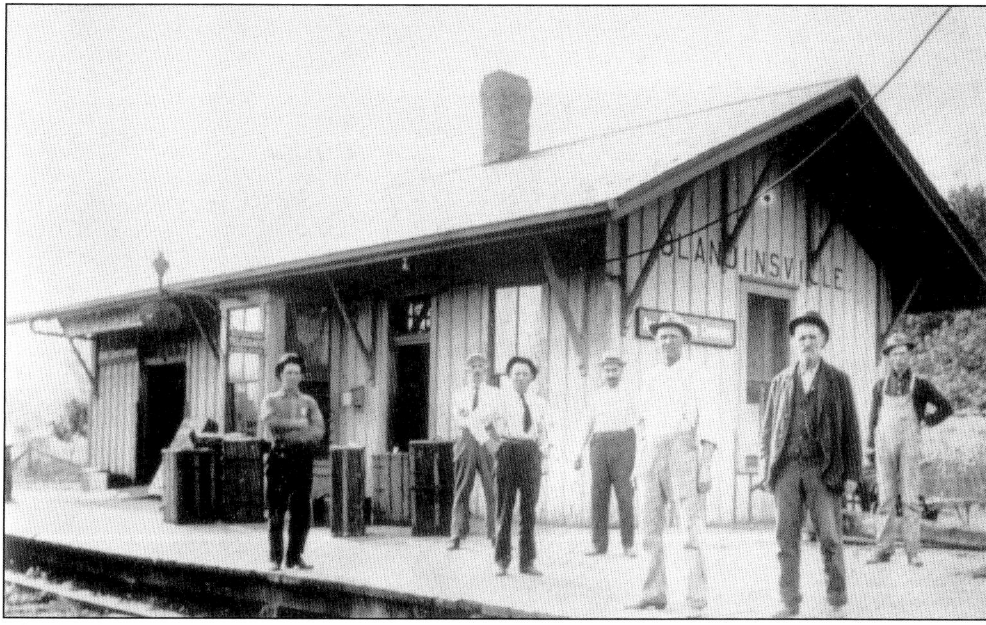

The development of Blandinsville was promoted when the Toledo, Peoria and Warsaw Railroad was constructed. It reached Blandinsville on October 25, 1866. During that postwar era, some brick stores were erected, and the town prospered as a farm center community. This image shows the Blandinsville depot in the early 20th century. It was located on the south side of the tracks, near the intersection with Bushnell Street.

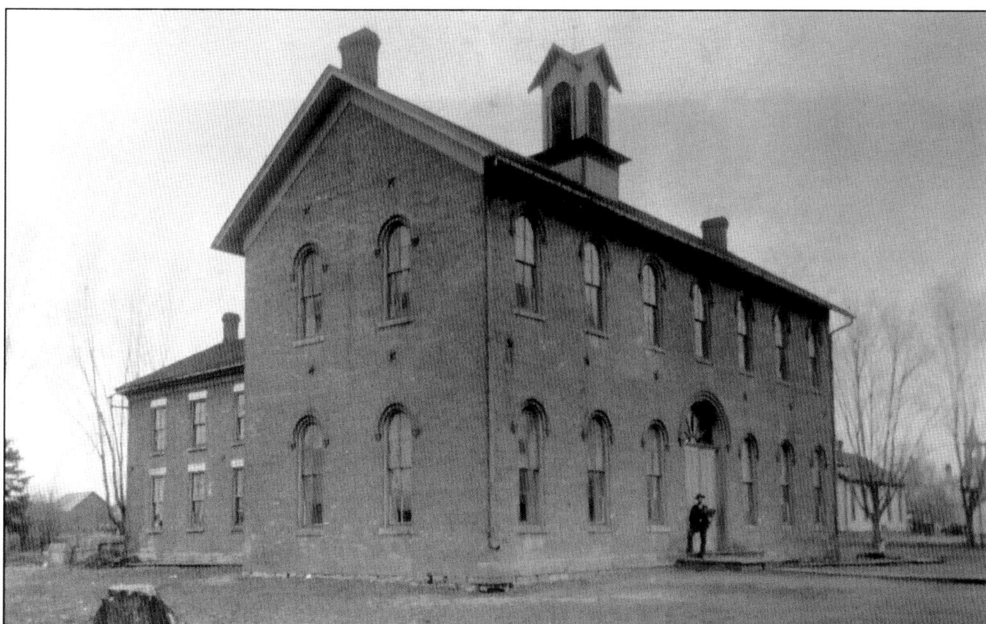

This photograph shows the old Blandinsville School, which was built by the United Brethren Church as a seminary in the mid-19th century. It had six rooms, and the high school classes were taught on the second floor. The building, which was torn down in 1905, was located one block west of Main Street, on the same land where the current high school now stands.

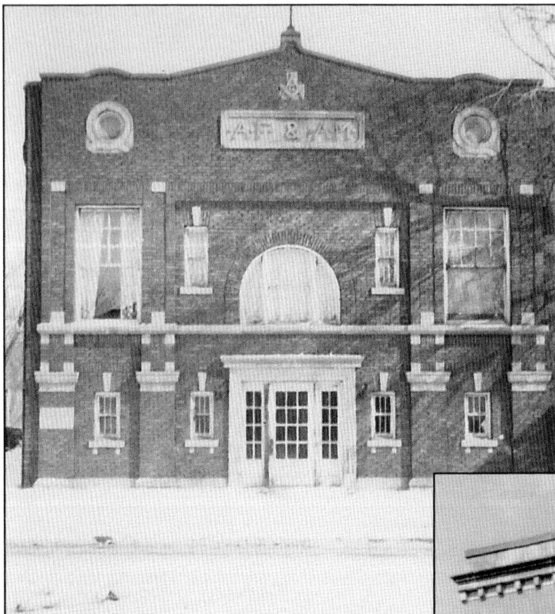

Two of the notable buildings on Blandinsville's Main Street are the Masonic Temple and the Union Bank. The temple was built in 1922, and the bank building, shown below, was constructed in 1913. At the time of construction, the latter housed the Huston Bank, which had been founded in 1895. The Blandinsville Masonic Lodge was established in 1857.

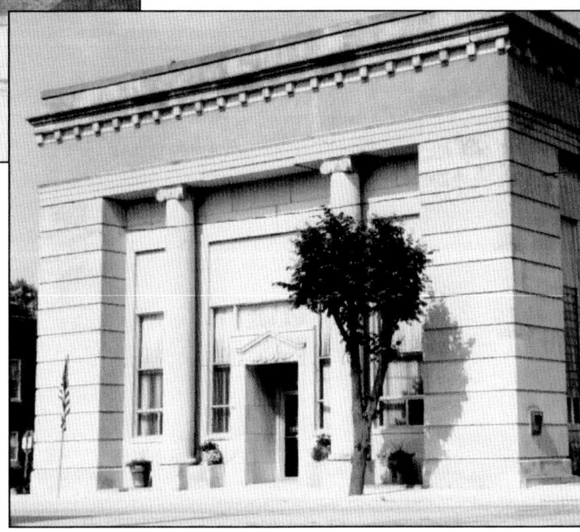

The early 20th-century photograph below shows the east side of Main Street, which was then a mixture of brick and frame shops. The building at the left was made of locally produced stone blocks. It was built in 1906 by E.E. Voorhees, a dealer in hardware, implements, and buggies. It is now occupied by a florist shop, My Sister's Place III.

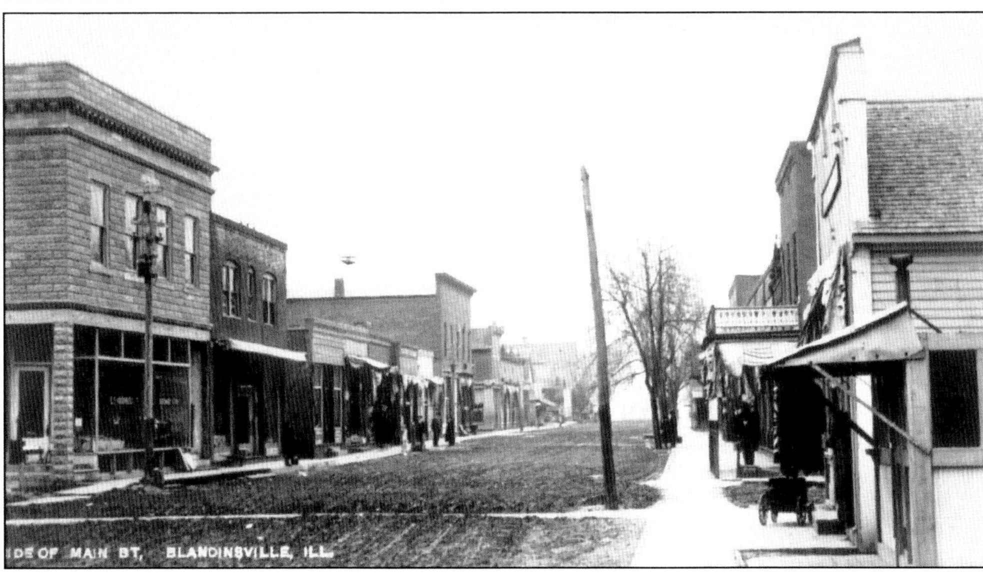

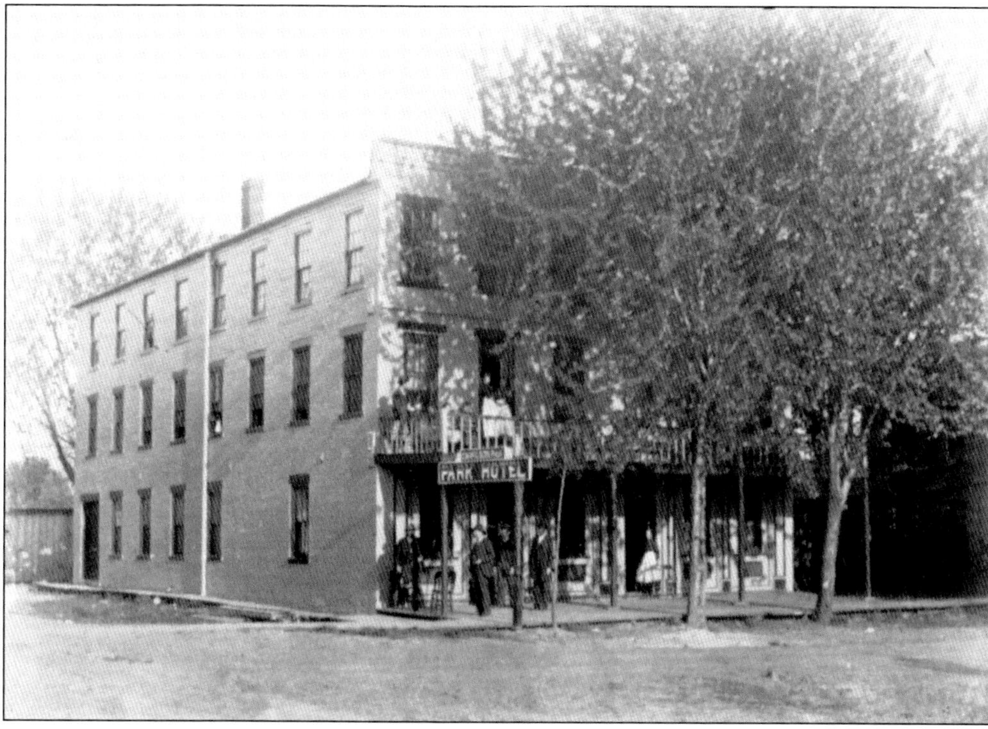

The Park Hotel was located east of the city park and north of the Blandin house. It was built by Thomas Davis in 1858. As the sign in this photograph indicates, the proprietor in the early 20th century was C.N. Wilson. The hotel was eventually torn down in 1914.

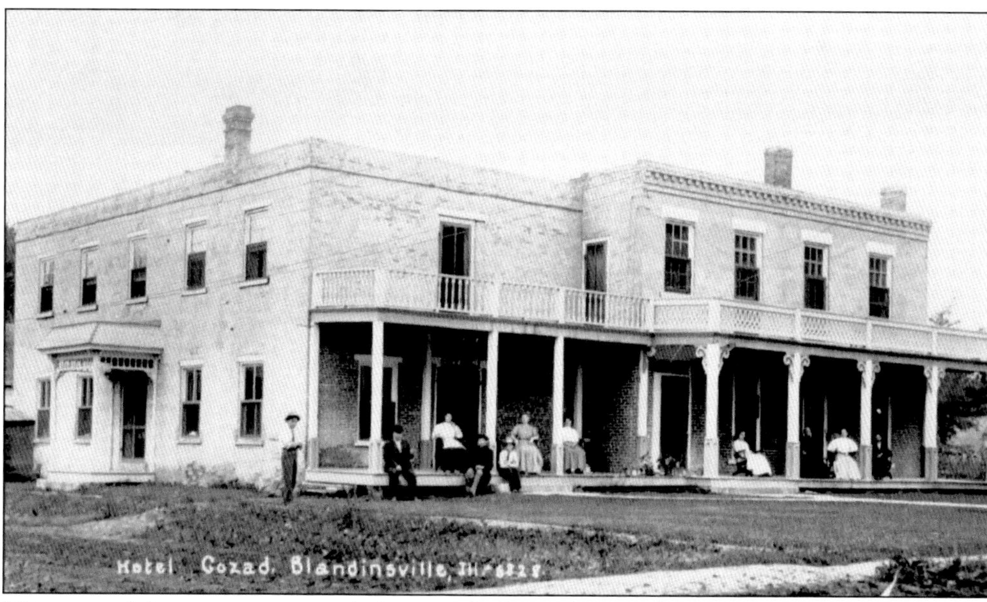

This turn-of-the-century postcard photograph shows the Hotel Cozad, with its long verandah, which was then owned by Martin W. Cozad. Originally known as the Meyers Hotel, the structure was built in the 1850s. Located on Main Street, it was later torn down, and the bricks were used to build the American Legion building, now the Hornbaker home.

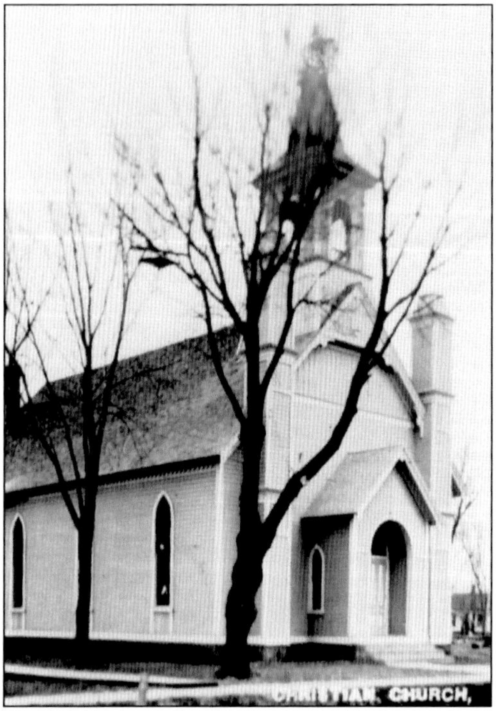

The Blandinsville Christian (Disciples of Christ) Church, located at 230 W. Washington Street, was originally a frame structure, as shown in this photograph. It was built in 1881 by a congregation that had been organized in 1849. The three-spired building was one of the most impressive examples of church architecture in 19th-century McDonough County.

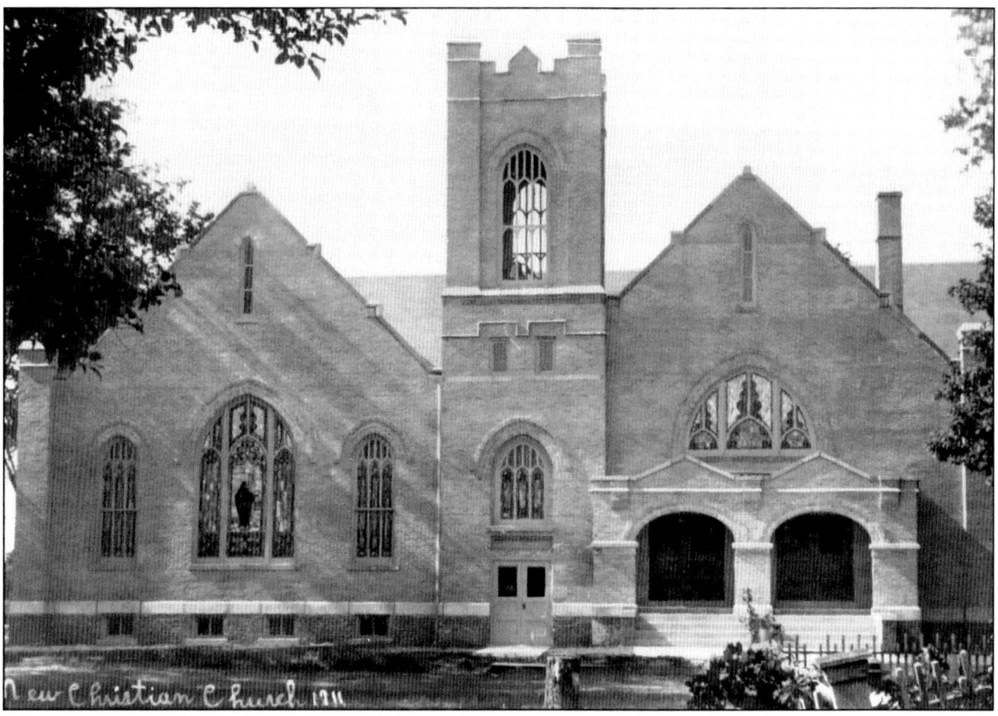

The current Christian Church, shown here on a 90-year-old postcard, was actually built around the old one in 1911. The left or west half of the brick building covered the framework of the 1881 church, and the right section was a new addition. The church has outstanding stained-glass windows. The large one at the left depicts the story of the widow's mite.

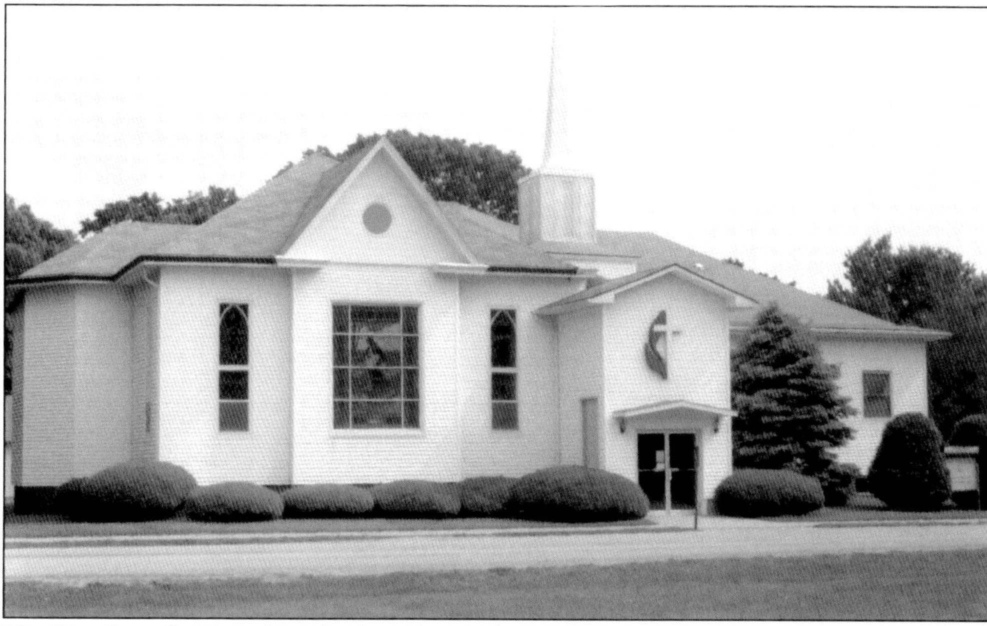

The Blandinsville United Methodist Church, located at the corner of Adams and Van Buren Streets, was built in 1878 and remodeled in 1906, when the stained-glass windows were added. The large window has an image of Christ the Sower. During the 1950s a fellowship hall, kitchen, and basement were added. The congregation was organized in 1848.

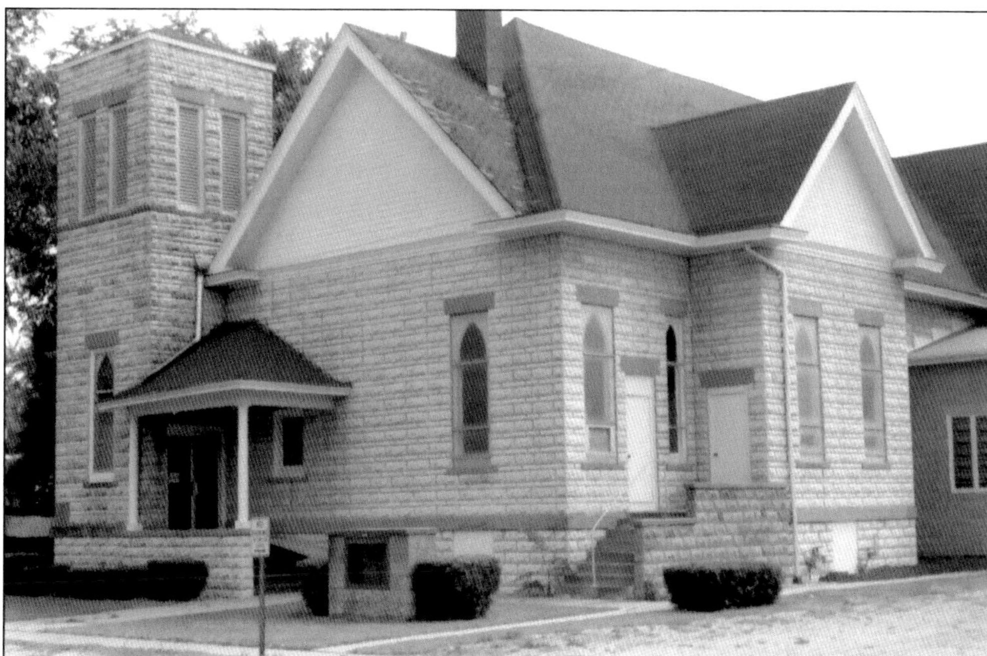

The Blandinsville First Baptist Church was organized in 1870, but its roots go back to the New Hope Baptist Church in Job's Settlement, founded in 1830. A frame church building was constructed on this site in 1872, and in 1909, it was incorporated into the cement block structure shown here. The church is located on Madison Street.

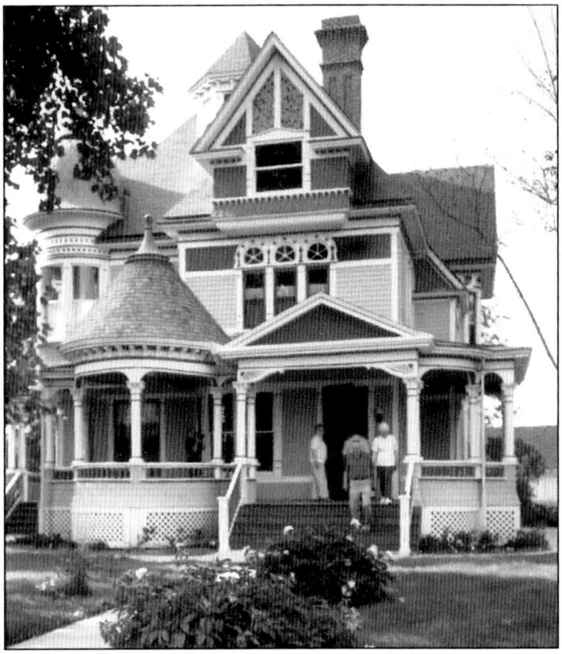

This outstanding Blandinsville residence, and one of the finest houses ever built in McDonough County, is the one now owned by Dr. and Mrs. Lawrence M. Kerr, located on Breckenridge Street. It was built in 1895 by lumber yard owner Frank Hicks, from plans drawn by George F. Barber and Co., a mail-order architectural firm in Knoxville, Tennessee. When the Kerrs acquired the building in 1989, it was in poor repair. They did extensive restoration, and this photograph shows visitors touring the renovated home.

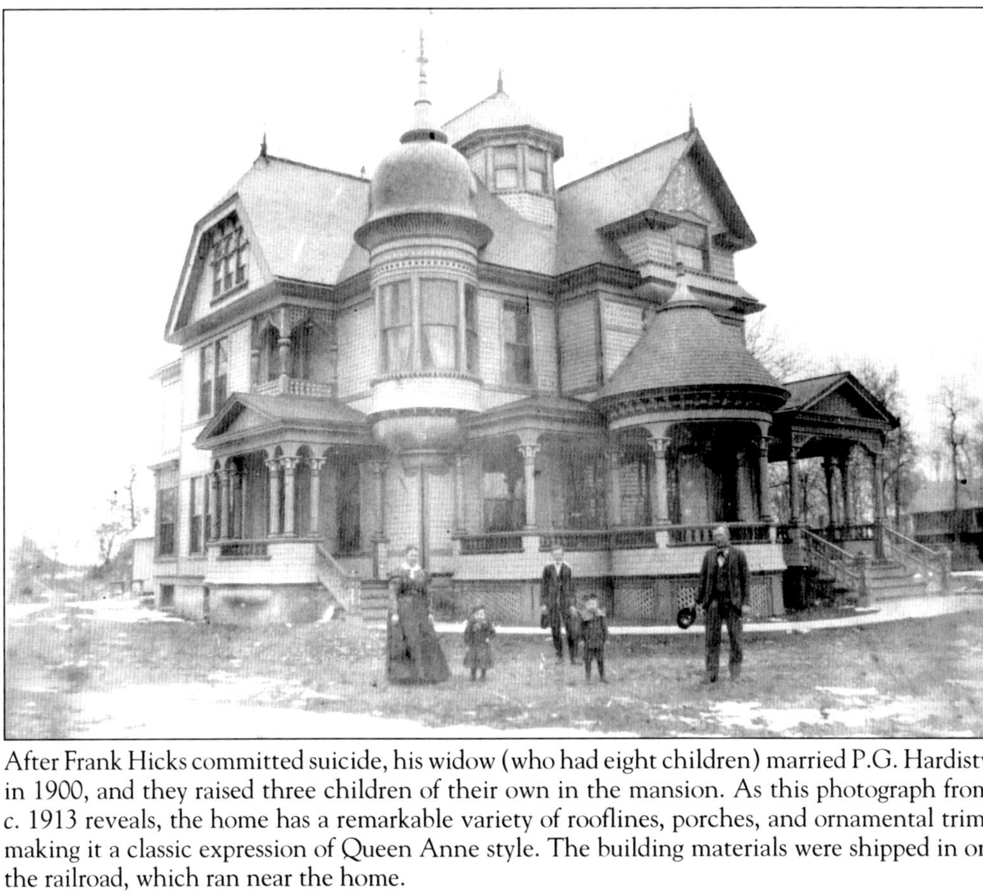

After Frank Hicks committed suicide, his widow (who had eight children) married P.G. Hardisty in 1900, and they raised three children of their own in the mansion. As this photograph from c. 1913 reveals, the home has a remarkable variety of rooflines, porches, and ornamental trim, making it a classic expression of Queen Anne style. The building materials were shipped in on the railroad, which ran near the home.

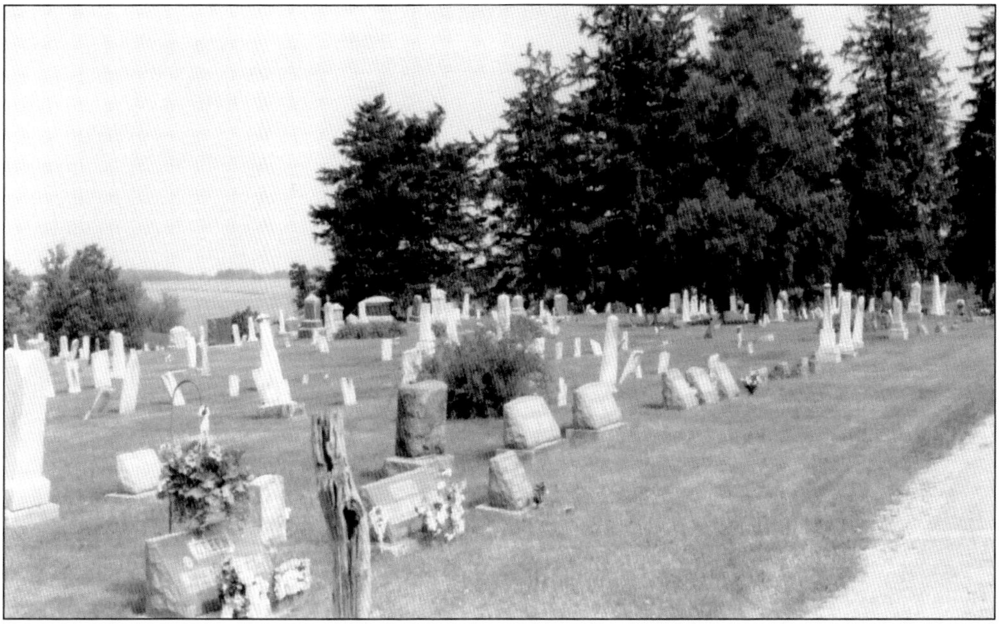

Blandinsville has two cemeteries of historic interest. One is the Glade City, or North, Cemetery, which has graves dating back to 1840. Included among them is that of Joseph L. Blandin, the founder of the community, who died in 1854. Located north of the railroad tracks, the cemetery has some 2,500 grave markers—far more than the town's total population today (800). This photograph shows the older section of the cemetery. "Glade City" was once a nickname for Blandinsville.

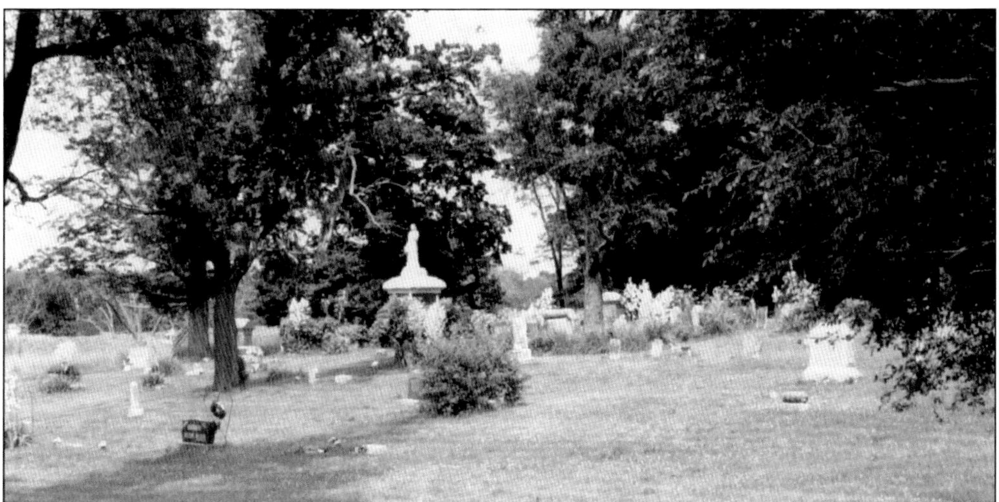

One half-mile south of Blandinsville is the New Hope, or Old South, Cemetery, which was established in 1837. It was developed in conjunction with the New Hope Baptist Church, once located there. Among the graves is that of Rev. John Logan, a noted pioneer minister who came to McDonough County in 1828. He moved to Job's Settlement in 1835 and died at Blandinsville in 1851. As this photograph shows, the lovely cemetery is dominated by the gravestone of Jacob and Catharine Hainline, which has a life-sized statue on a huge granite pedestal. The Hainlines owned an early farm in Hire Township.

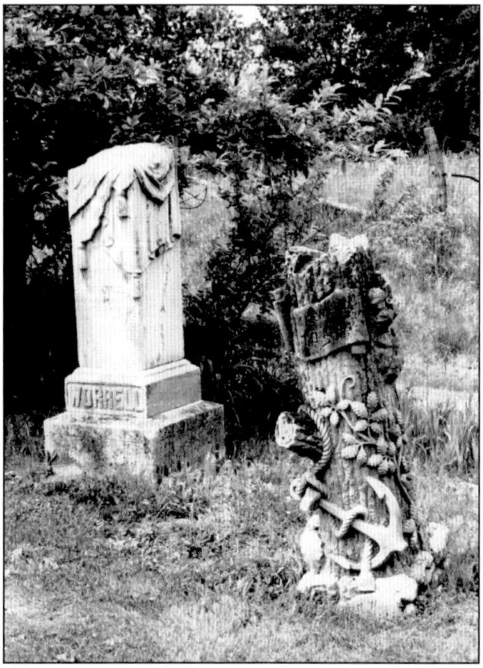

Wesley Chapel Cemetery, located at the intersection of roads Blackhawk Rd. and 00E, was developed in conjunction with a Methodist church, established there in 1848. The church is now gone, but the cemetery is still in use. Among the markers are these two, which are a study in gravestone symbolism. The shaft for Joshua Tipton Worrell, who died in 1890, is draped with a curtain, and on top of it is an open book—symbols of closure and God's plan as revealed in the Bible. On the right is the undated marker for Nathan W. Worrell. It is a tree stump with an anchor, signifying the death of living things and the security of being anchored in God. The banner simply offers a poignant good-bye: "Farewell to All."

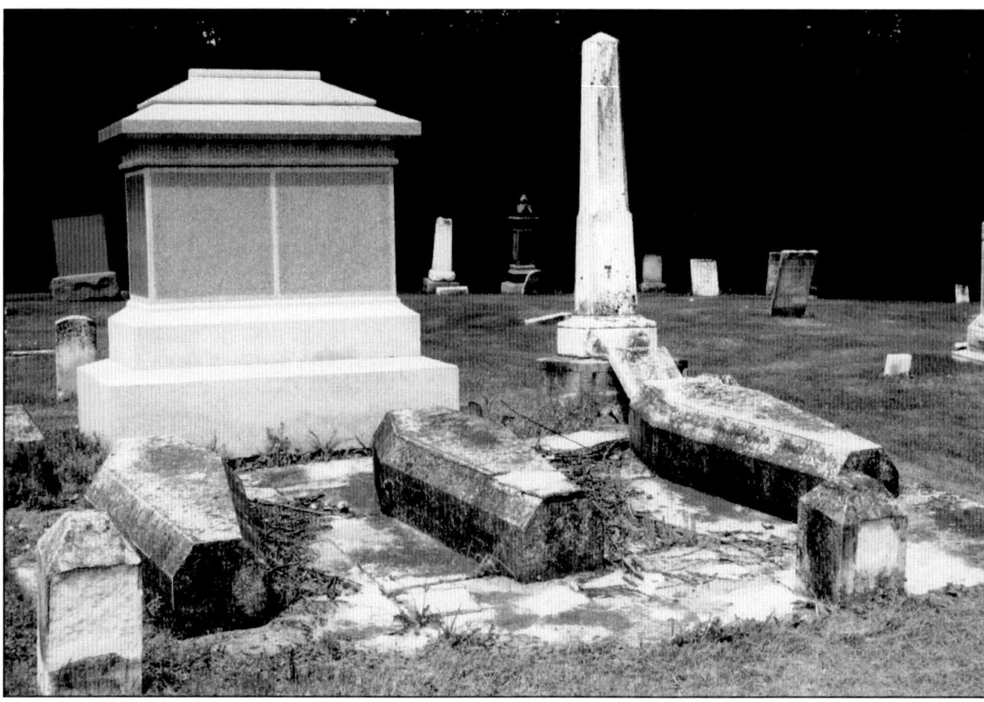

Just east of Wesley Chapel is Hillsborough Cemetery, at the intersection of roads Blueberry Rd. and 100E. A Baptist church built in 1850 was once located there, but again, only the cemetery remains. The most unusual grave markers are three coffin-shaped stones. The two at the left cover the graves of Edward and Mary Ann Wisslead, British immigrants who died in 1900 and 1886 respectively. The coffin stone at the right sits on the grave of Dinah Lawies, perhaps Mrs. Wisslead's mother, who died in 1878. The earliest gravestones at Hillsborough are from the late 1840s.

The Old Bedford Cemetery is in the northwest corner of the county on road Blackfoot Rd. It is associated with the Old Bedford Christian Church, organized in 1850. The present church building, erected in 1922, is a mile or so east of the cemetery. Three tall shafts for members of the Wassom family (John, wife Mary, and son Cyrus) tower over the small burial ground and tell a story of grief. Mary lost her husband, a wealthy farmer, on December 15, 1879, and five months later, her 35-year-old son died. On his marker she inscribed her sense of loss: "Tho' thou art gone, / And thy fair form lies mold'ring / In dust, still, dear son, / Fond memory clings to thee." She died two years later.

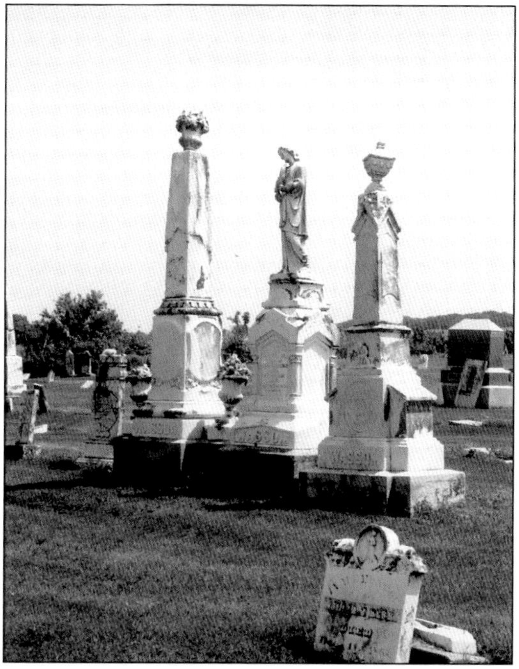

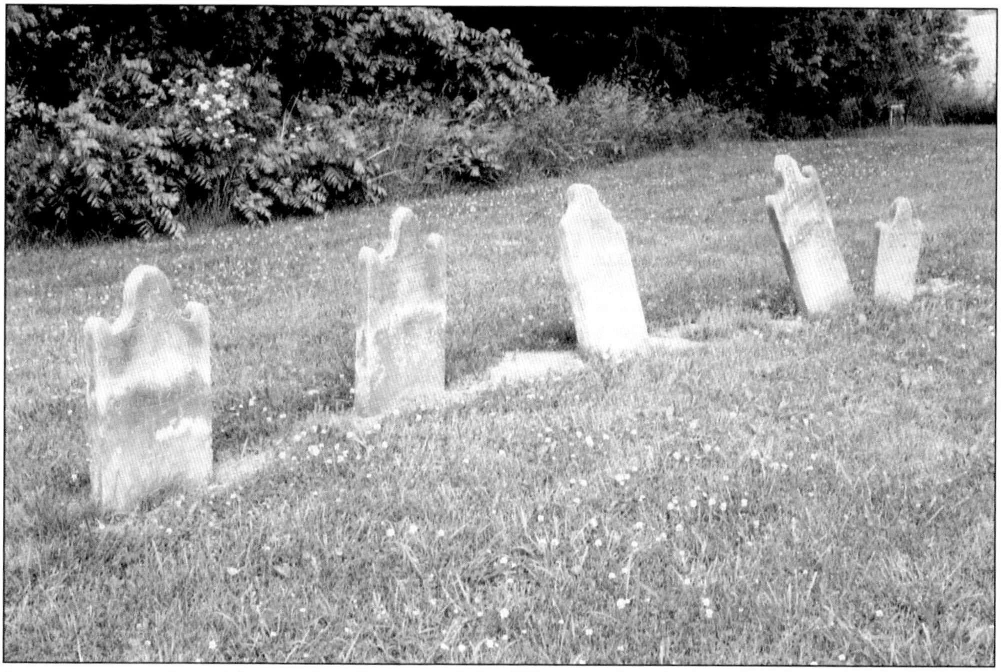

In contrast to the elaborate headstones of the Wassom family are these simple, headboard-shaped markers for the Vance family, located in Liberty Cemetery, between roads 200E and 250E, two miles north of Blandinsville. At the left is the marker for Nancy Vance, who died in 1841, and most of the others are for her children, who died before she did. The marker on the right is especially unusual: "In memory of / three twin sons / of John & Nancy / Vance born & died / June the 2d, 1832." The pioneers had no word for triplets—nor any way to save them. That triple death started this very old burying ground.

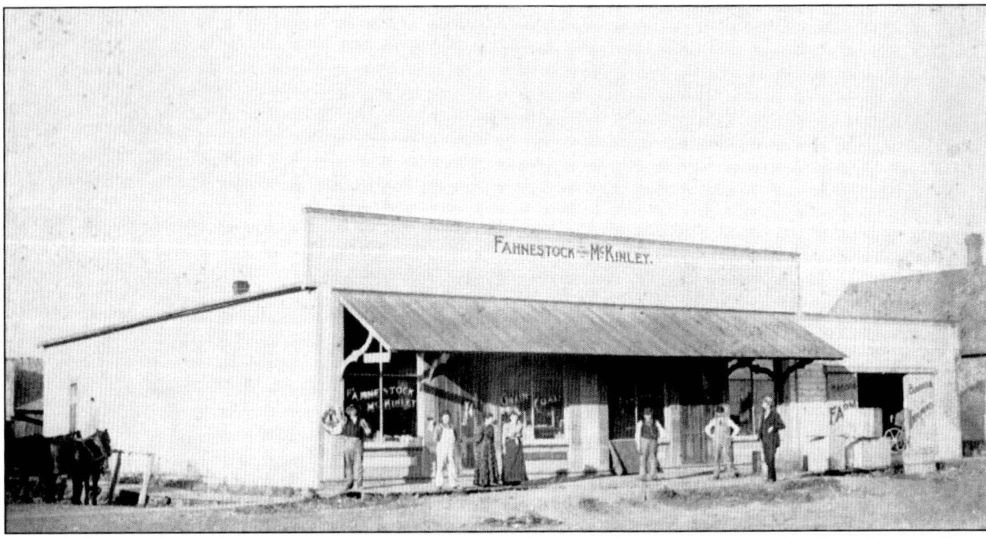

Established in 1867, Sciota was originally called Clarkesville in honor of the founder, William Clarke. It was platted along the Toledo, Peoria and Warsaw Railroad tracks, which had just been laid. Perhaps the biggest early business was C.D. Elting and Company, which sold groceries, hardware, and agricultural implements, and also bought and shipped grain. In 1884, that company built the largest store in town on Main Street. It was later sold to Charles Fahnestock and William McKinley and is shown in this photograph.

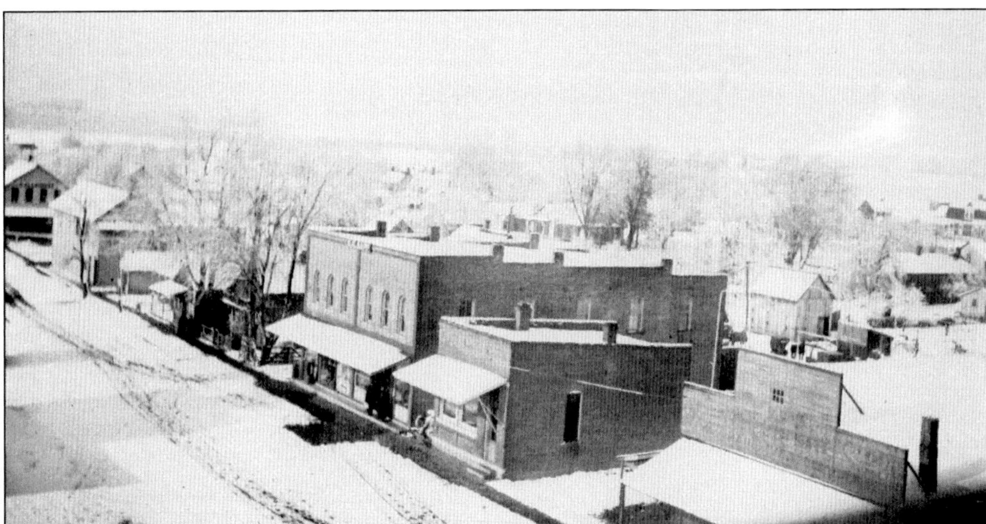

This winter image of Sciota shows E. Douglas Street looking west in the early 20th century, when the town had more than 300 residents. The large building in the center is E.E. Sapp's general store, and the smaller brick building to the right of it is the Sciota National Bank. Sapp also operated one of Sciota's three grain elevators, located across the street. In the lower right is George Elmer Bryan's store, established in 1912 in an old Christian church building, where the post office was also located until that building burned in 1931.

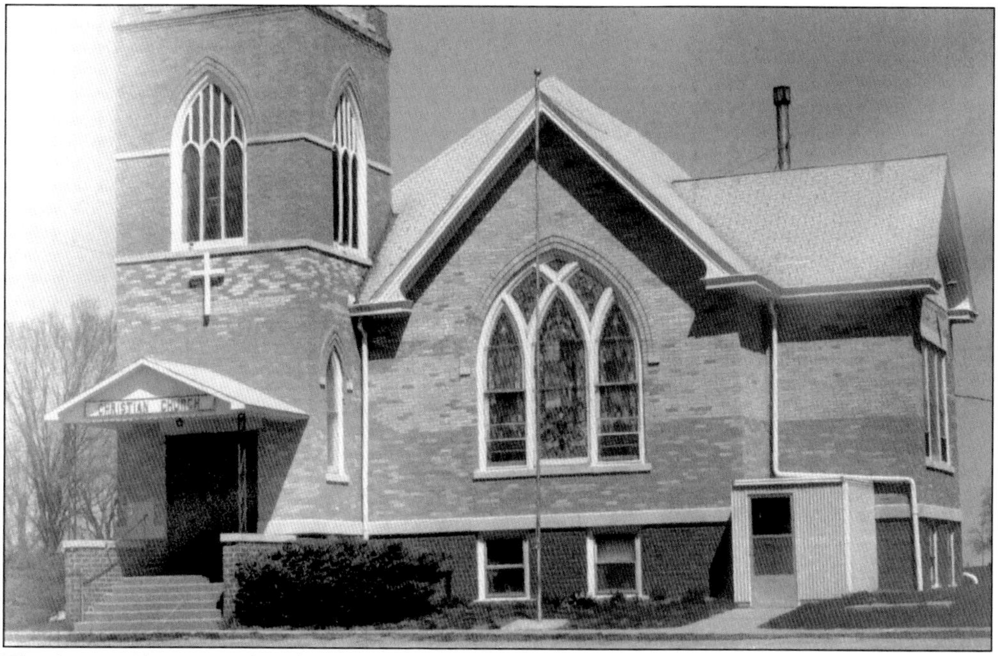

The Sciota Christian Church was organized in the 1850s at Walker Schoolhouse, near Walker Cemetery, but the meeting place was moved to Sciota in 1869, where the congregation built a frame church. The brick building shown here was erected at the corner of Buel and Seymour Streets in 1912, and an educational unit was added in 1961. Originally a Disciples of Christ congregation, the church has been an independent New Testament Christian group since 1968.

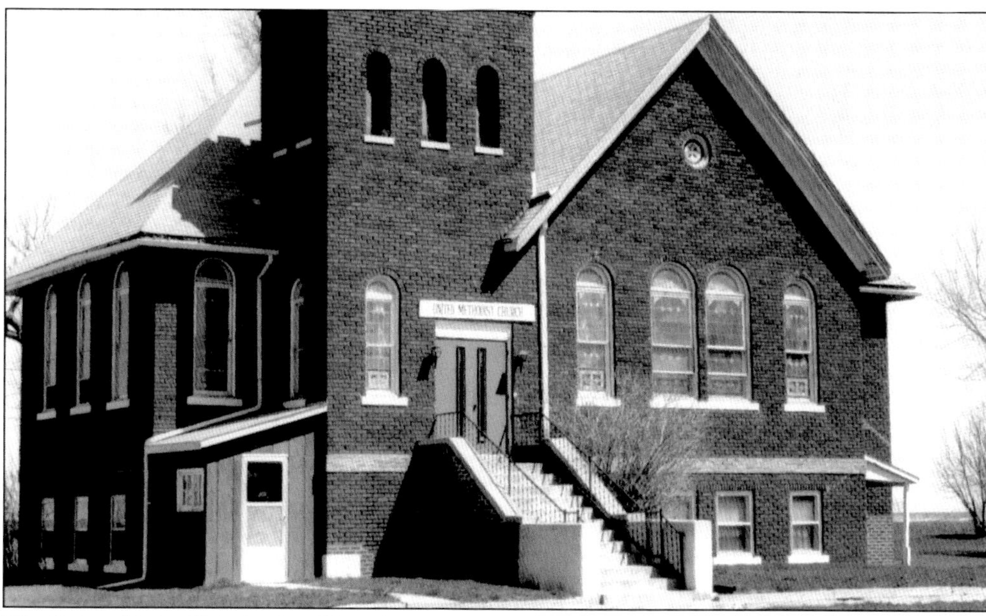

The Sciota United Methodist Church was organized in 1883, and the congregation met initially at the local Odd Fellows Hall. In 1887, they built a small frame church building, and in 1919, that structure was replaced by the brick one shown here, which cost $11,000. It was located on Seymour Street. That church was closed in 1999 and the building was razed.

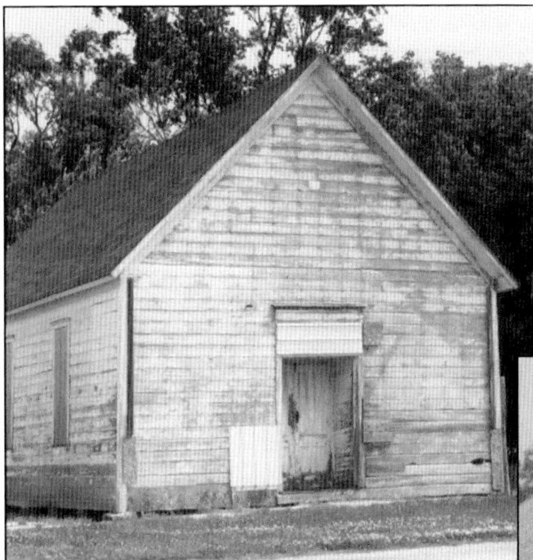

Two of the older frame buildings in Sciota are the town hall, shown at the left, and the post office, shown below. The town hall, erected by Henry Crane on E. Douglas Street in 1893, is no longer used, but the post office is. Located on Main Street, it was built in 1898 to be the office of Dr. R.F. Marrs, and it became the post office during the early 1930s. Since 1976, it has been a contract station of the Blandinsville Post Office.

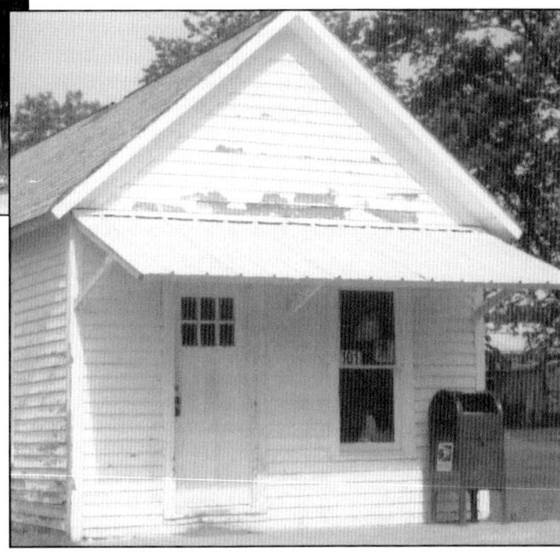

Organized in 1869, the Willow Grove United Brethren Church congregation erected a building in section one of Hire Township, at the intersection of roads 1750N and 550E. That 1872 structure was later replaced with the one in this photograph, which was dedicated in 1915. When the church later dissolved, the building was remodeled into a home for the George Mueller family.

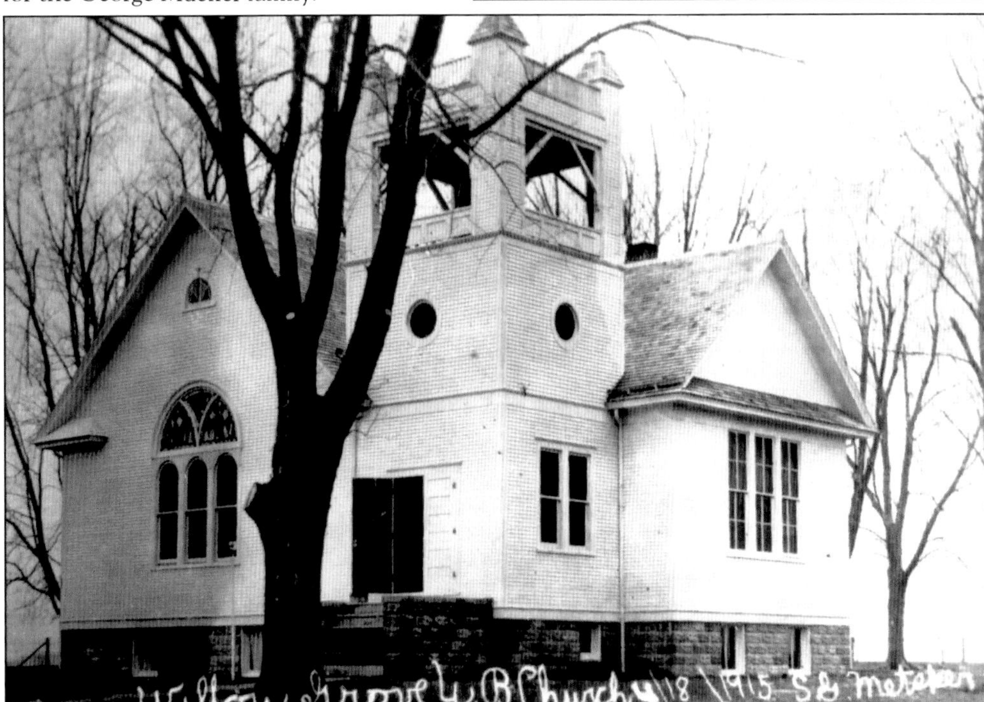

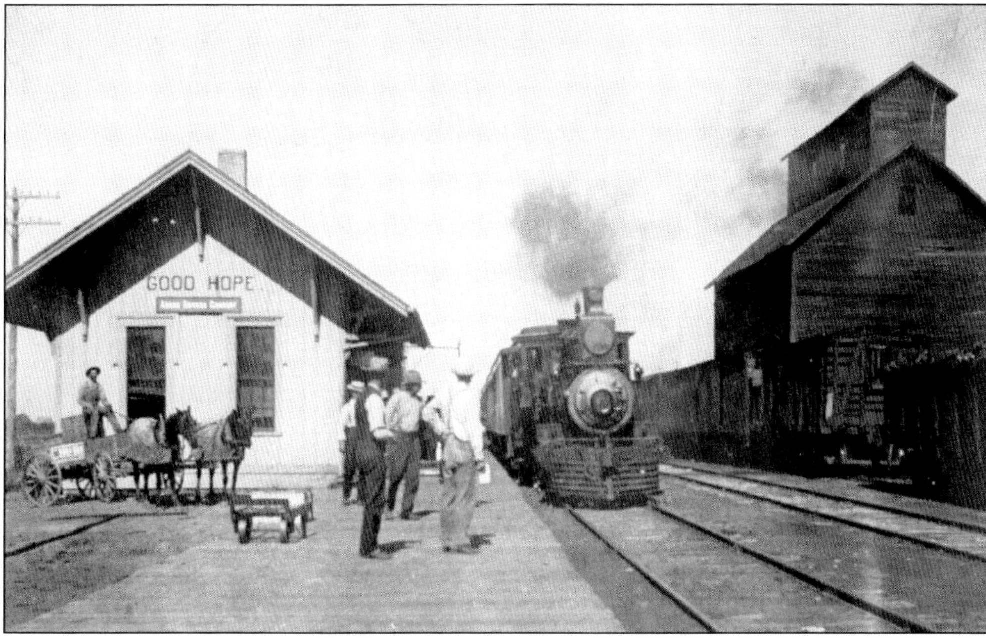

Like Sciota, Good Hope was platted along the Toledo, Peoria and Warsaw Railroad tracks in 1867 and was a shipping point for grain. This photograph shows the Good Hope depot and, across the tracks, a large grain elevator that was built in 1879. (An earlier one on that site was destroyed by fire.) The name "Good Hope" comes from an early post office, established in that area in 1858.

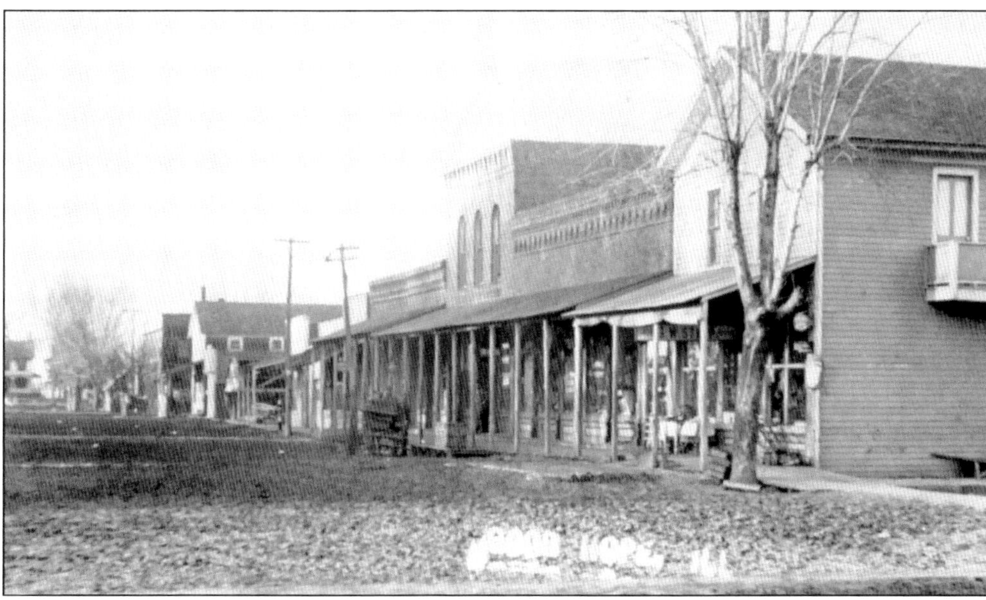

The business district of Good Hope was primarily on Chestnut Street, facing west toward the park. As this 1919 photograph reveals, there were a number of brick and frame shops, all with awnings to keep off the afternoon sun. Most of the businesses were either general stores or dry goods stores, although the town once had a furniture store, a lumber yard, and an automobile dealership as well.

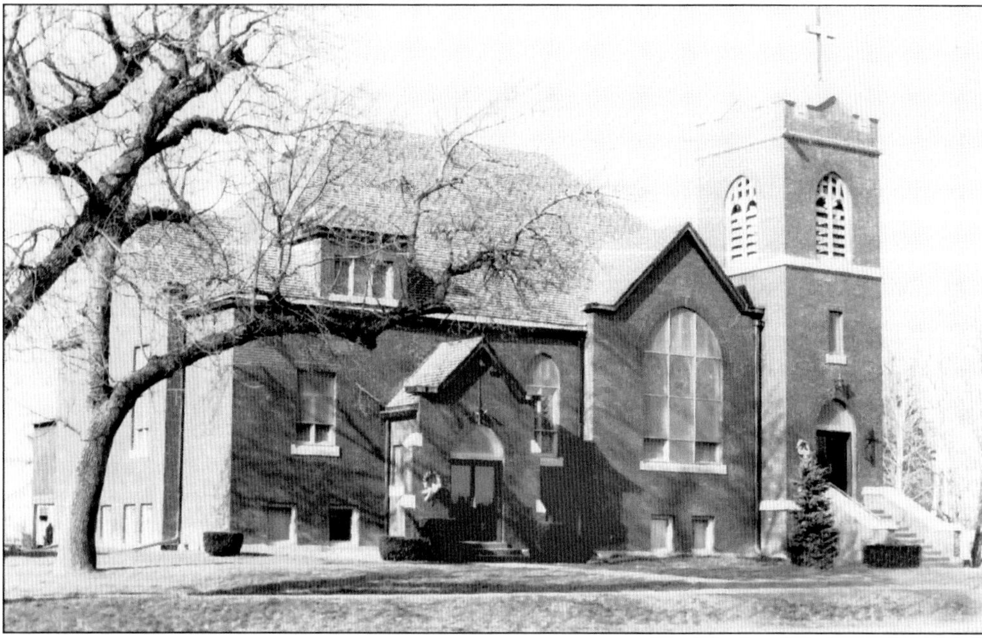

The Good Hope United Methodist Church was organized in 1866, northwest of where the village was later platted. When the town got started, the church building was moved there. In 1909, that structure was replaced by the present church building, shown here, which is located at 300 W. Main Street.

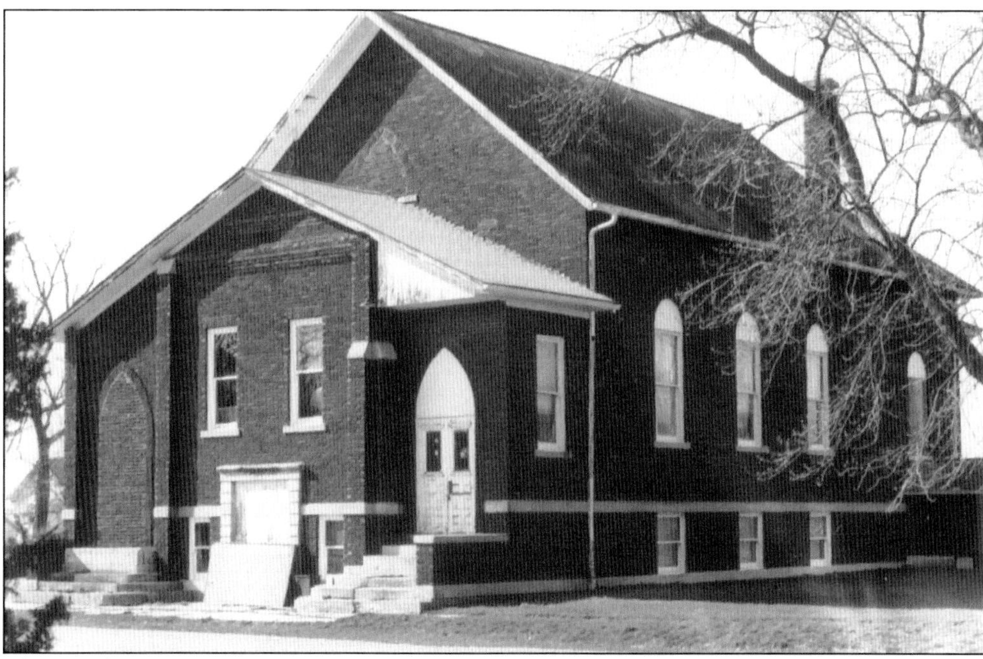

The Good Hope Presbyterian Church was organized in 1869, and a frame church building was erected at the corner of Ash and State Streets. That building was destroyed by fire in 1918, and the brick structure shown in this photograph was constructed on the same site. It was dedicated in 1921. The congregation disbanded in about 1937.

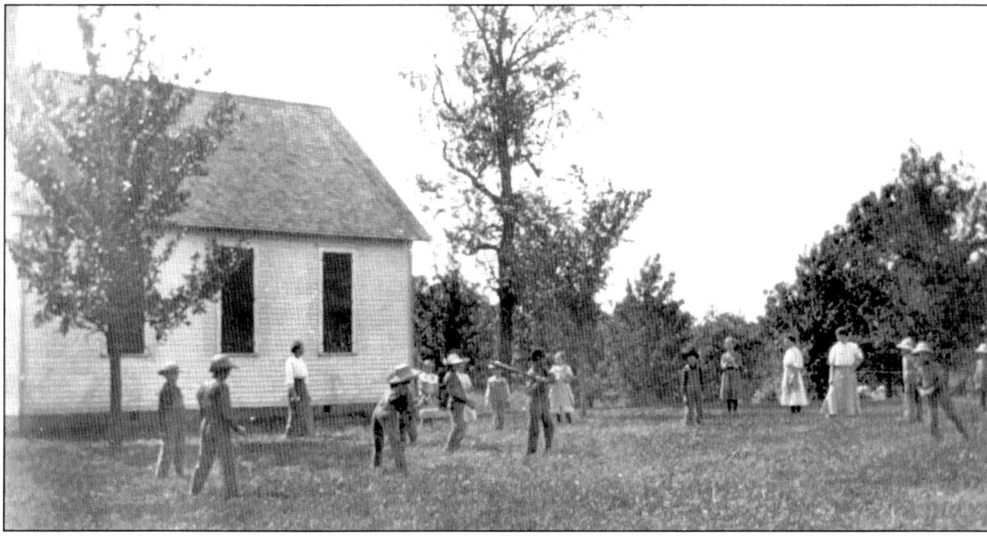

McDonough County had dozens of rural schools. One named Muddy Lane, in section 19 of Sciota Township, was named for a now-vanished frontier settlement. A frequently photographed school is Oak Grove or Guy School, shown here, which was located on the west side of section 17 in Emmet Township, on road 725E. The building was erected during the Civil War, in 1863. This 1910 photograph shows a baseball game at recess.

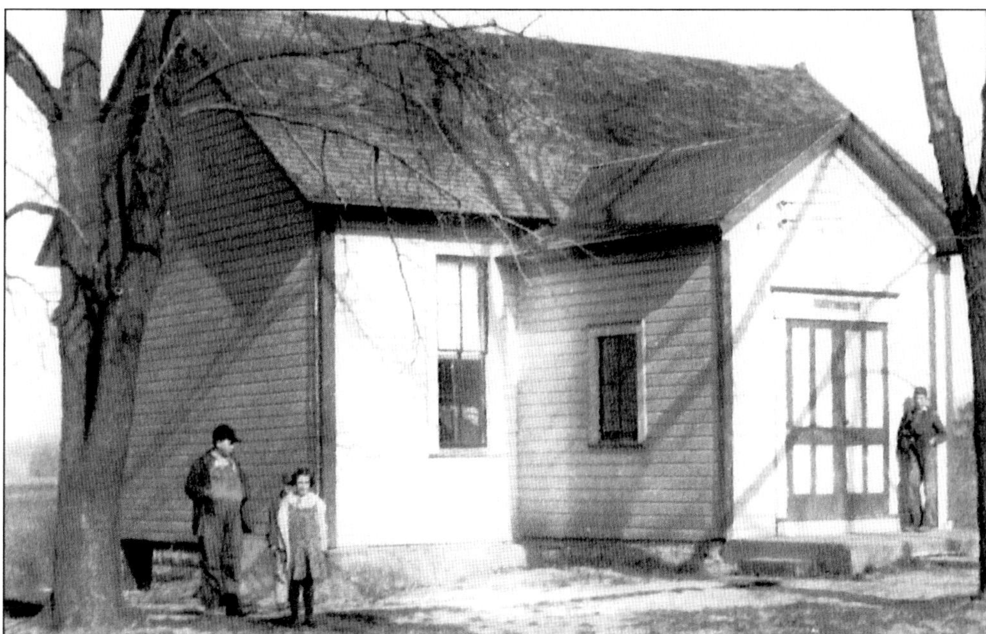

The Brickyard School, located one and a half miles west of Macomb and named for the nearby brickyard of James Chase, became a widely-known institution. Under President Alfred Bayliss, Western Illinois State Normal School had a strong focus on country school education, so in 1906 he agreed to supply a superb teacher, Mabel Carney, if the district officials would modernize their school building. They did so, and the result was a "model country school," which drew hundreds of visitors.

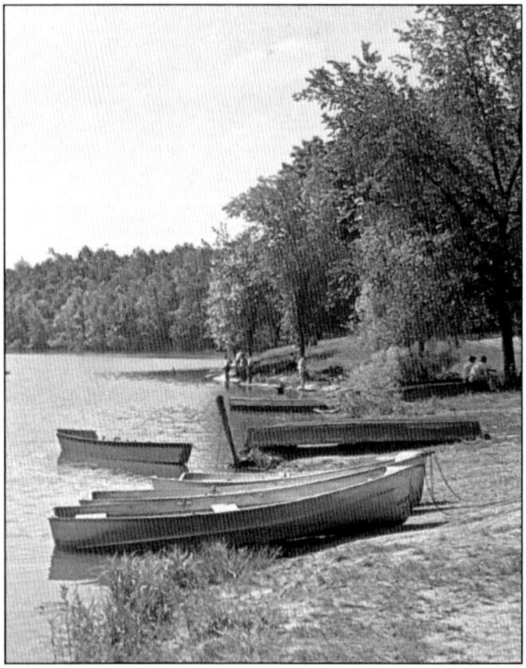

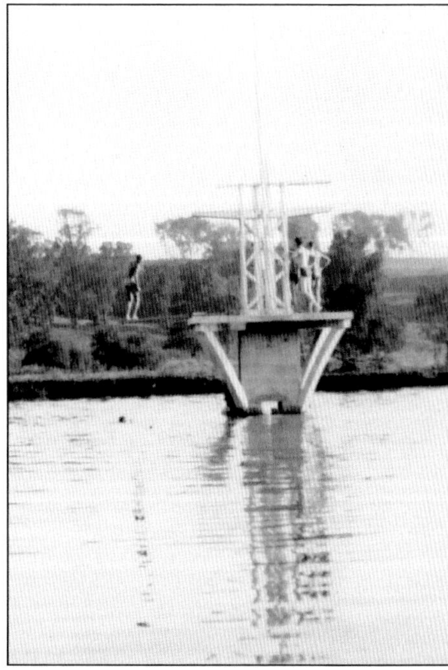

In response to water shortage problems, the City of Macomb purchased 250 acres along Spring Creek in Emmet Township, and in 1927, created a reservoir known as Spring Lake. A park was established there in 1929, and a new road was developed from Macomb to the lake. One photograph above shows boats at the lake in about 1930, and the other shows a swimming pool that was created by damming a section of the lake in 1933.

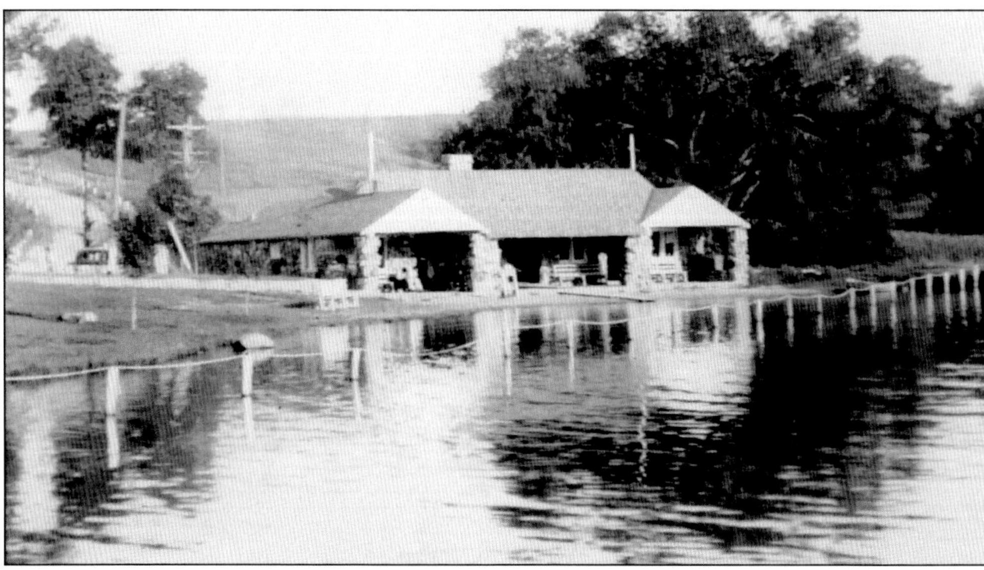

Various improvements were made at Spring Lake during the later 1930s by the CCC (Civilian Conservation Corps) and the WPA (Works Progress Administration). Among those was the creation of a fieldstone shelter house, shown in this photograph, at the foot of the entrance road to the park. When the lake was expanded in 1968, the shelter house was submerged. The lake now covers 200 acres in the 900-acre park.

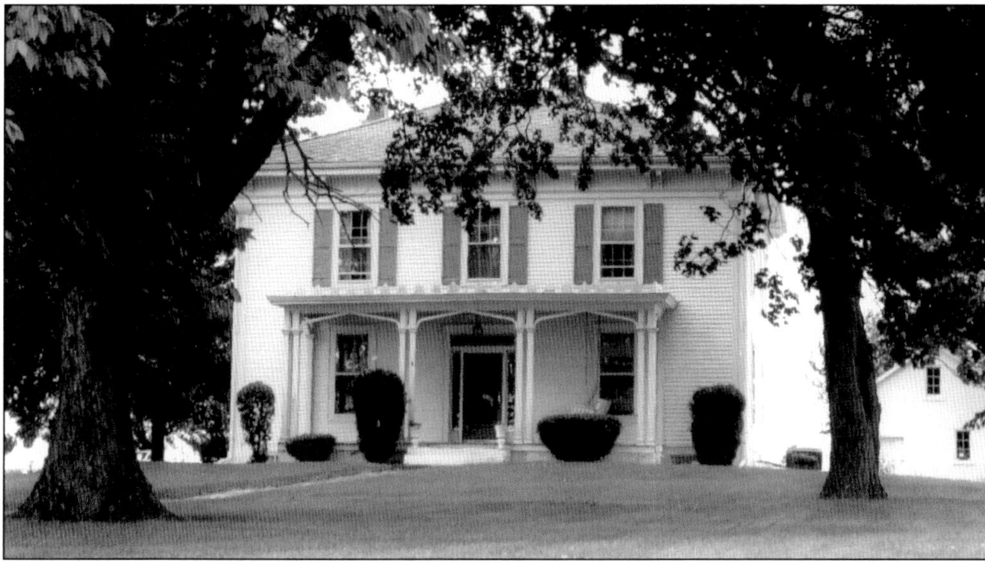

Abram Stickle, who had been born in Pennsylvania in 1787, came to Emmet Township in 1837 and built a two-story farmhouse there three years later. Located on the old Burlington Road (now Emerson Road), halfway between Beardstown and Burlington, his farm provided a stopping place for teamsters and became known as the Half-Way Farm. In 1866, Stickle built a second, larger home just southeast of the earlier one. That home, shown here, is now owned by Mr. and Mrs. Gilbert Peterson.

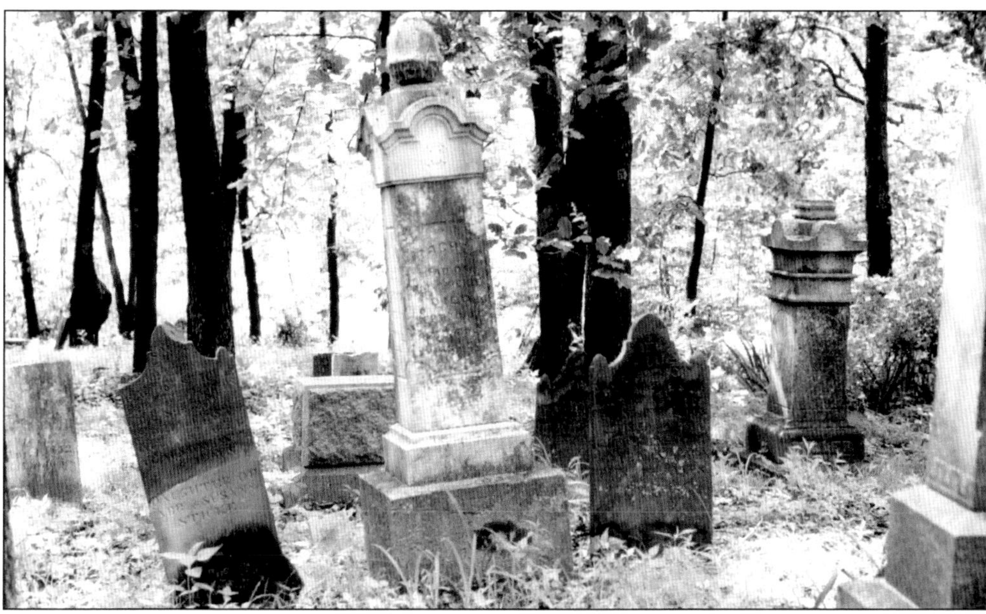

The Stickle Cemetery, three miles northwest of Macomb on Emerson Road, was started in 1839 when settler Abram Stickle lost both his 18-year-old daughter Rachel and his wife Susanna a few days apart on September 30 and October 2. Their headstones, at the left and right of the shaft that marks his death in 1872, even include the hour when they died, at "2 o'clock p.m." The well-engraved, headboard-style markers were probably the work of pioneer stone carver John Long. The cemetery was located southeast of the Stickle Methodist Episcopal Church.

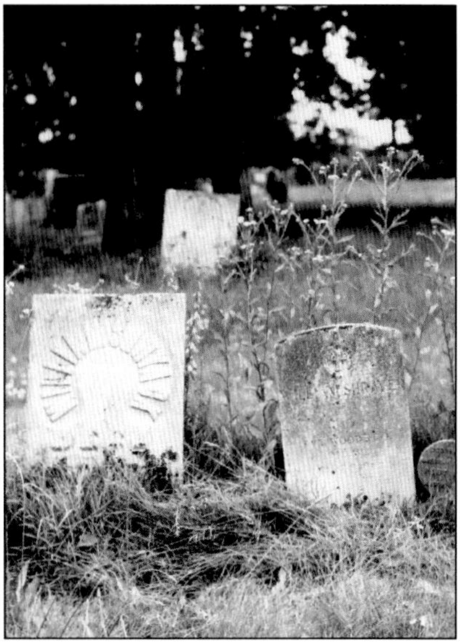

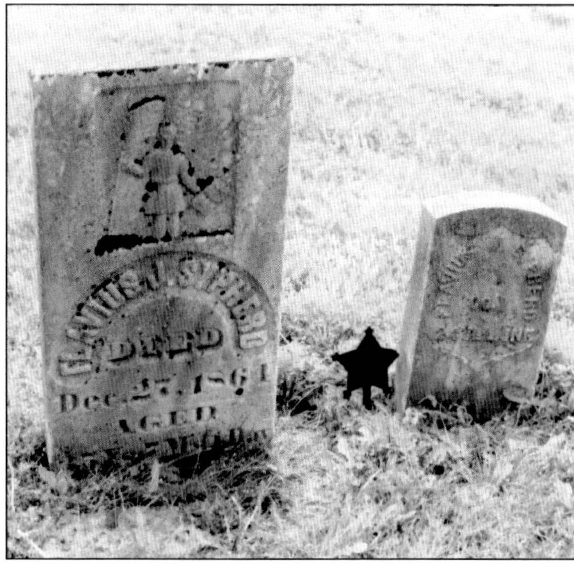

West of Spring Lake, near the intersection of roads 1650N and 725E, is the Walker Cemetery, on a hilltop where the Walker School was also once located. The cemetery was established in 1853, and among the burials are two War of 1812 soldiers. The left photograph shows the two markers for William Shryack, who served in the 1st Maryland Militia, and behind them is the headstone of William Wood, who served in the 2nd Ohio Militia. The other photograph shows the markers for one of the six Civil War veterans interred there: Flavius J. Sypherd of the 24th Illinois Infantry, who died in 1864.

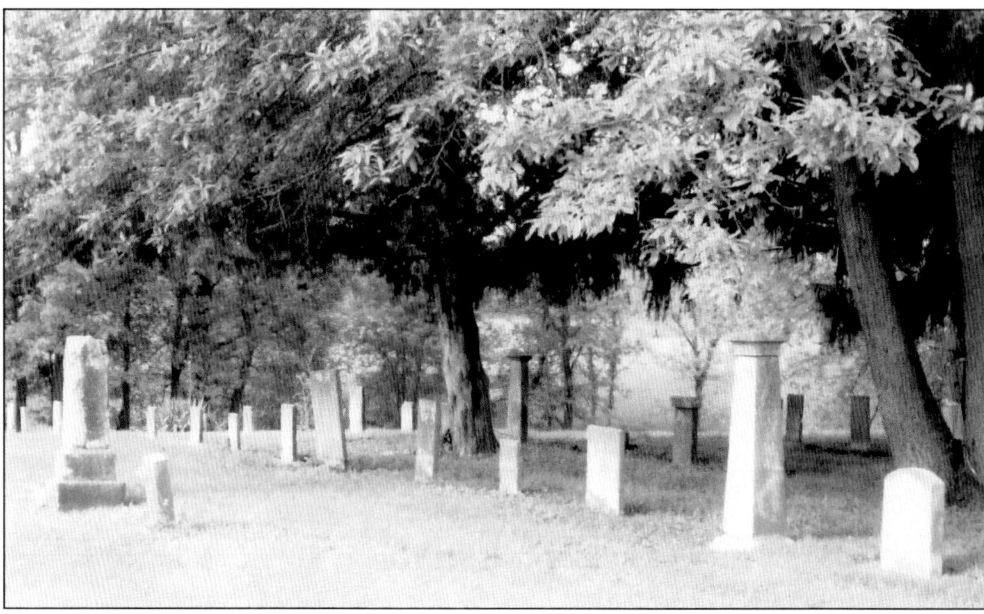

Spring Creek, or Sciota, Cemetery is located on road 1750N, just west of road 800E. The earliest burials in it date from the 1830s and 1840s, and some of those markers are shown here. At first a private cemetery, it became a public burying ground in 1867. Among the notable markers is one for Joel Hall, from Virginia, who fought in the War of 1812. Nine Civil War veterans are also buried there.

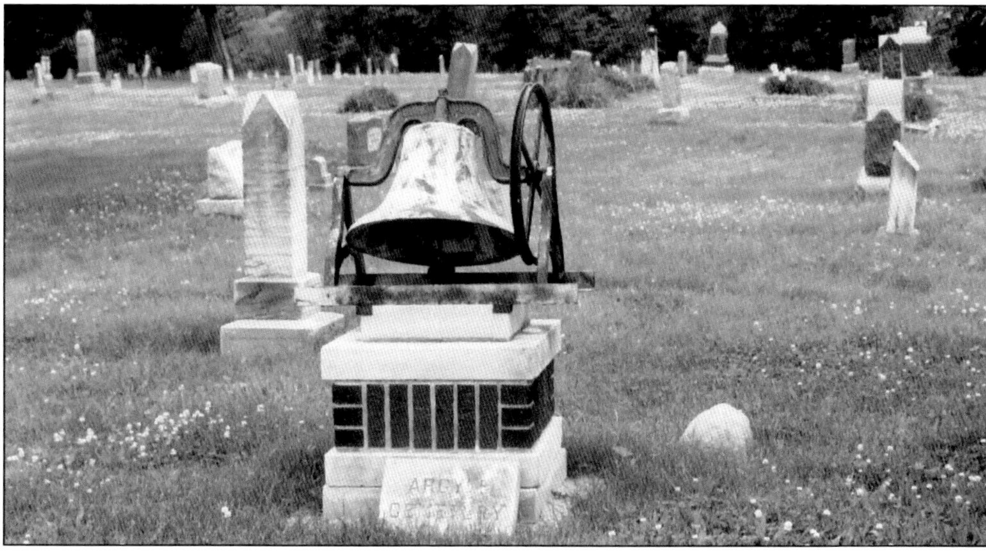

The Argyle Cemetery is adjacent to the Argyle Bible Church, north of Colchester on road 1250N, just off of road 500E. It was established in the 1830s and was used for many years primarily by Bersheba Cumberland Presbyterians, who erected a church there in 1854. As this photograph shows, the cemetery includes a bell that is a monument to that early church, which changed its name to Argyle Cumberland Presbyterian in 1884.

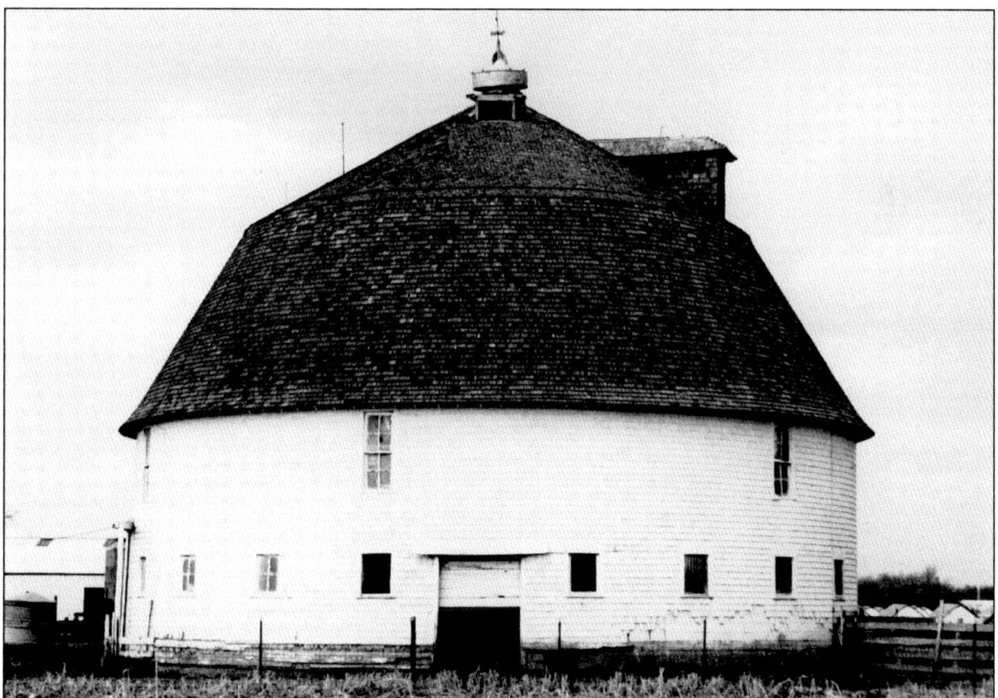

One of the notable barns in McDonough County is also located on road 500E, at the intersection with road 1200N. Built by Dick Carmack in 1914, this well-preserved round barn is owned by Kevin Kleinkopf. Discussed in several articles on barn architecture, it has been listed on the National Register of Historic Places.

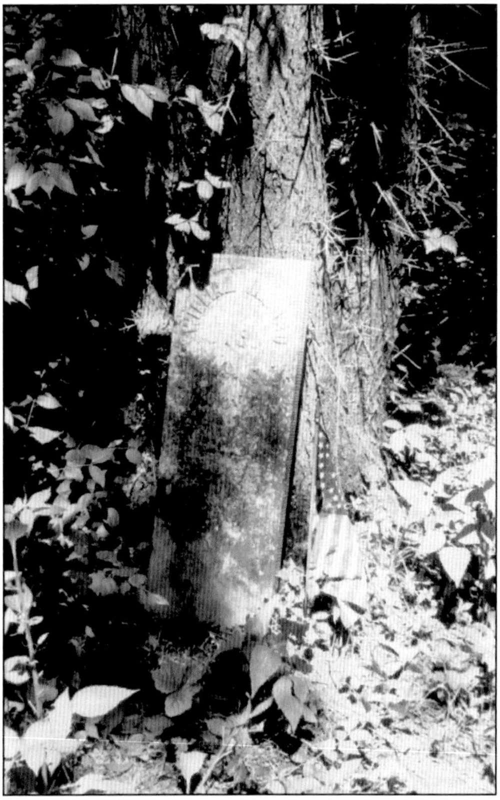

The Atkinson Cemetery, east of Argyle Lake on land now owned by the state park, dates from 1839, and it includes two burials of historic interest. One is the grave of William Willard, shown at the left. He was from Loudoun County, Virginia, and served twice in the Revolutionary War, during 1778 and 1781. He later came west with his daughter Mary and son-in-law John McCord. He died in 1846 at the remarkable age of 97.

Also in the Atkinson Cemetery is a headstone that simply says, "To the remains of Jack, the Black Man of John McCord, age 45 y." McCord had been raised in North Carolina and had lived for many years in Tennessee, where he apparently acquired Jack as a slave. When the McCords moved to Illinois in the 1830s, Jack came with them. He was then a youngster, for the 1850 census lists him as 25 years old. He died in about 1870. This photograph from the 1970s shows Glen Fentem, John McCord's great-grandson, and George Jones, who located Jack's marker in that remote, overgrown cemetery.

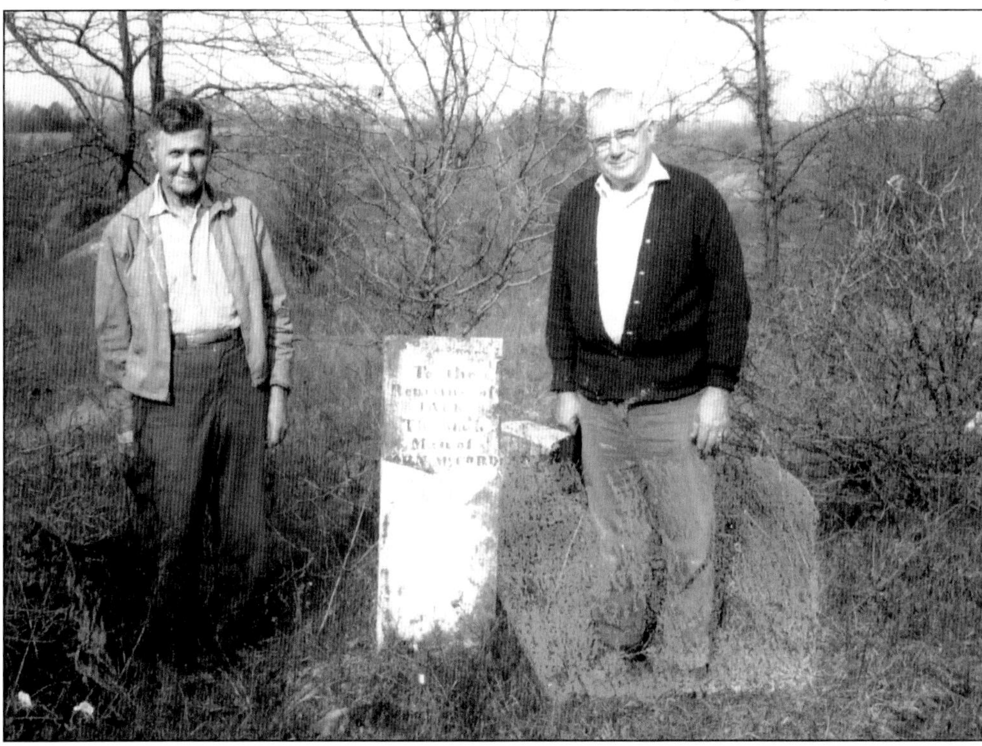

Three

THE NORTHEAST QUARTER OF THE COUNTY

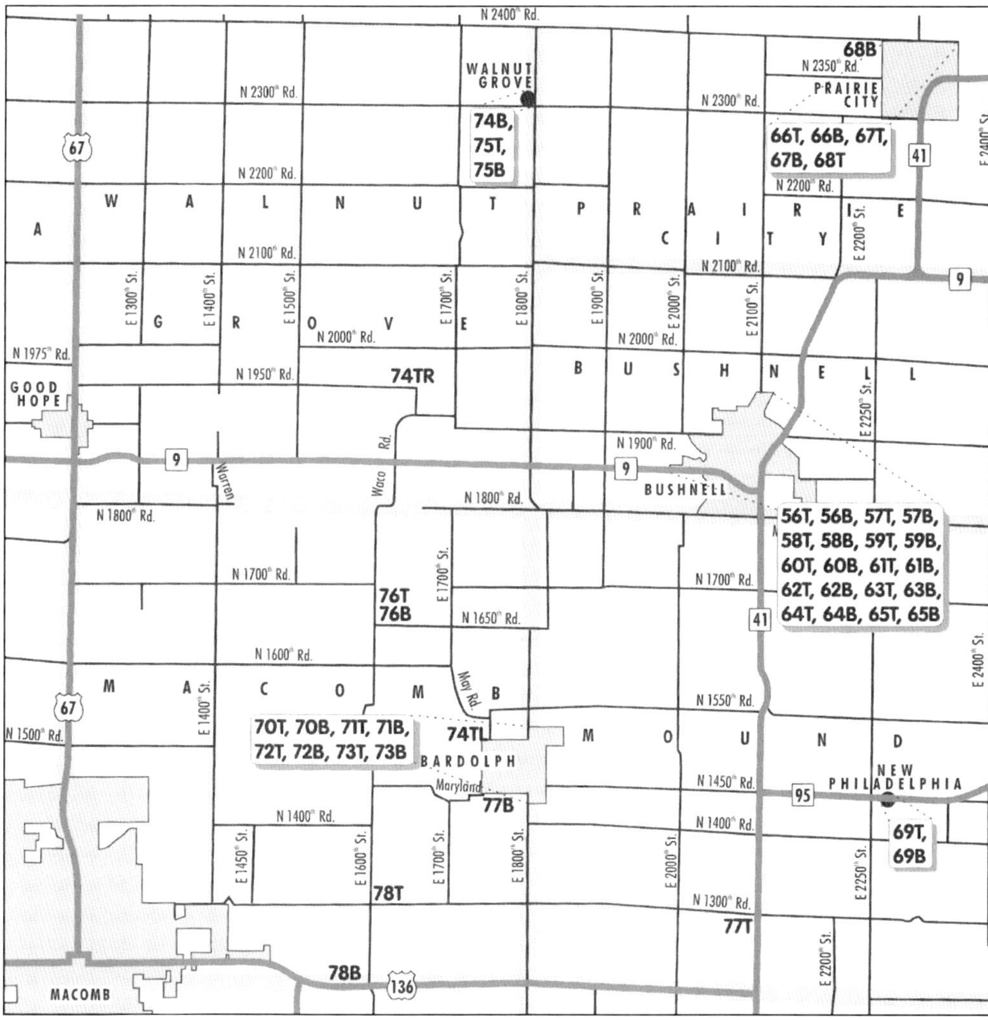

The development of the northeast quarter of McDonough County was also deeply influenced by the coming of the railroad, for Bardolph, Bushnell, and Prairie City were laid out in 1854, along the projected route of the Northern Cross (later the Chicago, Burlington and Quincy) Railroad. When it came through in 1855, significant growth began, and the towns became thriving farm-center communities. Walnut Grove was later platted along another line of the C.B.&Q.

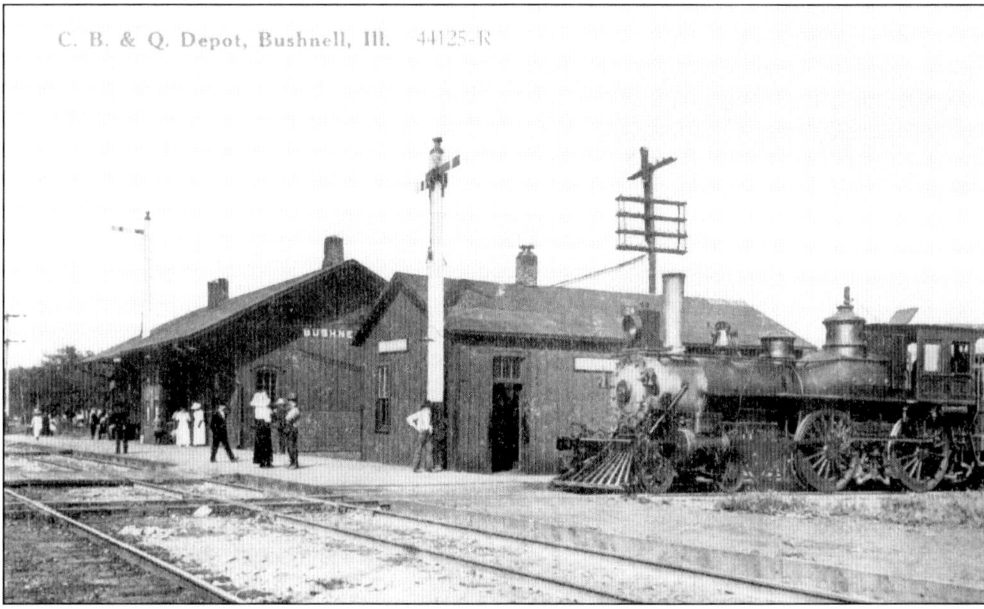

Bushnell was once a dynamic railroad town. It was, in fact, named for Nehemiah Bushnell, the president of the Northern Cross Railroad, which consolidated with the Chicago, Burlington, and Quincy Railroad in 1865. Two C.B.&Q. lines, Chicago to Quincy and Rock Island to St. Louis, ran through the town, so the company had several warehouses and many employees there. The C.B.&Q. Depot, where 16 passenger trains stopped every day in 1910, was located on E. Main Street. It was recently torn down.

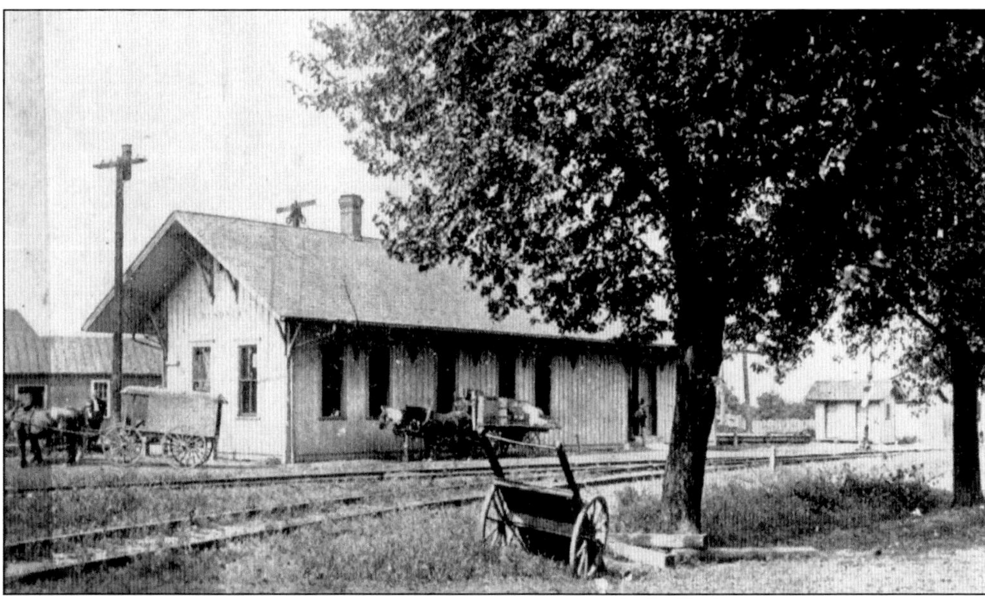

Another railroad, the Toledo, Peoria and Warsaw, came through Bushnell on an east-west route in 1867. By the early 20th century, there were four trains on that line stopping every day. The T.P.&W. Depot, shown in this early 20th-century postcard photograph, was located south of the C.B.&Q. station, just west of West Main Street. In the 1980s, it was moved to Hamilton to be part of a railroad memorabilia exhibit.

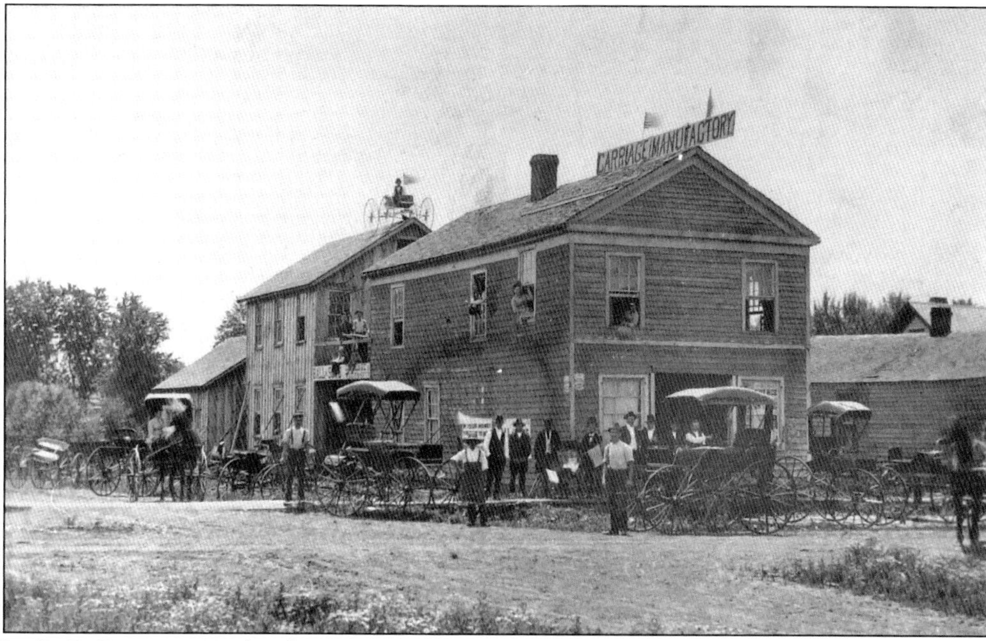

Ira D. Ball came to Bushnell in 1863 and became one of the town's earliest carriage and wagon makers. For many years he was in partnership with his four sons under the name "Ball and Sons." This 1878 photograph shows their factory, located on the southeast corner of Gridley and E. Main Streets. The earliest building is in the rear, and the second one is in front. In 1888, as their business grew, they constructed a third building to the right of the second one.

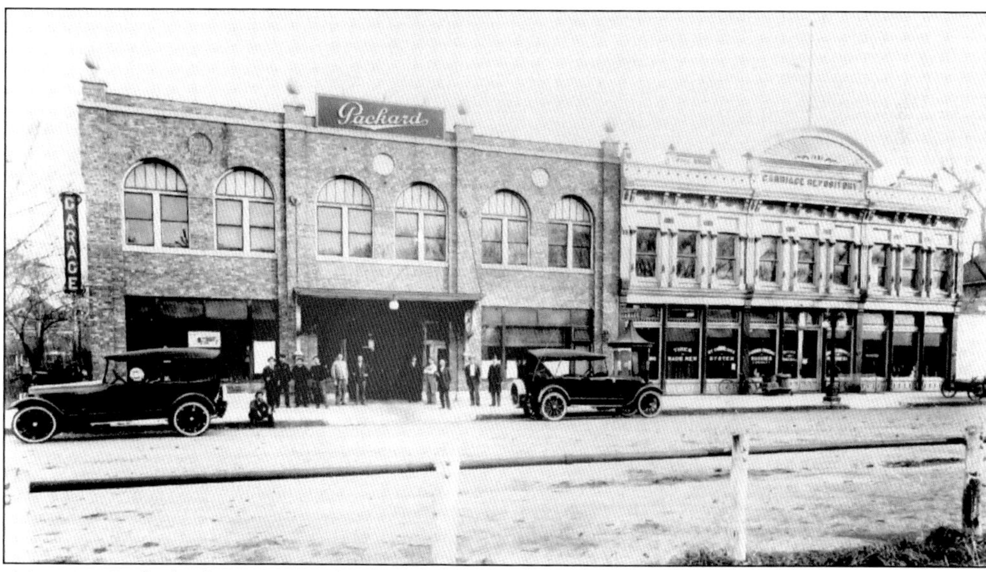

After Ira Ball died in 1908, the business was known as "Ball Bros." By 1915, when this photograph was taken, it had been sold and was a Packard dealership. The brick building at the left had been built around the early frame structures. The building at the right, labeled "Carriage Repository," had been built in 1890 by the Ball brothers as a showroom. It was later used as the Bushnell USO and as a recreational center. Both buildings are now owned by Midwest Control Products Corp.

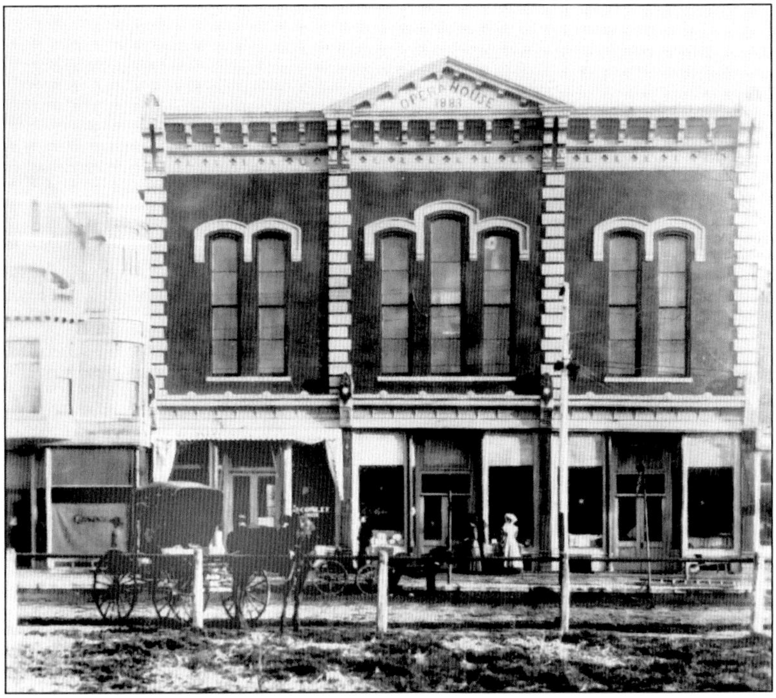

One important cultural asset of early Bushnell was the Opera House, built on E. Main Street in 1883 by R.S. Randall, H.L. Randall, and S. Houghton at a cost of $22,000. It featured a stage 60 feet wide and offered lectures, musical shows, and vaudeville acts. The Opera House functioned until the 1920s. The building still stands and is owned by Ace Hardware.

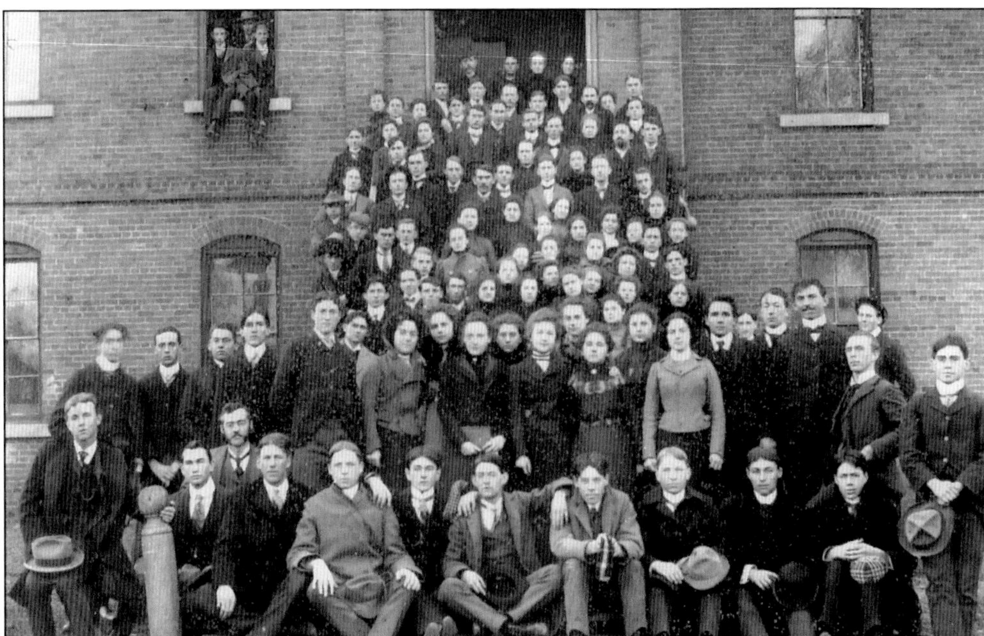

Western Normal College was founded by J.E. Chandler in the early 1880s. He built the brick structure shown in this photograph at 750 E. Main Street. In 1888, W.M. Evans and W.W. Earnest took over the institution and added three buildings, including two dormitories on Twyman Street. The college had several hundred students by the mid-1890s, but declined with the coming of state-supported normal schools, including the one that opened in 1902 at Macomb. The main WNC building has been razed, but the dormitories still stand.

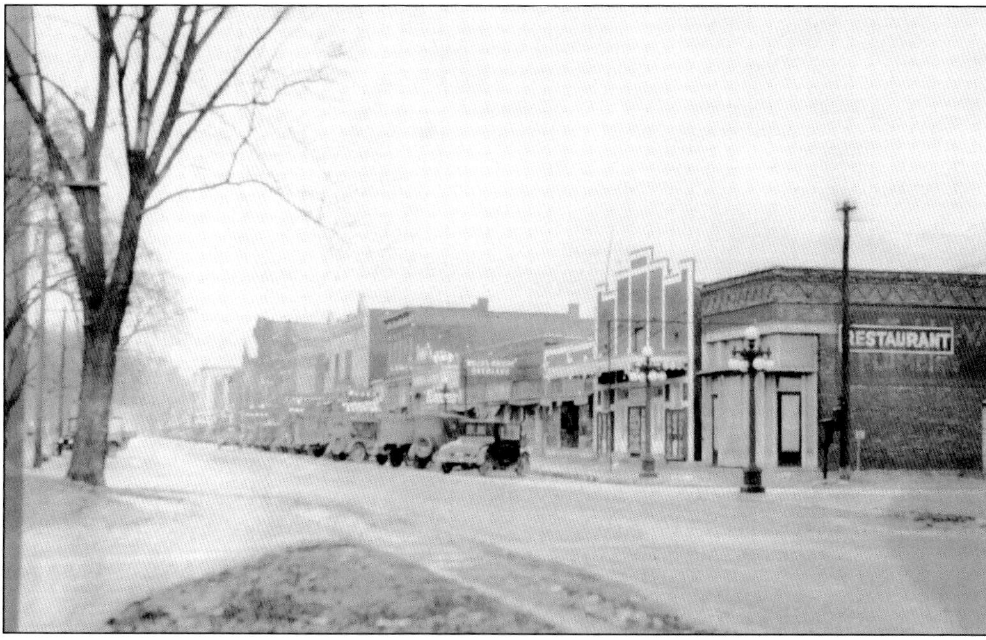

This 1930 photograph of E. Main Street looking north shows the Rialto Theater, which opened in the early 1930s and contributed to the decline of the Bushnell Opera House. The theater still stands, but it ceased operating in the 1950s. Although the Rialto was successful for a time, Bushnell was starting to decline by the 1930s, as automobiles and hard roads made the county seat convenient for shoppers.

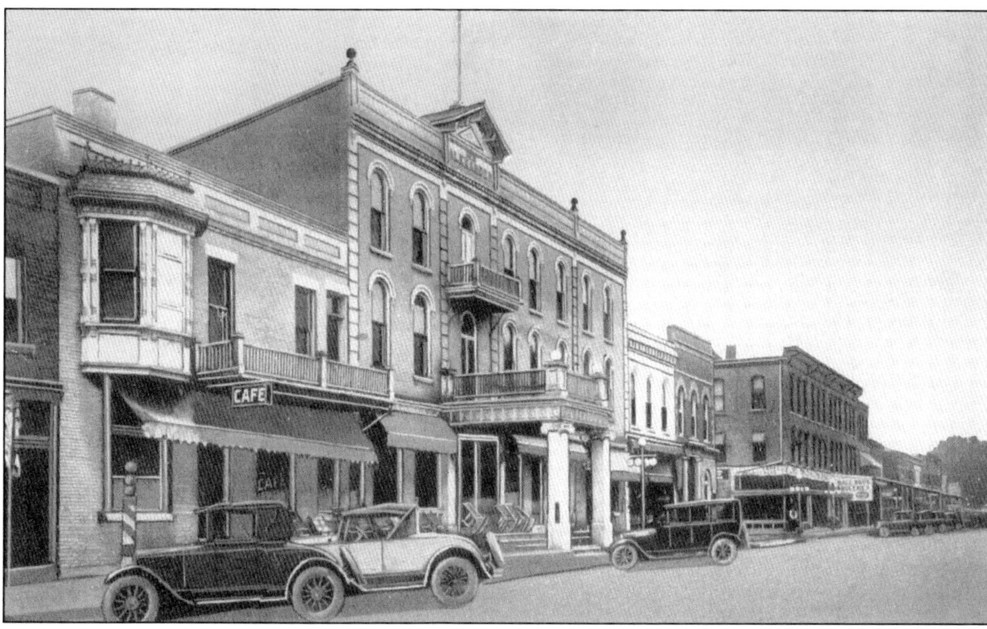

This postcard image, also from about 1930, shows W. Main Street. The large building was the Bushnell Hotel, which had been built prior to 1890 by S.A. Hende. It later had other owners, including the Korn family, and it eventually closed in the 1960s and was demolished in the 1970s. As the small sign indicates, there was a café next door.

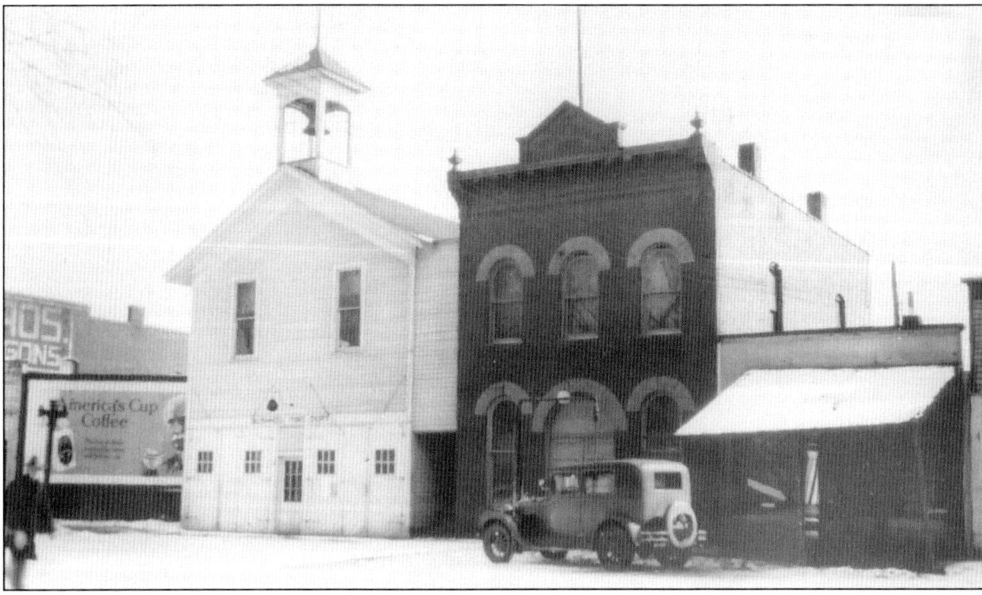

This 1930s photograph shows the old fire station, on the left, and the city hall on E. Main Street. The Bushnell Fire Department was organized in about 1871, but at that time it was a volunteer agency known as the Alert Hook and Ladder Company. This frame building went up soon afterward. The city hall was constructed in 1888.

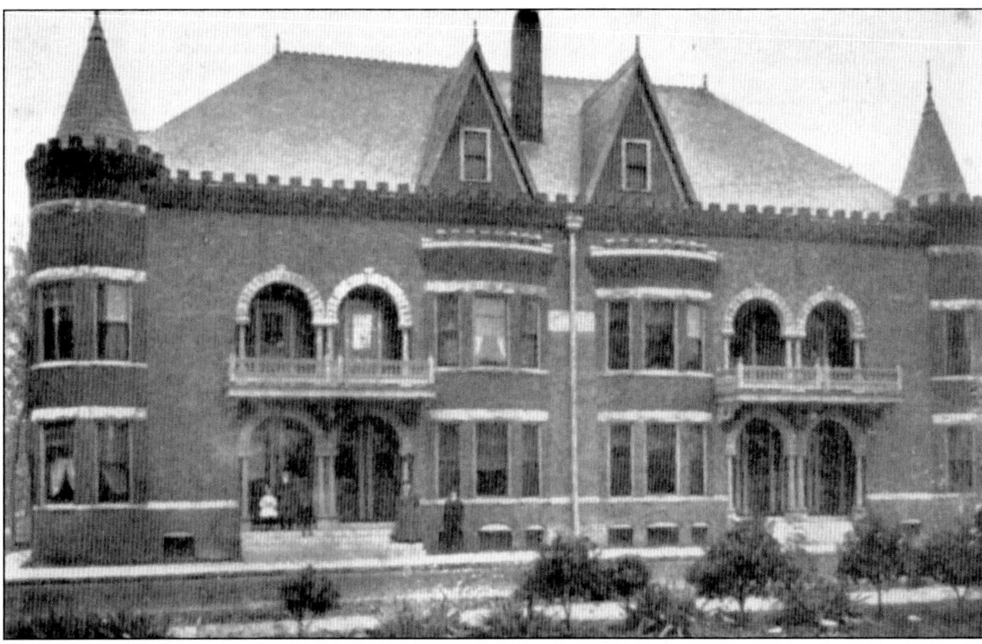

A very impressive addition to Bushnell was "Cole Flats," an apartment building constructed in 1904 at the corner of E. Hail and N. Crafford Streets by James Cole. An early Bushnell merchant and grain dealer, he developed much of the northeast section of town, and in 1860, he built the Cole Building at the corner of E. Main and Hail Streets. At that location in 1906 he started the First National Bank. The Cole Building was torn down in 1954, but his once elegant apartment building remains.

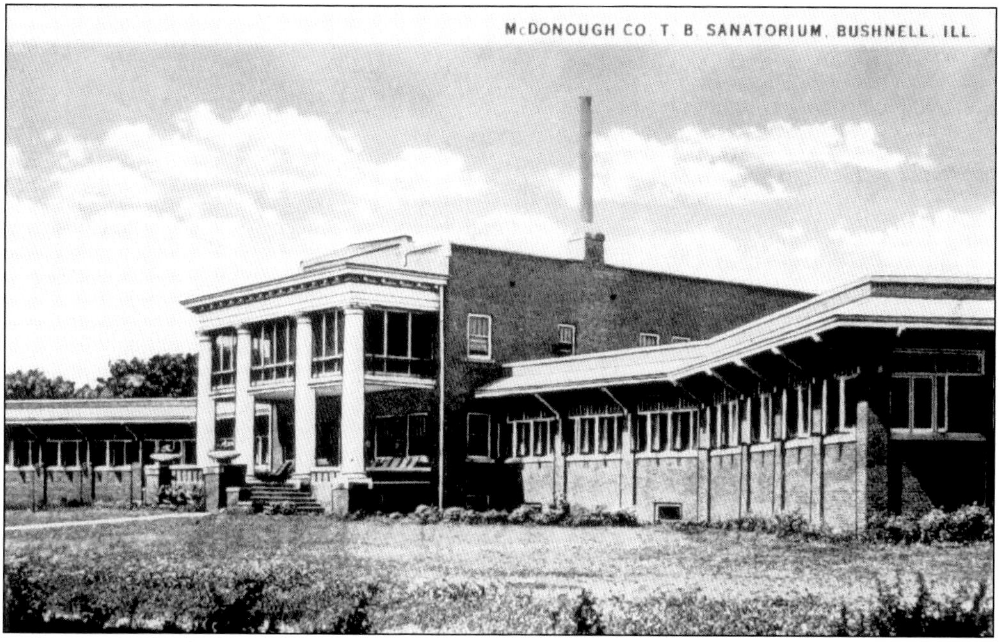

An important 20th-century structure was the Elmsgrove Tuberculosis Sanitarium, which opened in 1926. It was located in the center of the 25¢ Fairground racetrack, west of the business district. In 1958, after medical progress eliminated the need for TB sanitariums, Elmsgrove became the McDonough County nursing home. In 1977, The Elms, as it was then called, was moved to a new building in Macomb, and the structure shown here was demolished.

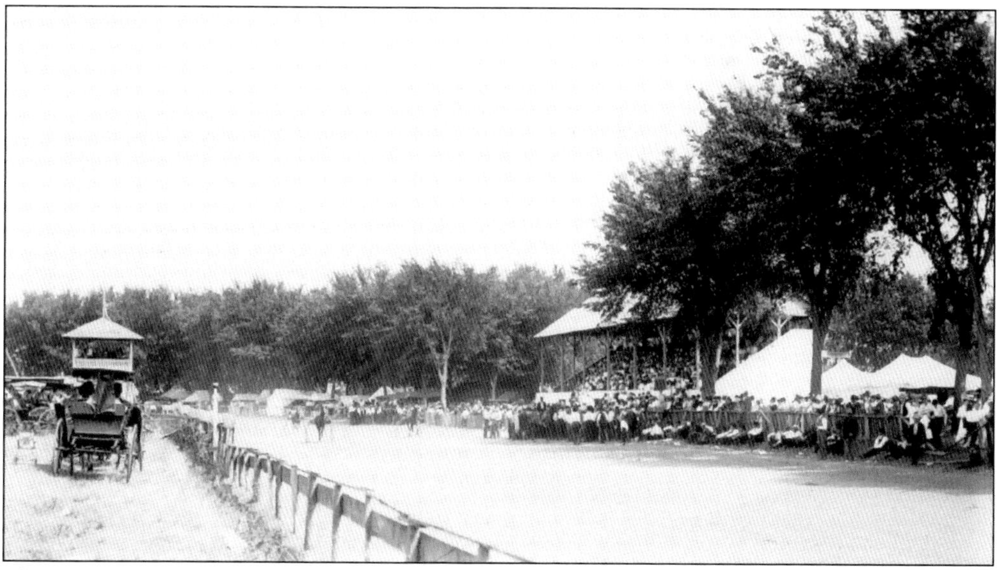

This photograph shows a trotting race at the 25¢ Fairground's half-mile racetrack, located west of town. That activity was the main attraction of the "Big 25¢ Fair," held every summer starting in 1879. The fairgrounds included a Women's Building, where ladies competed for prizes in needlework, flowers, and foods, as well as barns where livestock could be kept and shown. After the Great Depression began and a big barn on the grounds burned in July 1930, the fair was discontinued.

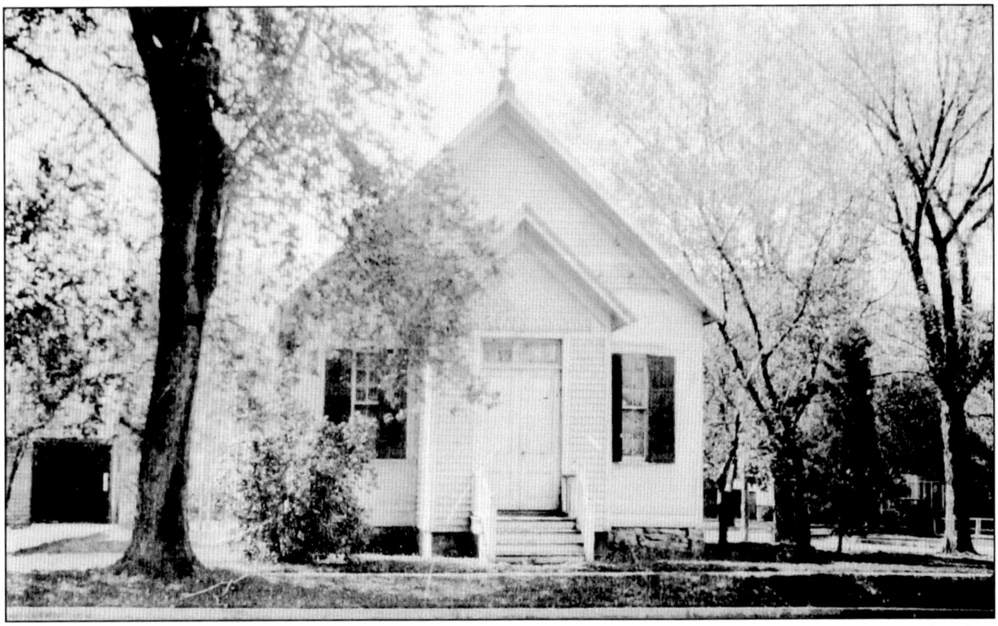

Perhaps the earliest 19th-century church building in Bushnell was the German Methodist Episcopal Church, located at the corner of W. Hail and Jackson Streets. The church was organized in 1857, and this building was erected later that year. That congregation was disbanded in 1906, but the building was still occasionally used for a number of years. This photograph was taken in 1930. The church was finally torn down in the 1950s.

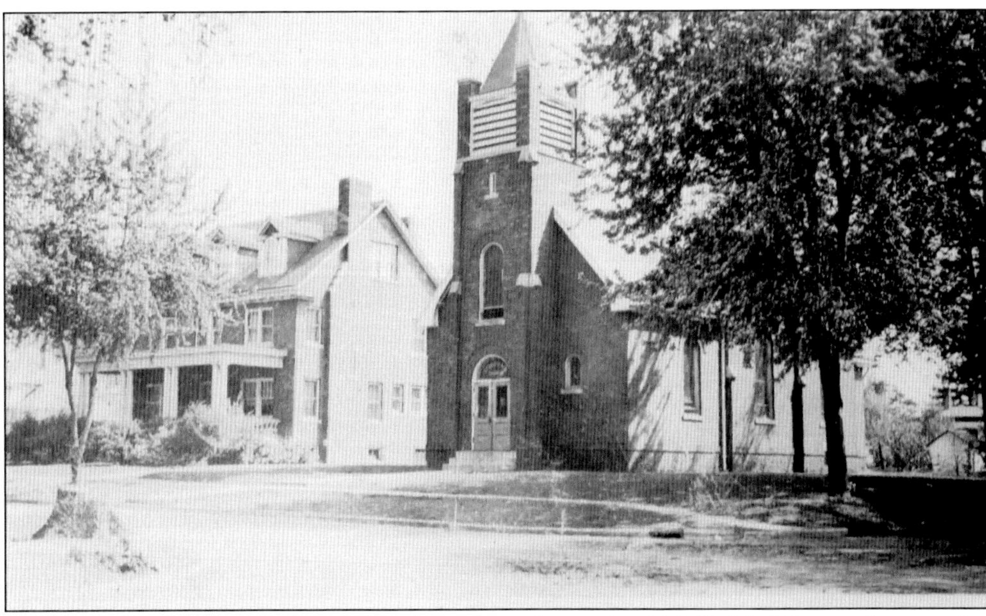

The St. Bernard Catholic Church has always been located at 376 W. Hail Street. Organized in 1877, the congregation purchased the old Third Ward school building and held services there until the brick structure shown here was constructed on that site in 1907. Standing next to it in this 1930 photograph is the handsome, two-story rectory, which was built in 1916. The current St. Bernard Church replaced this one in 1953.

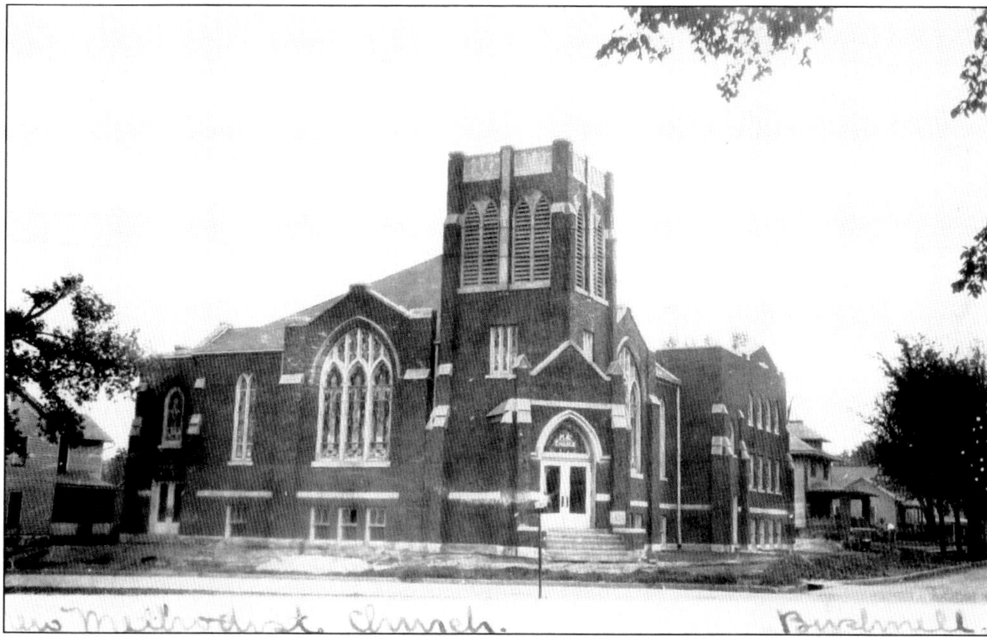

The Bushnell United Methodist (formerly Methodist Episcopal) Church was organized at the home of merchant James Cole in 1856. One of the early ministers was pioneer preacher Milton Haney. A frame church building was erected at the corner of Crafford and Hurst Streets in 1863, and it was replaced by a brick structure in 1884. On February 4, 1923, that church was destroyed by fire, and the one shown here was erected on that site in 1925.

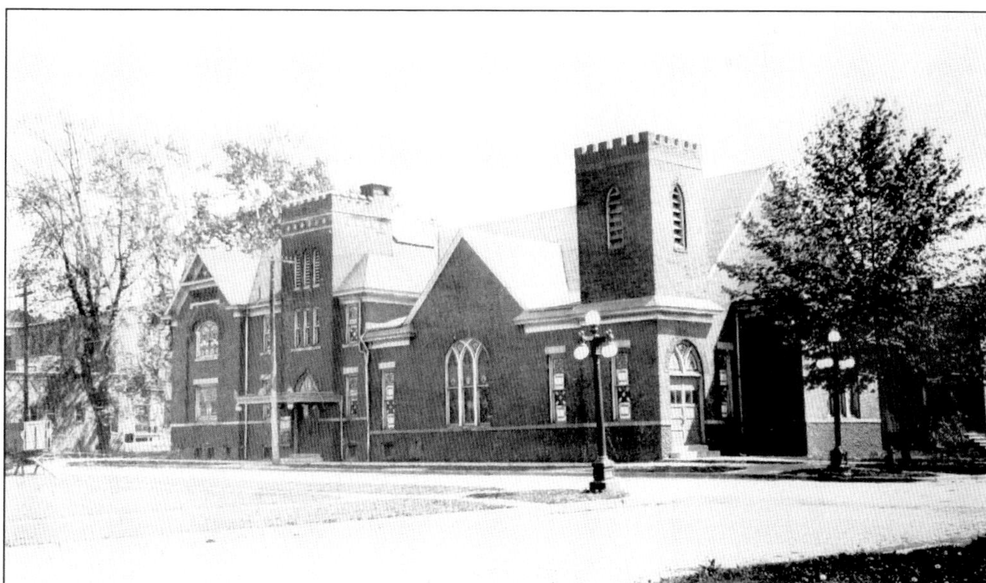

The Bushnell First Presbyterian Church was organized in 1857 but was soon disbanded. In 1868, it was launched again, and during the following year the congregation built a frame building on Dean Street. In 1903, it was moved west to the adjacent corner lot, turned to face the west, and remodeled as a brick structure. In 1917, a large addition was made on the east side, running along Hurst Street. This photograph was taken in 1930.

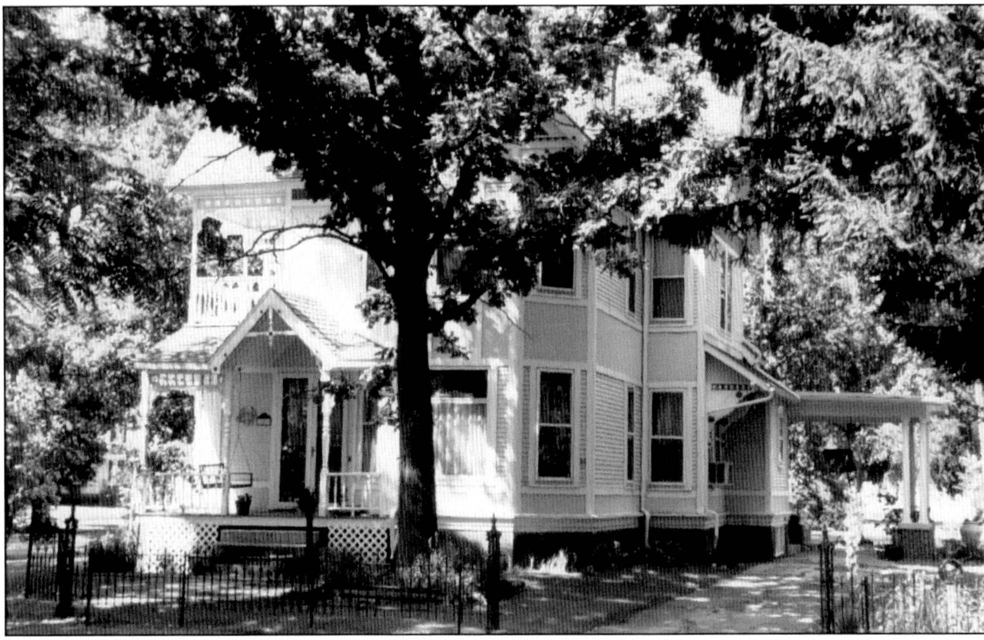

Bushnell has a number of lovely older homes. This one at 287 W. Hail Street was built in 1892 by contractor J.O. Justice for James H. Smith, a wealthy farmer. The latter's name is inscribed in the cement on the front of the top step. The elegant house, with its decorative porches, was designed by George F. Barber of Knoxville, Tennessee, and cost around $4,000. Owned by Mr. and Mrs. Daryl Boden since 1994, this home faces Bushnell's West Park, which has other sizable older homes around it. Three other Barber homes are also located in Bushnell.

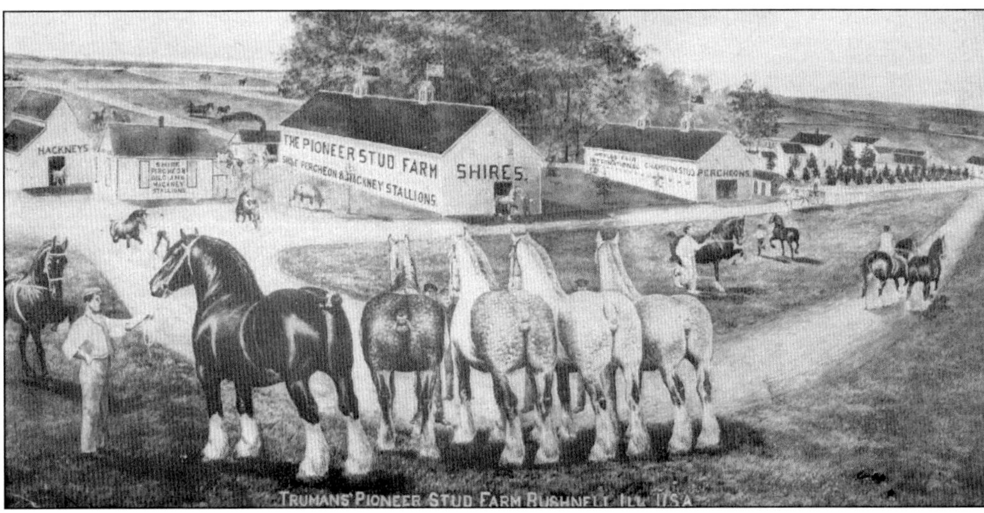

The once-famous Truman Pioneer Stud Farm was started in 1878 by English livestock dealer Jonathan Hall Truman, and it was later operated by his five sons, four of whom moved to Bushnell. Originally located on W. Main Street, the business was moved in the 1890s to a 100-acre tract with a dozen buildings located south of town. The importing and breeding operation was fabulously successful, earning a national reputation. The Trumans organized the Bushnell Horse Show in 1908, and it drew huge crowds to town every year until cars and mechanized farming caused horse breeding to decline. The large barn shown in this postcard painting is still standing.

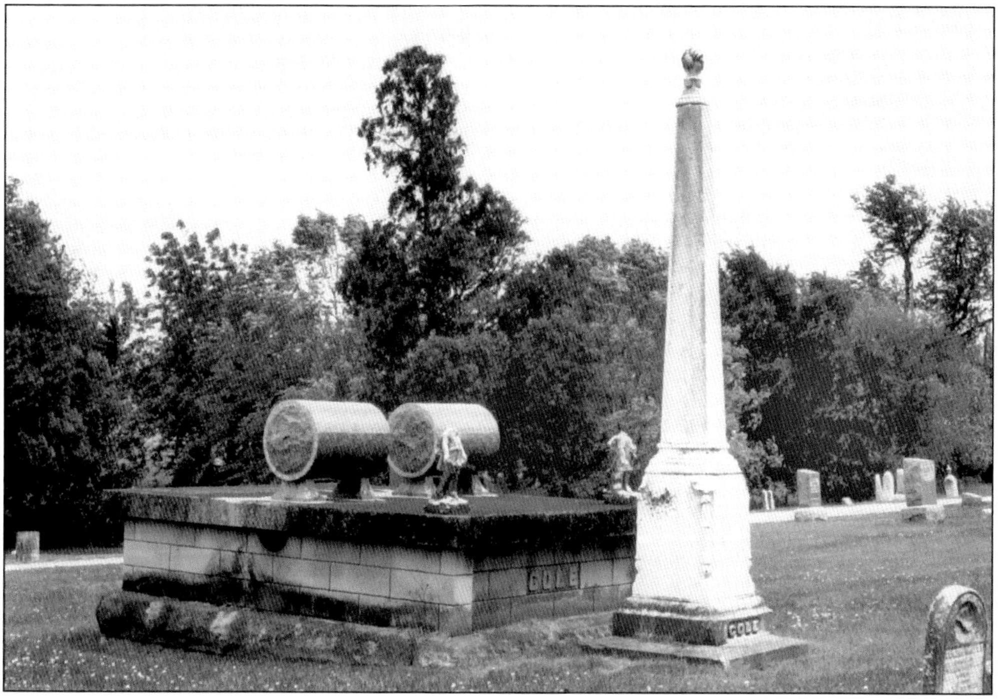

Bushnell Cemetery was laid out in 1863, southeast of the business district, and a mausoleum was constructed there in 1914. One very elaborate grave marker is for merchant, banker, developer, and mayor James Cole and his wife, Eliza. It includes a tomb with two round headstones and two small (now headless) statues on it, as well as a white obelisk. Cole's headstone refers to his public achievements: "James Cole 1824–1909. His deeds are recorded in history." His wife's headstone seems to respond: "Eliza J. Cole 1827–1907. Her deeds are recorded in our hearts."

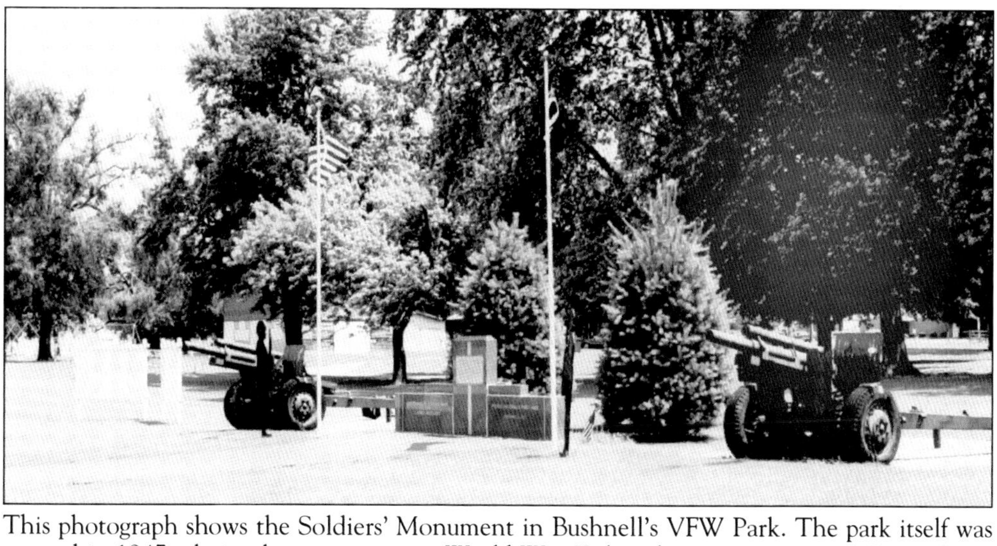

This photograph shows the Soldiers' Monument in Bushnell's VFW Park. The park itself was created in 1947, obviously in response to World War II, but the monument was "Erected and dedicated in memory of all who have served and to those who gave their lives in the service of our country in all conflicts," as stated on the stone marker in the center. At the left is an "Honor Roll" that lists local soldiers who were in the service in 1944.

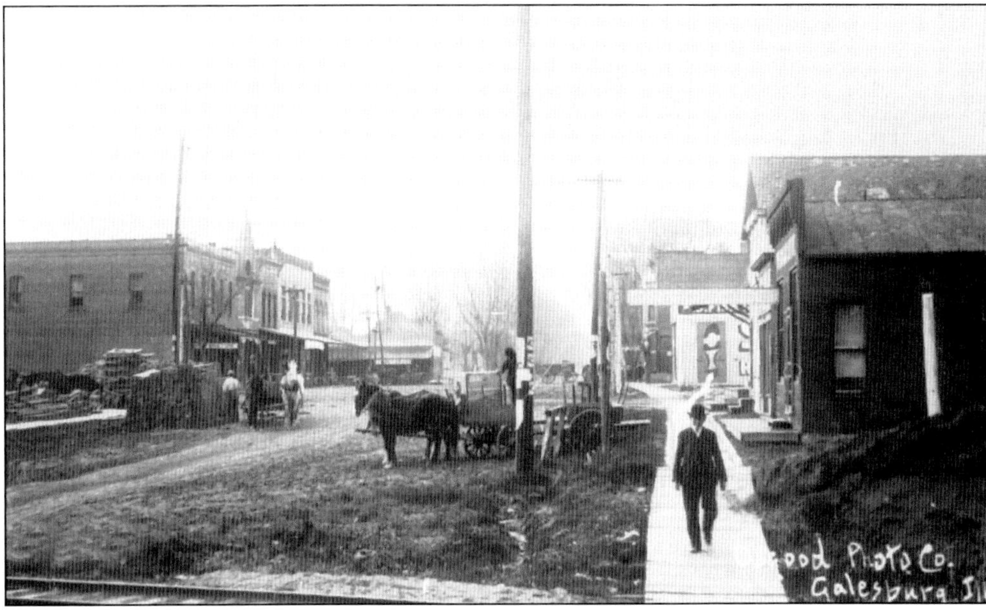

The first store in Prairie City, established by Alonzo Barnes and J.R. Parker, opened in 1854, the year that the town was platted at the point where "the old state road" intersected the proposed railroad line. By 1880, the town had some 800 hundred people and more than two dozen businesses, including a hotel, a bank, a lumber yard, a jewelry store, two drug stores, and two wagon manufacturers. This turn-of-the-century photograph shows Main Street looking east.

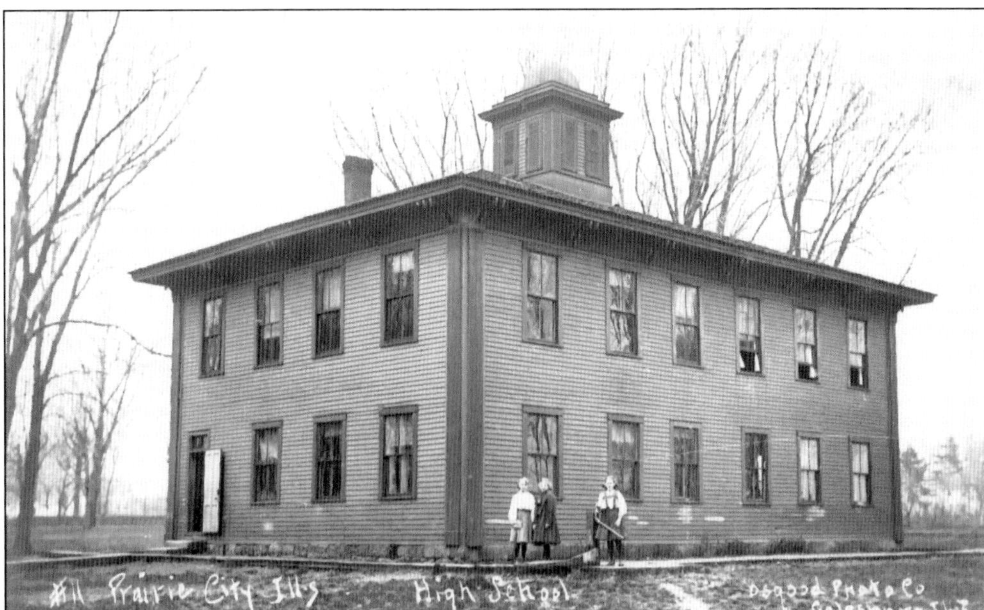

This postcard photograph shows Prairie City Academy, which was constructed in the late 1850s. By 1860, it had about one hundred students, many of whom came from surrounding areas and boarded in the new community, which then had well over 1,000 people. When the community declined in population after the Civil War, the academy was closed. The building later served as the high school.

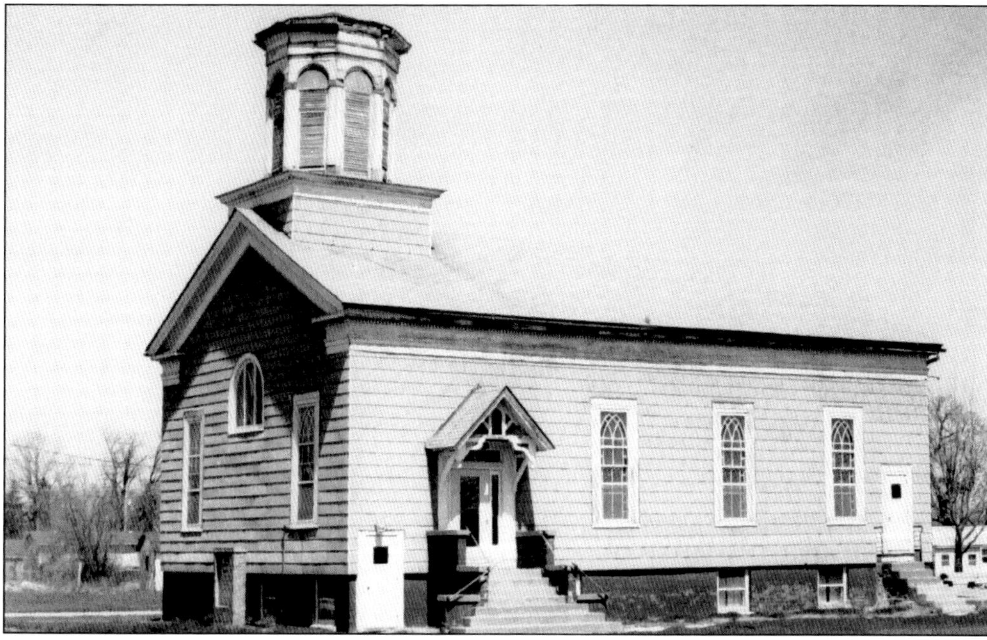

Prairie City Methodist Episcopal Church was organized in 1856, and this building was erected in 1858 at 45 N. Clay Street. It was remodeled in 1908 and again in 1925. After a fire in 1956, the structure was again renovated. The church was active until 1985, and then the building was sold. Used briefly as the Prairie City Community Church, it is now the Jeff Zeisler residence.

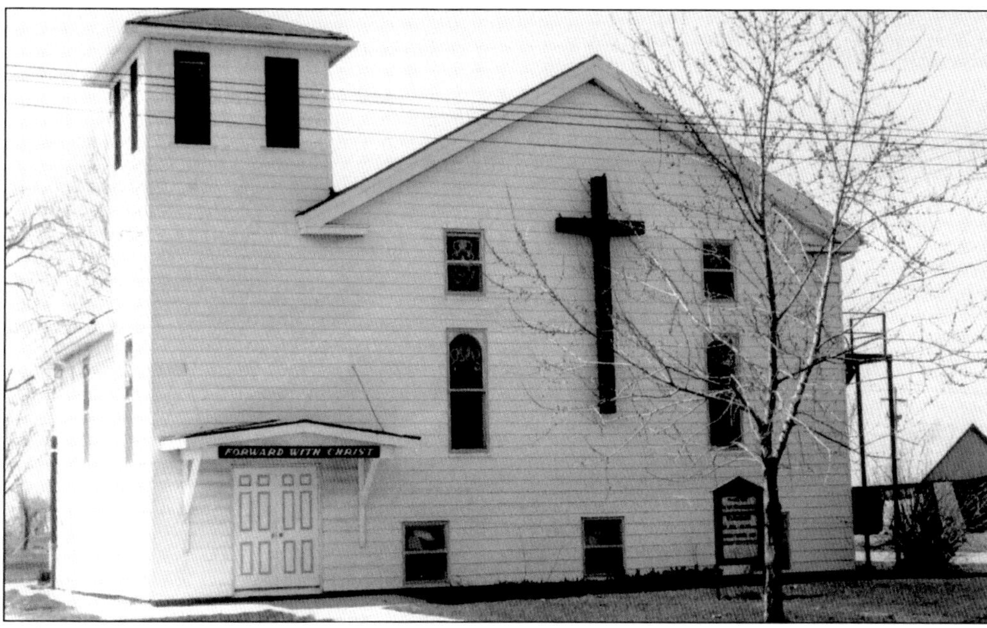

Before Prairie City was platted, the Presbyterian congregation was organized at the George Kreider log cabin, five miles northeast of there, in 1841. Known as Pleasant Prairie Presbyterian Church, it was reorganized in 1851, and five years later the congregation erected a building in Prairie City, at Clay and Columbia Streets. That was enlarged in 1868 and remodeled in 1926. This photograph was taken in 1989.

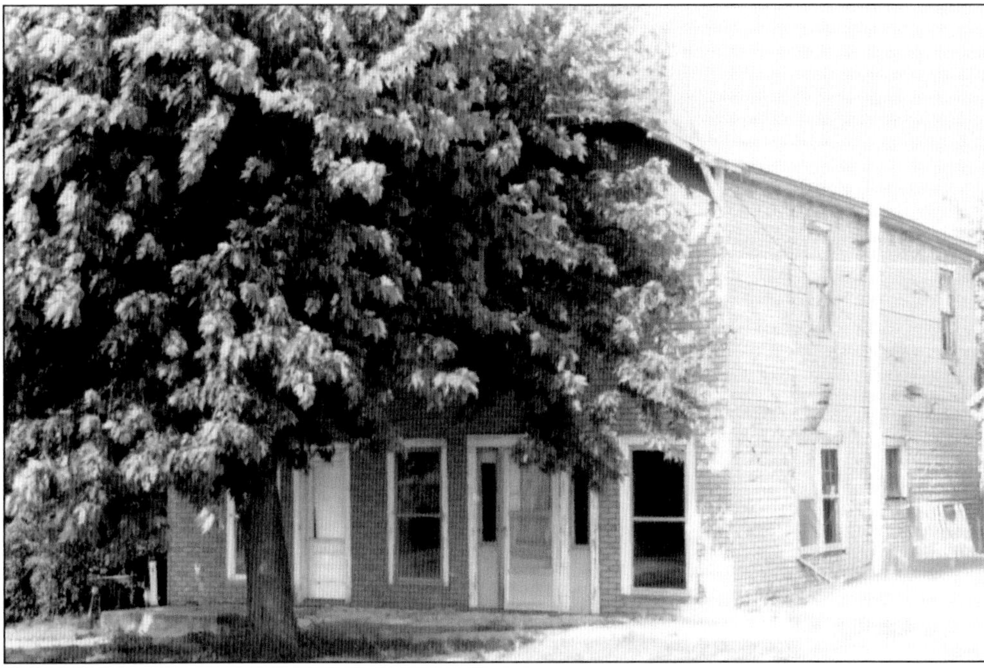

This building, photographed in 1975, was once the Eldon James Drug Store. Starting in 1937, it was also the site of the Decker Press, which became well-known in the 1940s. James Decker, the grandson of Eldon James, published books by scores of poets, including famous figures like Edgar Lee Masters, August Derleth, and Kenneth Rexroth, but he ran into financial trouble and had to sell the press in 1947. Ervin Tax then operated it with James's sister Dorothy. Spurned by Tax, whom she loved, Dorothy killed him and herself with a rifle in 1950, and the press died too.

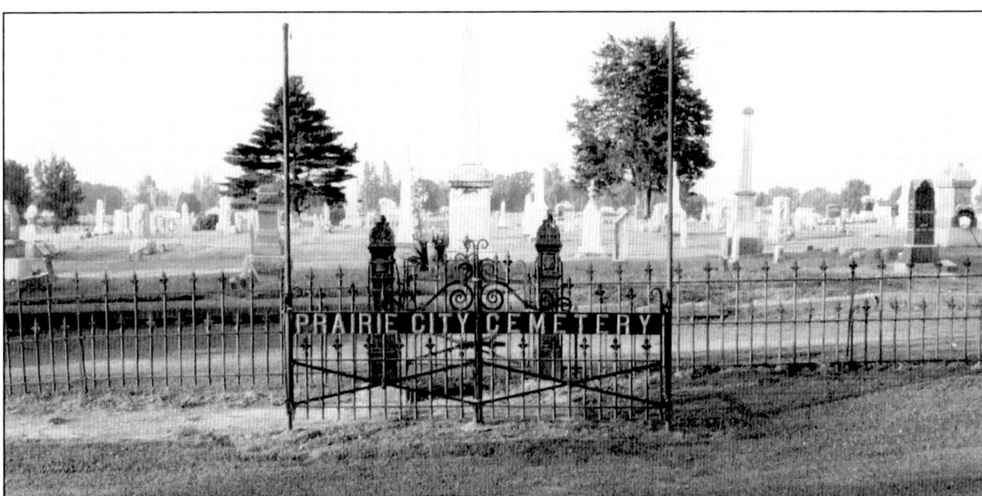

Prairie City Cemetery, northwest of town on road 2400N, was laid out in 1874 and is still in use. The old iron fence in front gives this attractive burying ground a Victorian look, and along the fence (but not shown in this photograph) is the last 19th-century hitching rail still standing in McDonough County. An older Prairie City Cemetery, now unused, is just over the county line, one mile east. Among its few markers are ones for War of 1812 soldier Ephriam Tipton, who died in 1869, and Civil War soldier Mathew McComb, who died on Christmas Day 1863.

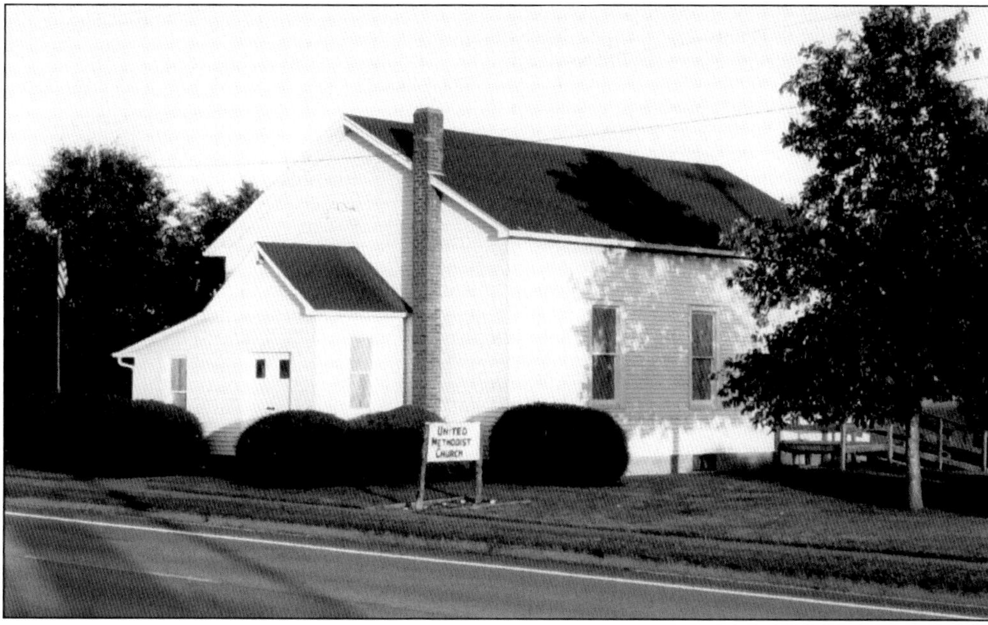

The New Philadelphia United Methodist Church, located on Route 95, dates only from 1968, when the Methodists merged with the United Brethren, who had bought this building in 1930. But the structure itself is much older. Built in 1864 by the Mound Christian Church in section 26 of Mound Township, it was moved to town in 1888 and was renamed the New Philadelphia Christian Church. The building was remodeled before and after that church disbanded in 1930.

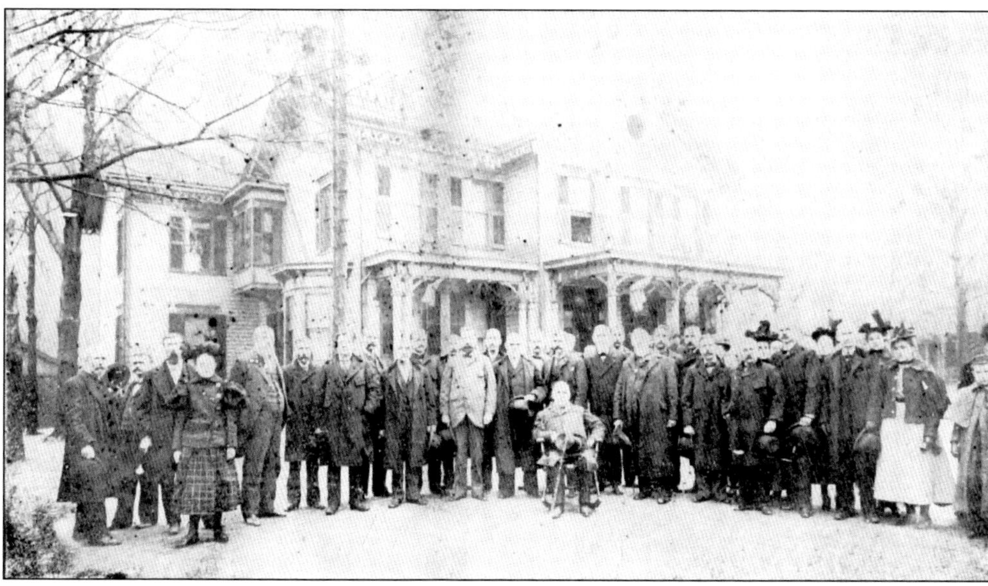

New Philadelphia was first platted one mile south of its present location in 1858. When the T.P.&W. Railroad came through one mile north, the town was moved and was re-platted along the tracks. By the 1880s, the village had several businesses—including the hotel shown here. Located north of the railroad tracks on Main Street, it was built in 1877 by J.H. Nebergall, who lived there himself and also sold groceries in an adjoining building. The people in the photograph are unidentified.

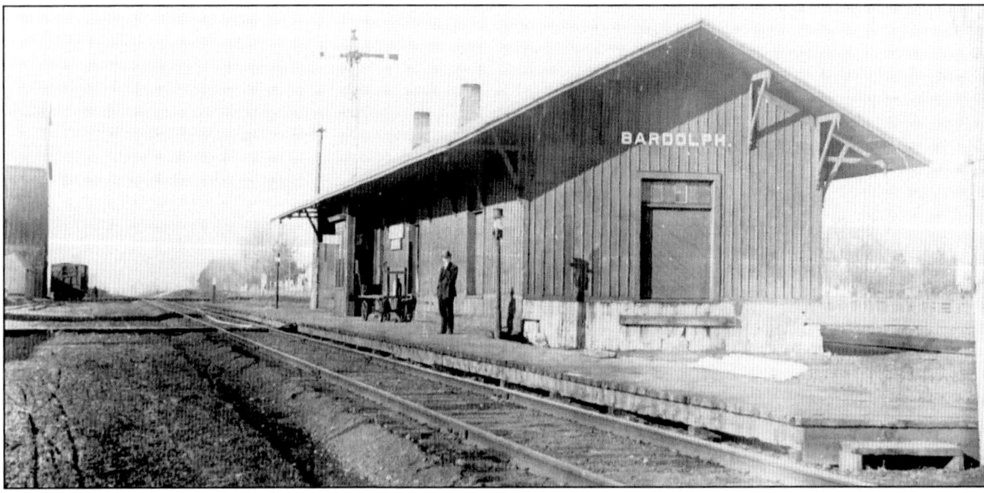

In 1854, a year before the Northern Cross Railroad came through, banker W.H. Randolph of Macomb platted Bardolph, which was then named "Randolph." Since Illinois already had another town named Randolph, the name was changed. The depot shown here was constructed in 1856, and soon Bardolph became an important shipping point for Mound and Macomb townships.

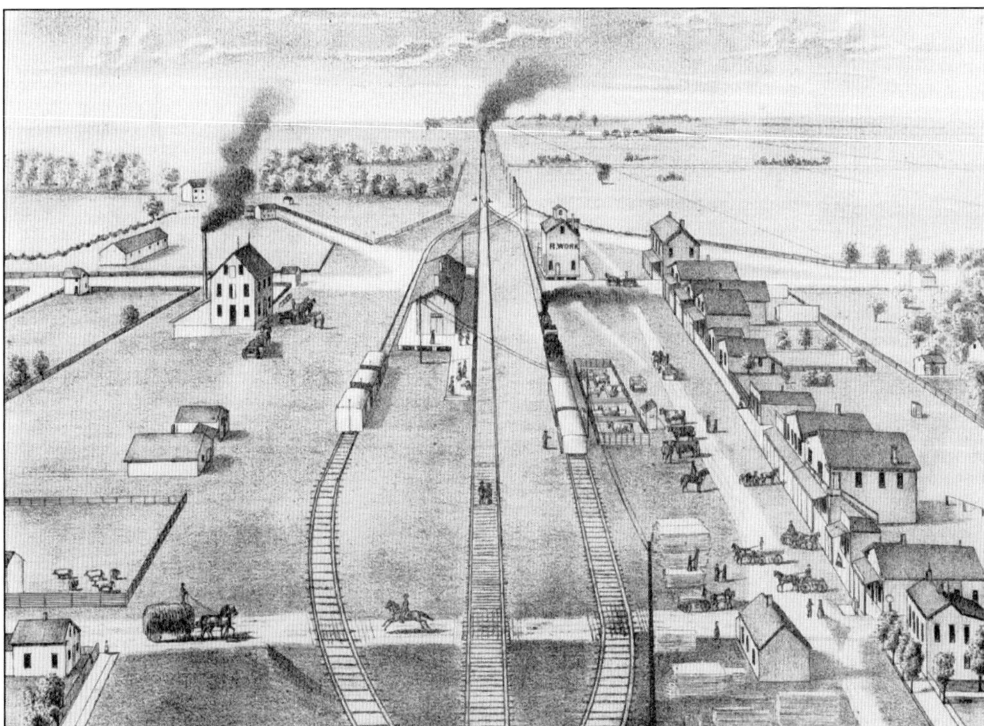

This remarkable 1871 lithograph shows that Bardolph, like so many communities in the county, still looked like a frontier town after the Civil War. The railroad had built livestock pens along the tracks in the late 1850s, and the elevator was owned by grain and livestock dealer Robert Work. Behind the depot was a pottery established by William Cleveland and his son in 1870. Many of the shops shown here, east of the tracks, and others built later were destroyed by four devastating fires, in 1893, 1896, 1901, and 1903. The last one led to arson charges against a local merchant.

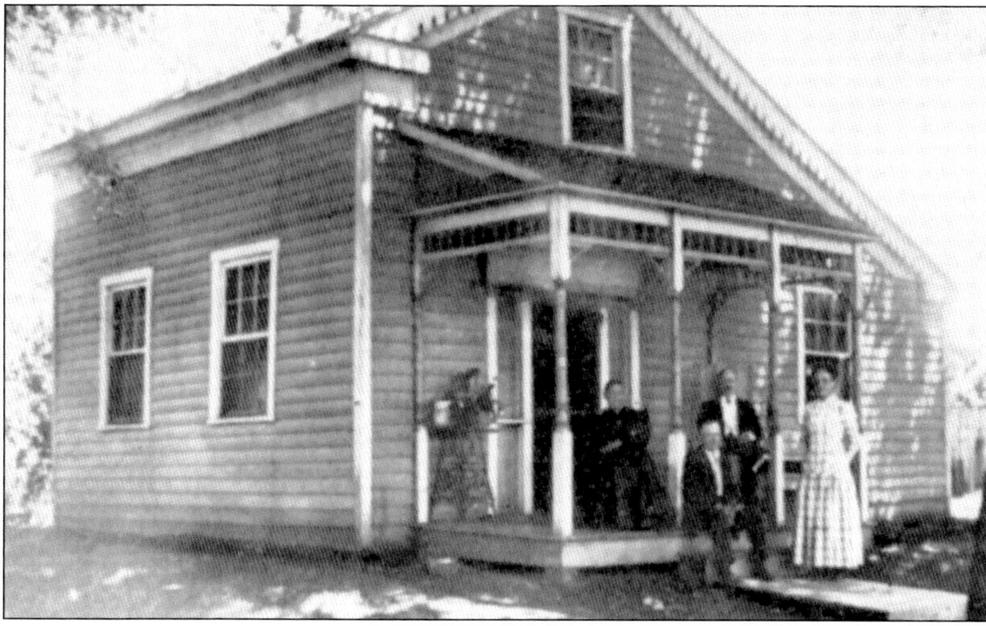

There were settlers in the Bardolph area before the railroad came. The Creel, Harris, Hoagland, and Jackson families, and several others, came in the 1830s and settled in what came to be called Wolf Grove. There were several short-lived log schools there but no shops. T.J. Creel and Belle Hoagland came as children with their parents and later married in 1854. They moved into this small house that year and lived in it until they died—he in 1902 and she in 1918. By then, the old house symbolized the pioneer heritage of Bardolph.

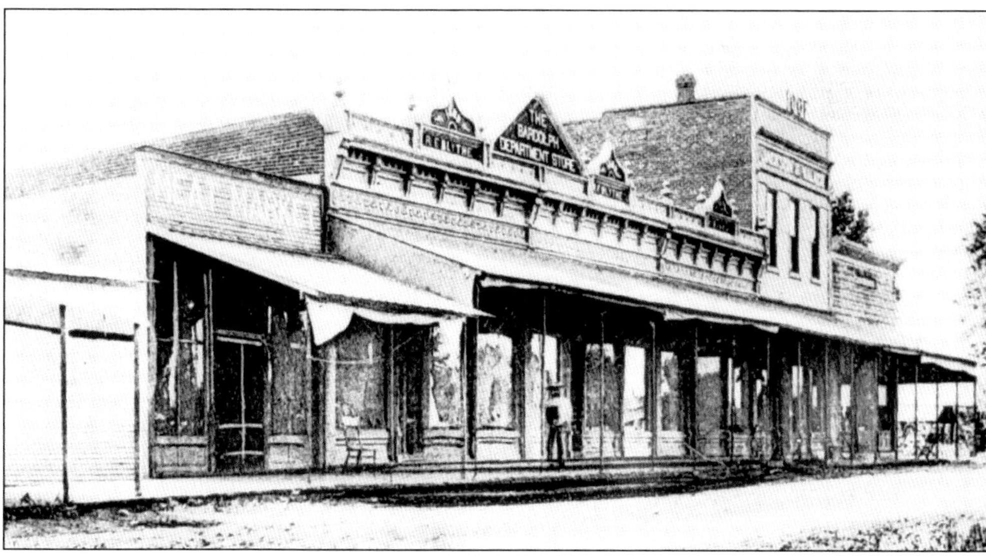

This postcard photograph of Main Street (now Broadway) dates from 1909. The buildings shown here include the meat market owned by Ronald Landis, R. Frank Blythe's Bardolph Department Store, the Bardolph State Bank, the two-story Odd Fellows Hall (which had Elmer Jackson and Glenn Walker's Bargain Store on the lower level,) and the Casner and Sons store. The bank building (later the post office) and the adjacent Odd Fellows Hall (built in 1904) are now apartment buildings but look very different. The other buildings are gone.

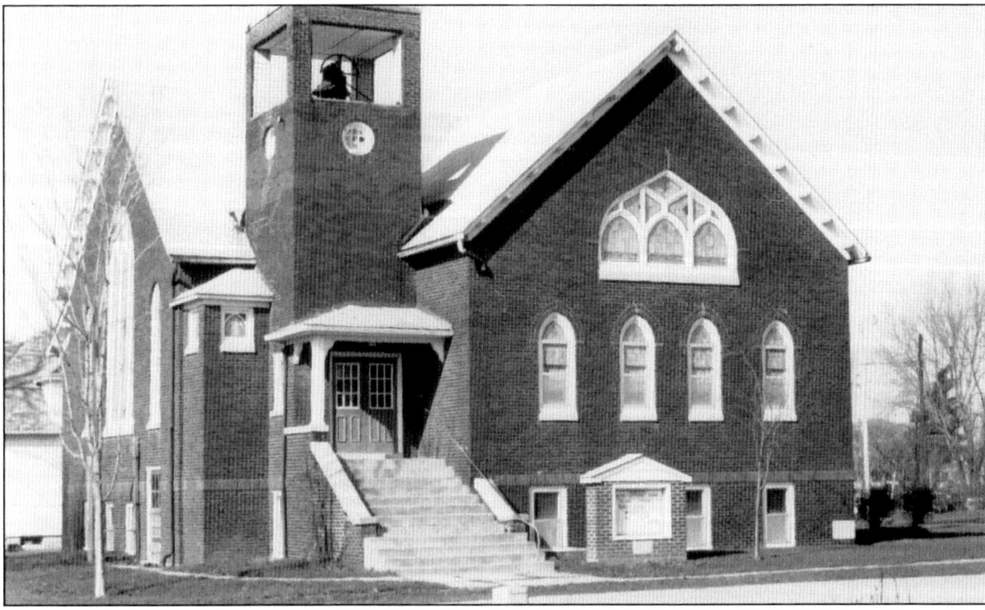

The Bardolph Methodist Episcopal (later United Methodist) Church was organized in 1837 at Wolf Grove. Services were held in various homes and schoolhouses until 1867, when a frame church building was erected for joint use by the Methodists and Cumberland Presbyterians. (The latter group disbanded in about 1881.) In 1915–1916, that structure was swapped for a Model T Ford, moved to another site, and replaced at Jackson and Spruce Streets by the brick building shown in this 1989 photograph. The congregation was disbanded in 2000, and the building was razed. A brick monument marks the site.

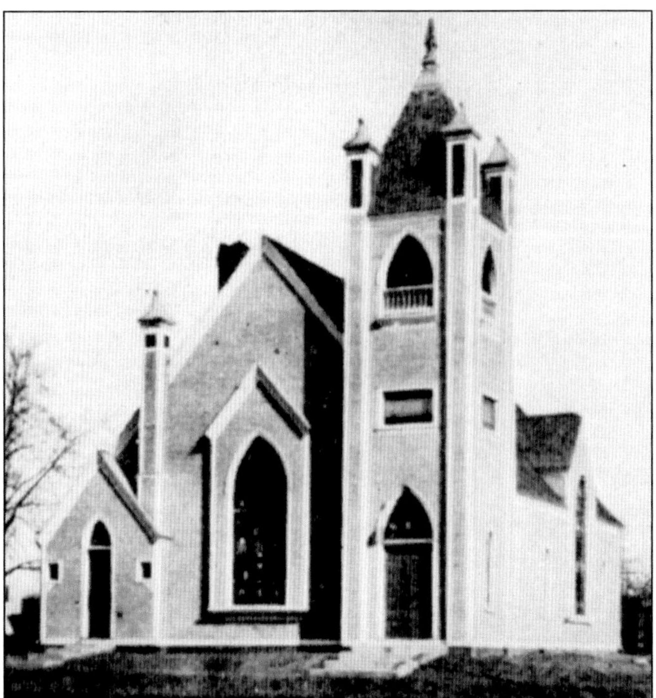

The Bardolph Presbyterian Church was organized in 1852 at the Wolf Grove schoolhouse. A two-story frame church building was erected in 1853 and was replaced by a larger one in 1868. That burned in the 1893 Bardolph fire, and a third building, shown here, was constructed later that year. It is still standing at Jackson and Elm Streets, but was altered and is now in poor repair. In 1992, the congregation joined with two others to form Scotland Trinity Presbyterian Church, located on Route 67.

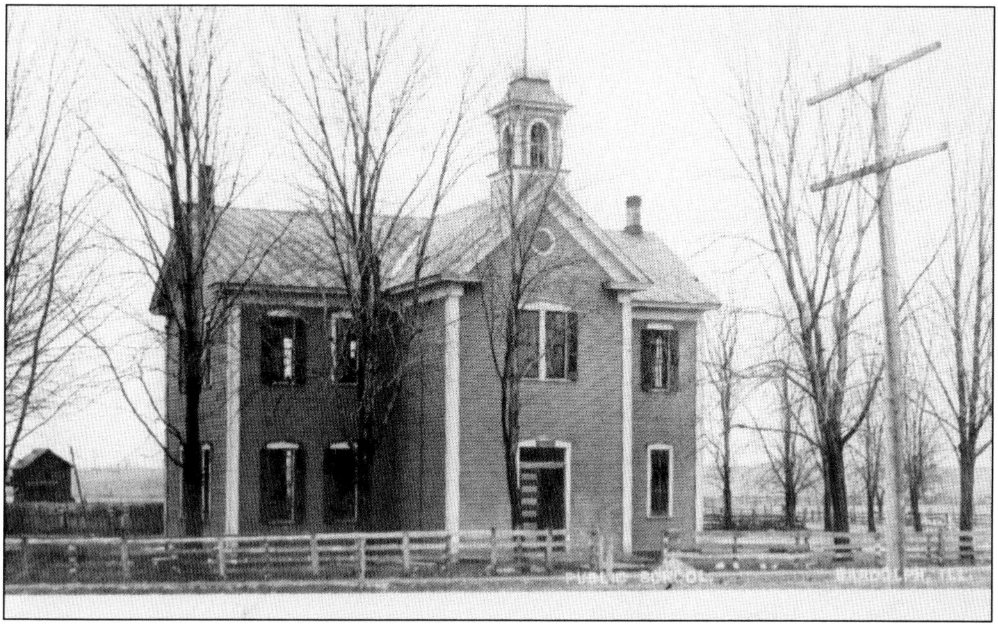

At Wolf Grove and early Bardolph, school was taught in log buildings, but in 1860, a two-story frame schoolhouse was erected. That building was replaced in 1874 by the one shown here, which housed primary, intermediate, and high school departments. Because high school courses were infrequent, classes graduated only every few years. The building was closed in the early 1920s. A new high school and grade school were built in 1919 and 1922.

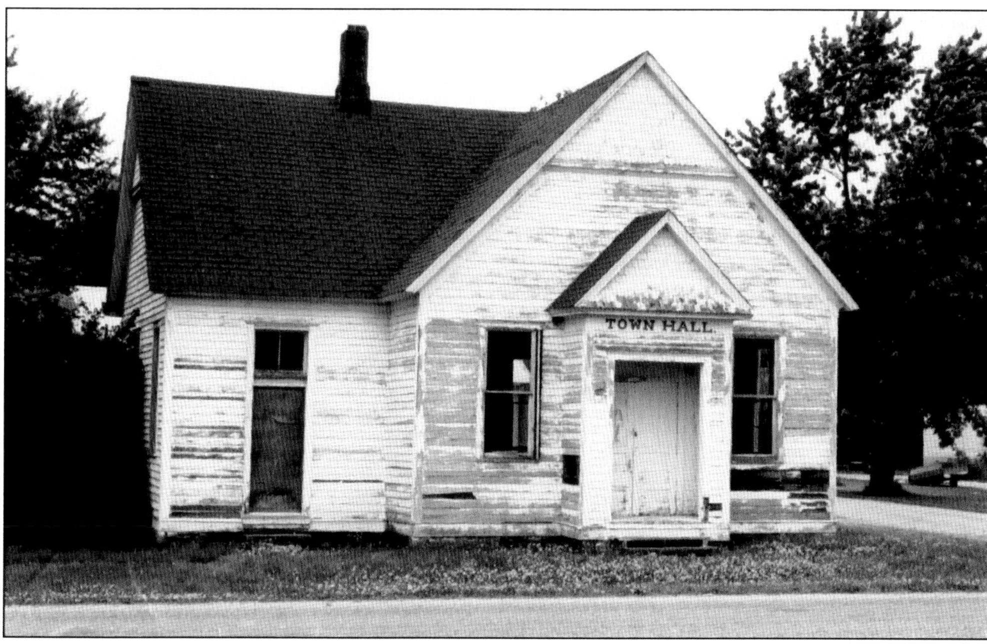

The Bardolph Town Hall, located on Chestnut Street, was built before the turn of the century, and it was originally painted gray with white trim. The building was used for community meetings until June 2002, when this photograph was taken. It is the only public or business building that remains essentially unaltered from the era when Bardolph was a thriving town.

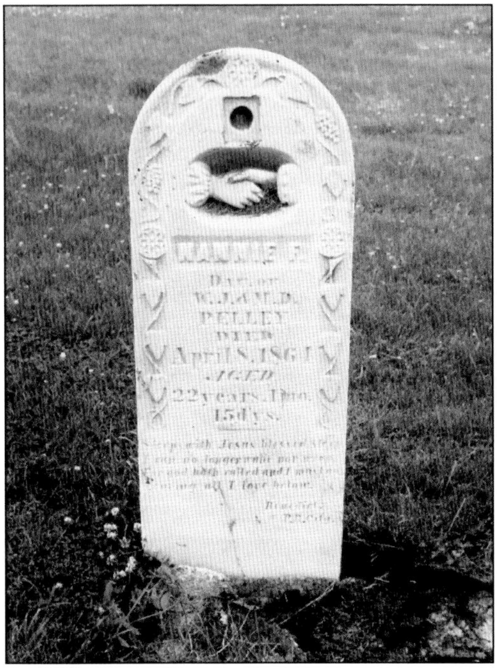

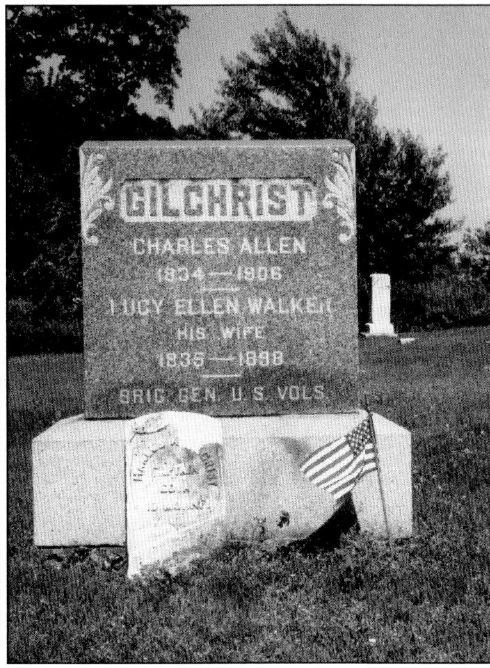

The Bardolph Cemetery, located northwest of town, has markers dating back to 1837. Included among them is this attractive headstone for Nannie F. Pelley, who died in 1864. Inscribed on it is a poem that expresses her ambivalence about death: "Sleep with Jesus, blessed sleep, / I can no longer wake nor weep, / For God hath called and I must go, / Leaving all I love below." The poem is mysteriously signed, "Benedict. / P.R. City." North of Bardolph and west of Bushnell on road 1950N is the Arbogast, or Pearce, Cemetery, which also has markers dating from 1837. Among them is the headstone of Charles Allen Gilchrist and his wife. The only Civil War general buried in McDonough County, he served in the 10th Missouri Infantry.

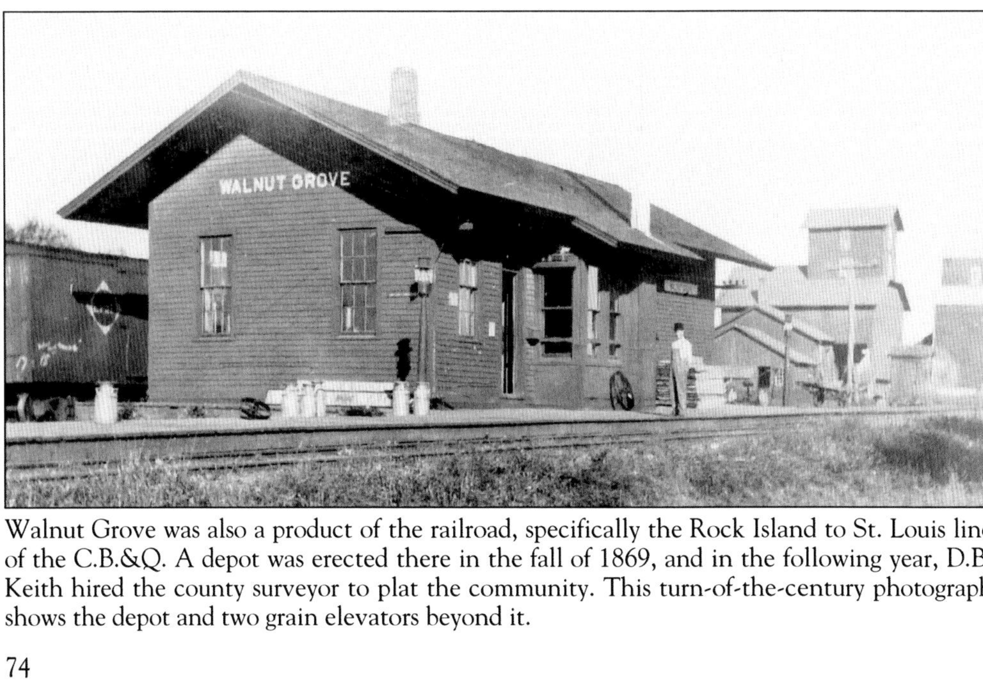

Walnut Grove was also a product of the railroad, specifically the Rock Island to St. Louis line of the C.B.&Q. A depot was erected there in the fall of 1869, and in the following year, D.B. Keith hired the county surveyor to plat the community. This turn-of-the-century photograph shows the depot and two grain elevators beyond it.

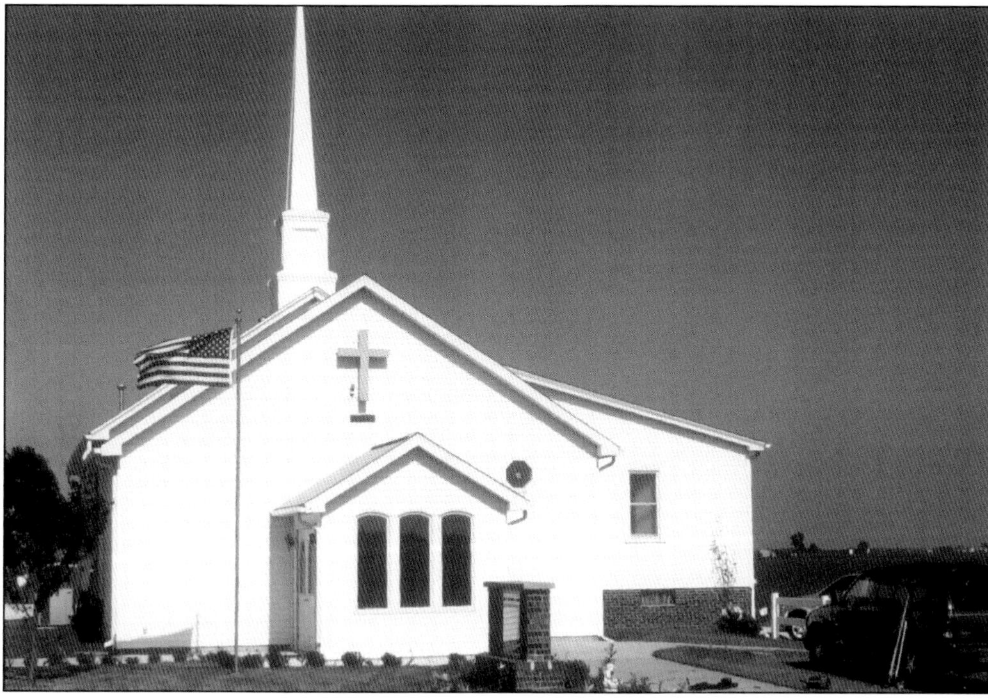

Walnut Grove Methodist Church was originally the Pleasant Mound Methodist Episcopal Church, which was organized in 1858 at the Union schoolhouse. That same year, a church building was erected a mile or so north of where Walnut Grove would later be platted. In the first decade of the 20th century, that structure was moved into the community. After it burned down in 1935, the church shown here was built and dedicated in 1937.

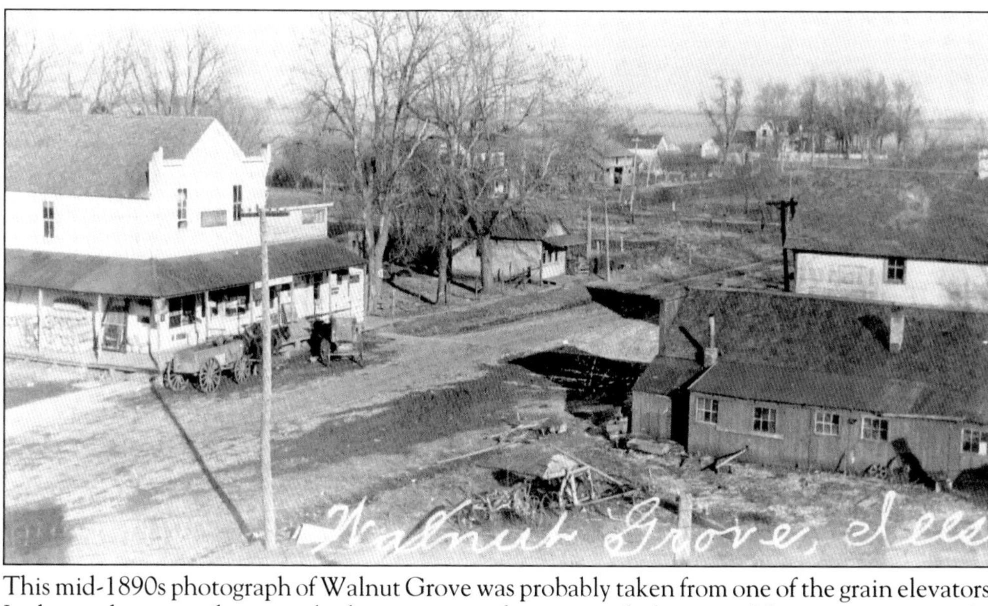

This mid-1890s photograph of Walnut Grove was probably taken from one of the grain elevators. It shows the general store, which was operated successively by several businessmen over the years. In the 1890s, George Tucker owned it. Walnut Grove also had a feed mill, two blacksmith shops, and a post office. At the right is Charles Raymer's blacksmith shop.

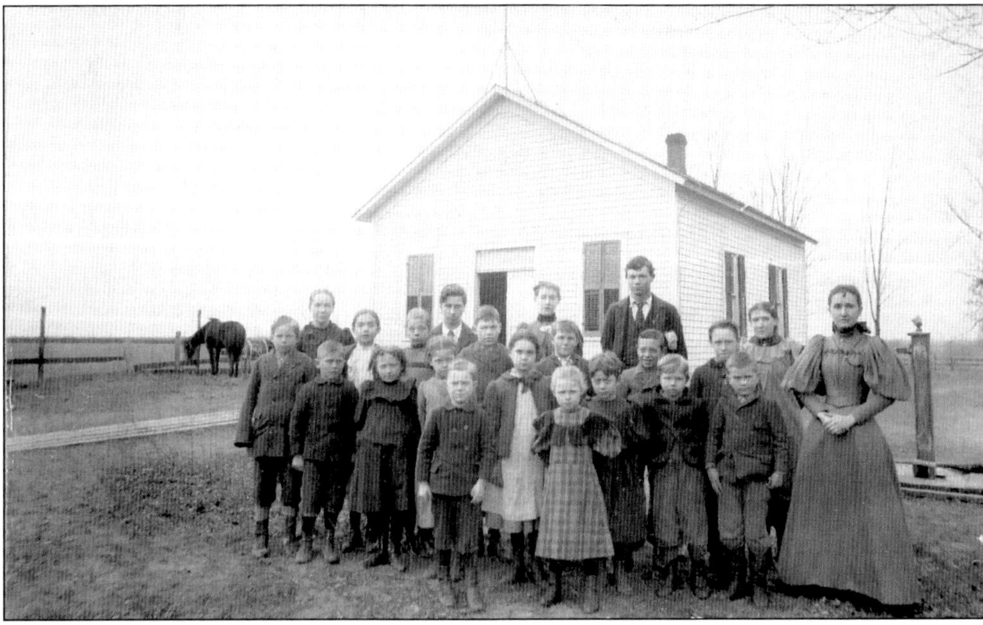

There were many rural schools with names like Prairie, Railroad, and Possum Hollow in the northeast section of the county. This 1897 photograph shows Mt. Solan School, which was located in section 11 of Macomb Township across the road and a little north of the Jerusalem Church. The teacher was Mattie Simpson.

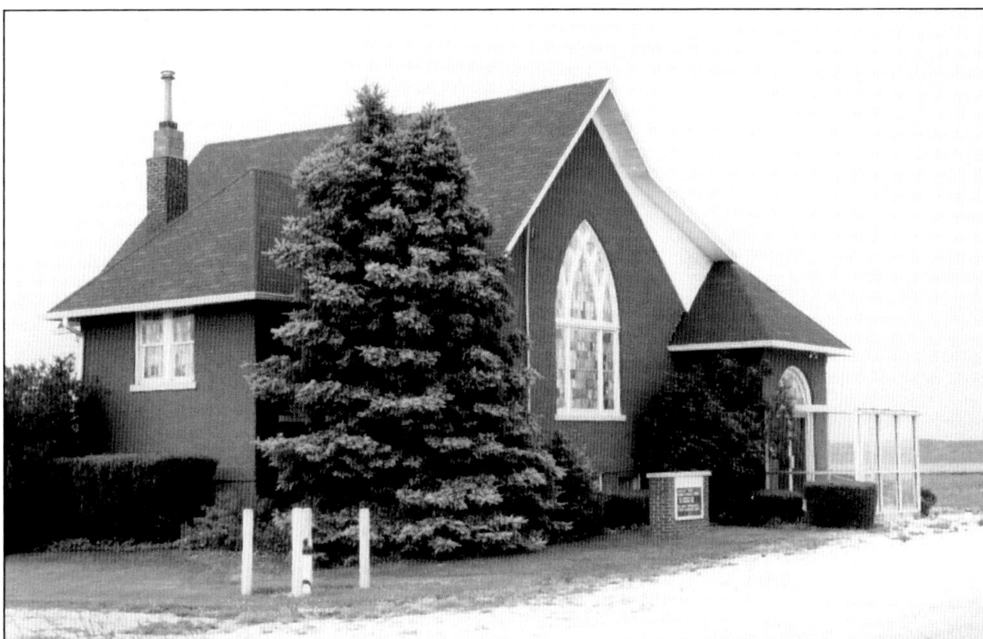

The Jerusalem United Methodist Church was organized in 1867 as the Jerusalem Chapel of the United Brethren Church. A frame church building was dedicated the following year, and it was replaced with the present brick structure in 1918. Remodeled in the 1960s, the church is located on road 1600E just south of road 1700N.

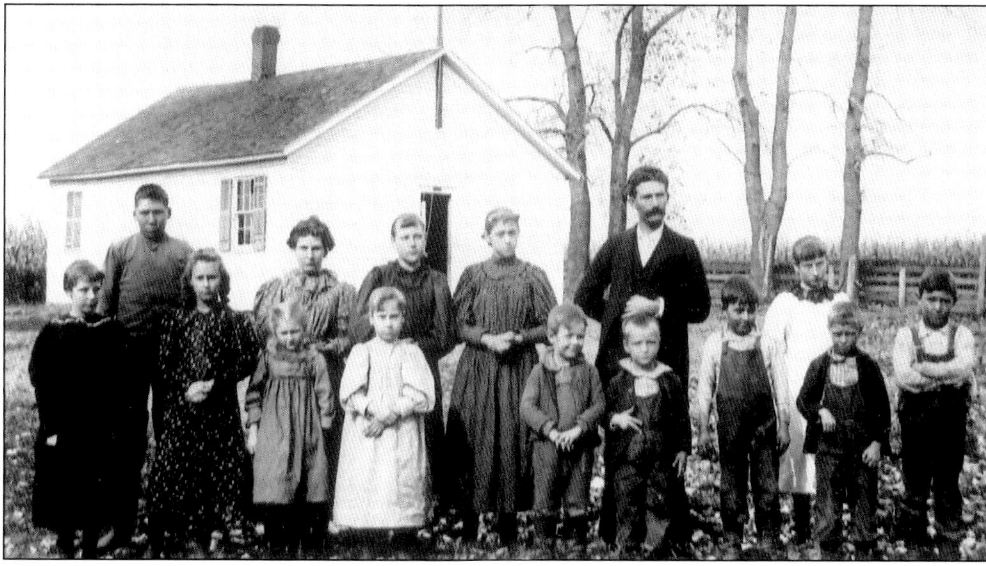

This photograph of Cottonwood School, located in section 33 of Mound Township at the intersection of road 1300N and Route 41, was taken in 1895, when the teacher was Albert Warfell. The school burned in 1899, and a sturdy brick one was erected to replace it. On June 24, 1924, that building and the nearby Cottonwood Free-Will Baptist Church were destroyed by a tornado. A third Cottonwood School was then built, and it was used until 1943. The building was torn down in the early 1980s.

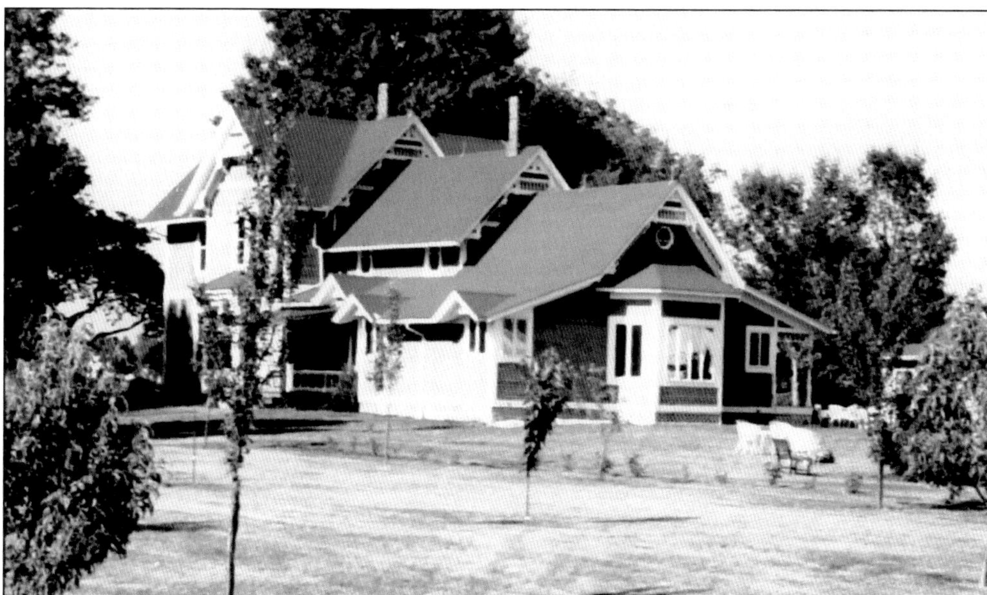

The most elegant 19th-century farmhouse in the county is located southwest of Bardolph on road 1450N. It was built in 1882 by Robert Work, who raised and imported livestock and was a grain dealer. The Queen Anne-style farmhouse had been vacant for 15 years when Dr. and Mrs. Lawrence M. Kerr bought it (with 125 acres) in 1984 and restored it, adding a third gable-roofed section in back, as shown in this rear view. The three main barns also remain, and the Kerrs have added four others.

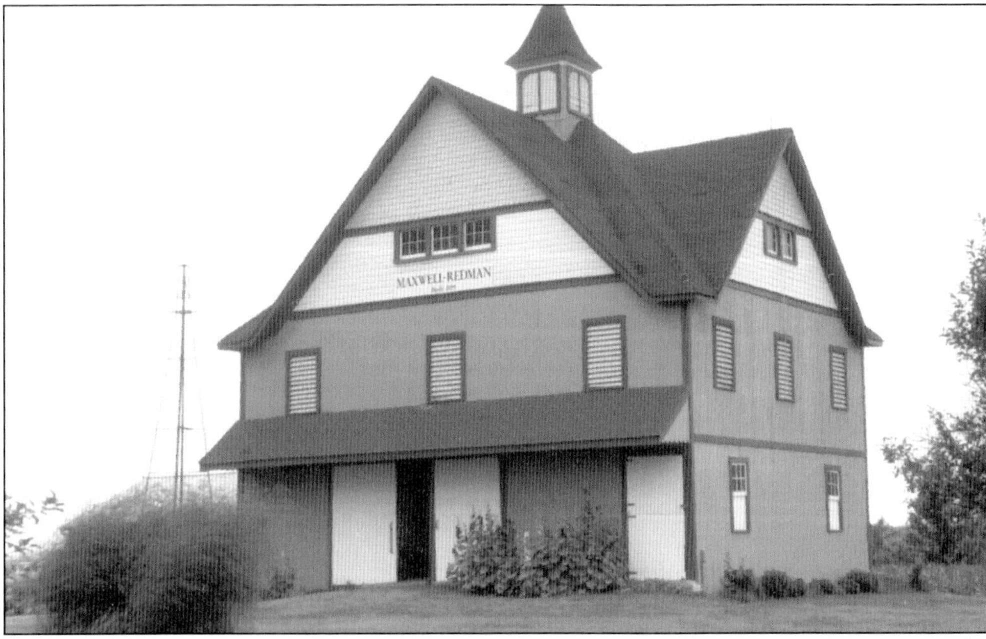

McDonough County is noted for its cross-gabled barns, built by contractor Newt Willis of Table Grove. The one in this photograph, located at the intersection of roads 1300N and 1600E, was erected in 1895. Willis also built the farmhouse in 1890, and it still stands as well. The farm has been owned by Mr. and Mrs. Gerald Redman since 1945, and the barn now contains an extensive exhibit of antique hand tools.

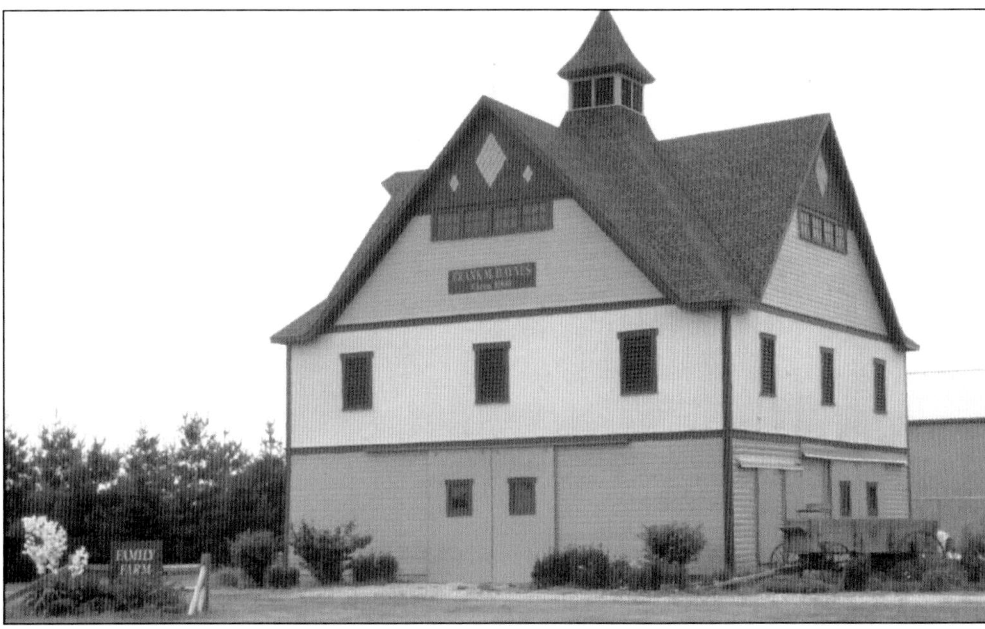

Another attractive Newt Willis cross-gabled barn is located on Route 136 at county road 1600E. The farm where it stands has been in the family of owner Charles H. ("Chick") Flack since 1857, and his great-grandfather, Frank Haynes, had the barn built in 1890. The farm is rented and maintained by Mr. and Mrs. Dean Ruebush.

Four

THE SOUTHWEST QUARTER OF THE COUNTY

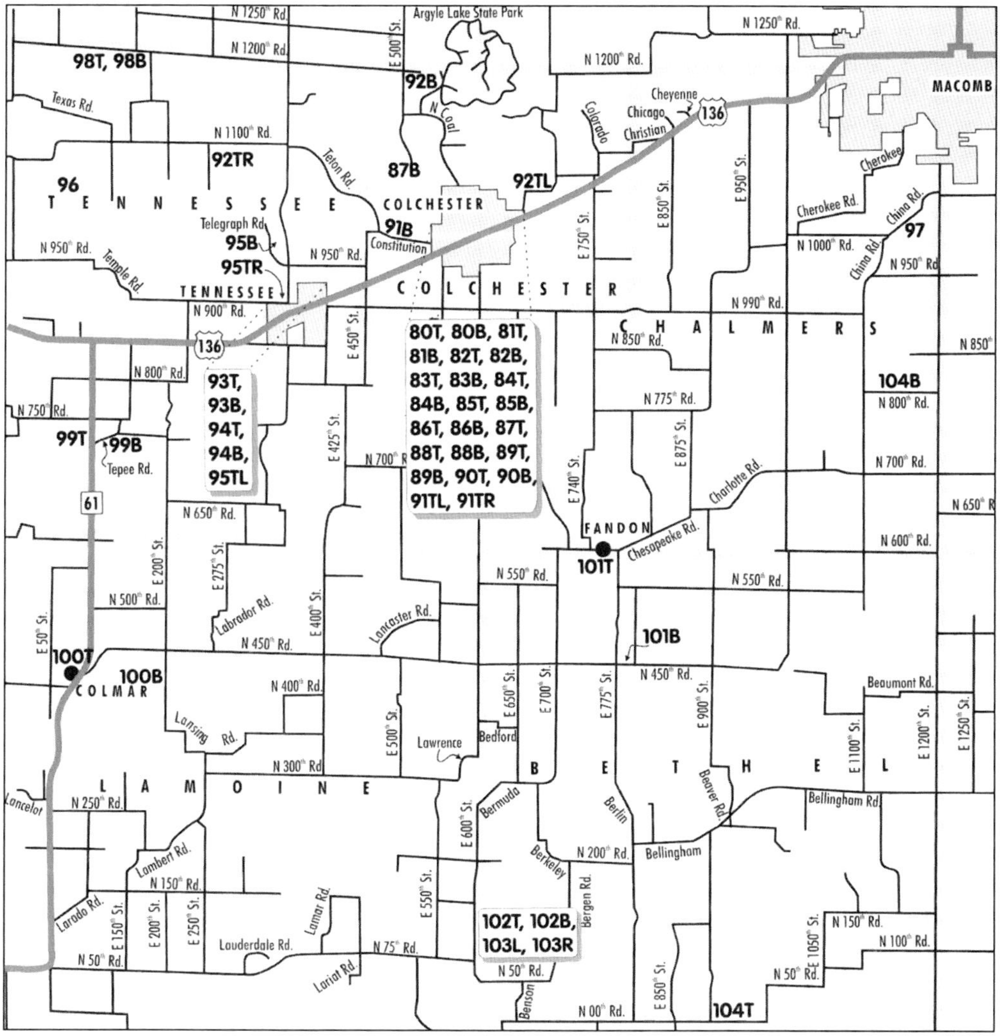

In the southwest quarter of McDonough County, the only community with a business district is Colchester and it has just 1,500 people. Like Tennessee and Colmar, it was fostered by the Northern Cross (later Chicago, Burlington and Quincy) Railroad, but only Colchester, a mining town, grew significantly. The landscape to the south is not familiar to most county residents, but it has many streams, small valleys, and stands of timber. It was settled largely by southern upland pioneers, and it was less prosperous than the rest of the county. In recent years, it has acquired a small Amish population.

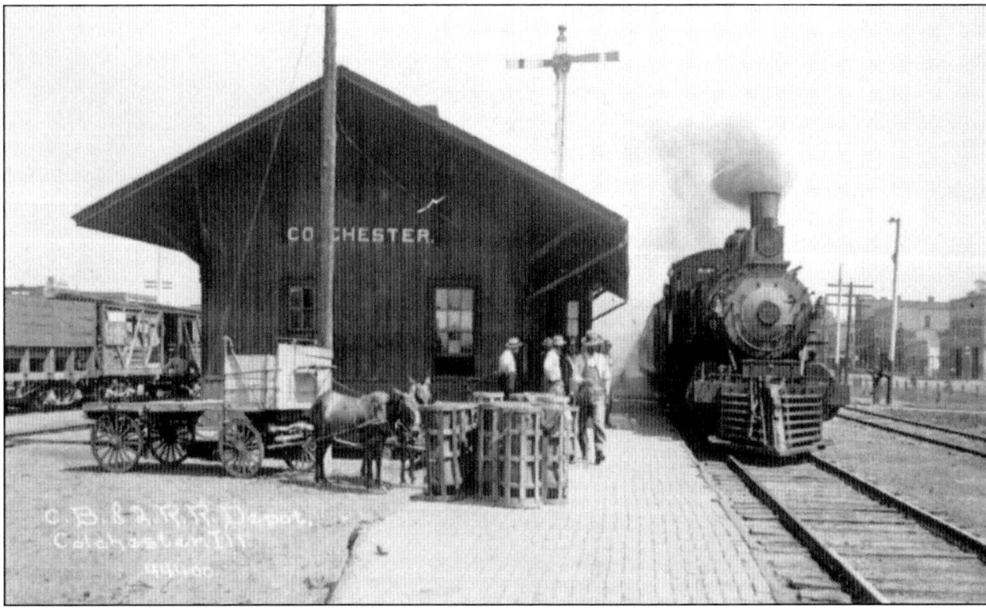

Pioneer coal mine operator James Roberts convinced the railroad to build a depot within a mile or so of the mines along the Lamoine River, and that was the start of Colchester, which was platted in 1855. The first depot was replaced by a larger one in the early 1870s, and it is shown in this early 20th-century photograph. By the 1880s, Colchester was shipping out 80,000 tons of coal a year, and 20 passenger and freight trains stopped there every day.

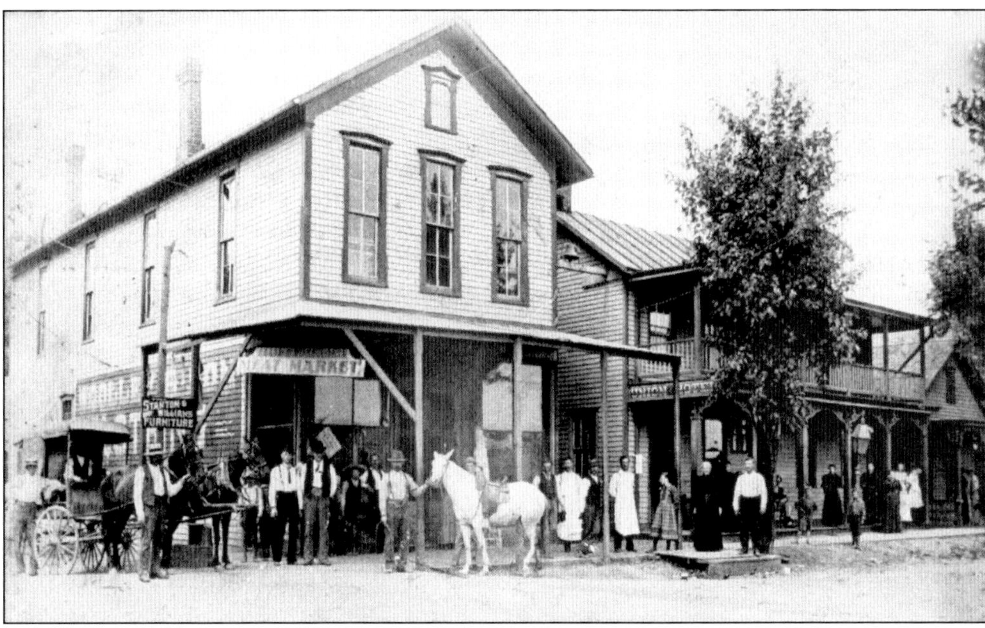

This 1889 photograph shows the Ellis and Dunsworth Meat Market, on the left, and the Union Hotel, located on Depot Street. Built in 1869, the hotel had a dining room, a sample room (for salesmen to display their goods), a dozen guest rooms, and a second-story verandah. After 1883, it was also the location of the Colchester Independent. Welsh immigrant J.D. Trew was the hotel proprietor.

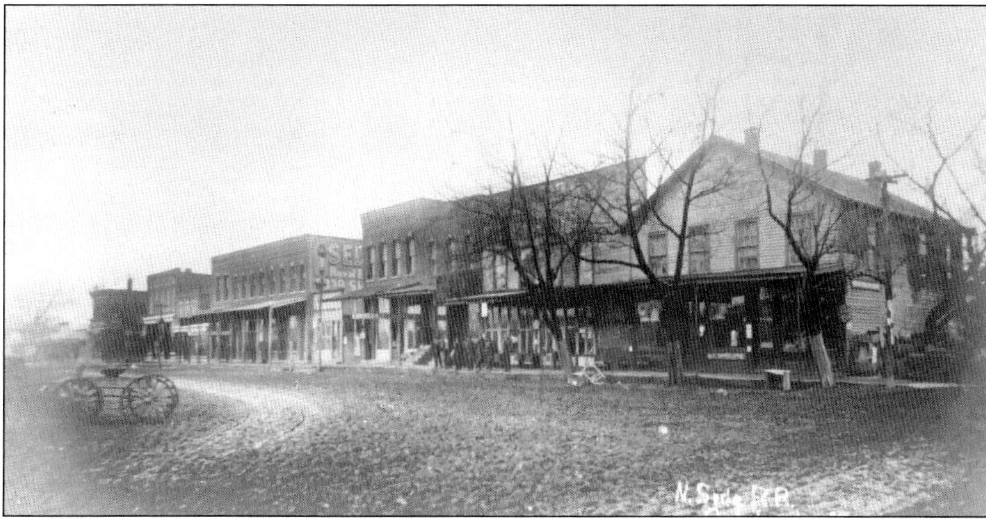

This 1890 photograph shows a long section of Depot Street. The large frame building on the right was the Abram Newland General Store, built in the late 1860s. Like so many of the Colchester coal miners, Newland was from England. He had come with his parents to Colchester in 1856, and after working in the mines and serving in the Civil War, he became a merchant, Methodist minister, and mine operator.

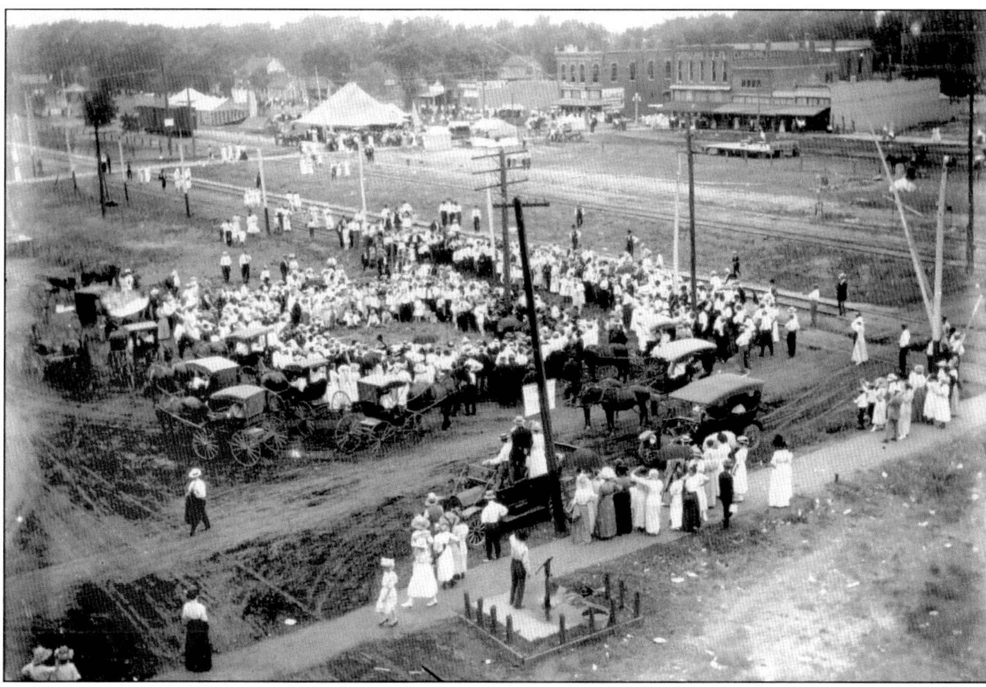

The Colchester Miners' Friendly Society, a kind of insurance club, was organized in 1867, and soon the members developed the most important annual event in the town's history: the Miners' Picnic. Commonly held in a grove south or west of town, it was a massive celebration of community to which local residents—and later all people—were invited. By the 1880s, activities were also held in the business district, as this 1912 photograph shows. It looks northwest, across the railroad grounds, to Depot Street.

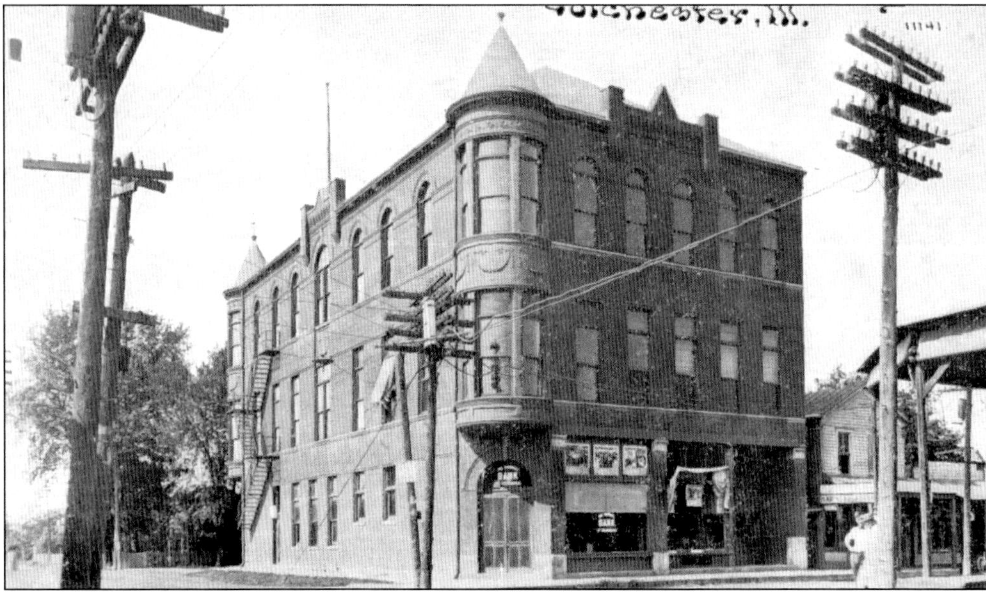

This postcard photograph shows the huge Fraternity Building, which was constructed in 1901 at the corner of Coal and Macomb Streets. The first floor was soon occupied by the Colchester State Bank, and the second and third floors were used by Colchester's various fraternal organizations. Built at a time when Colchester was starting to decline, it symbolized the town's determination to succeed in the new century. It was eventually razed in 1972.

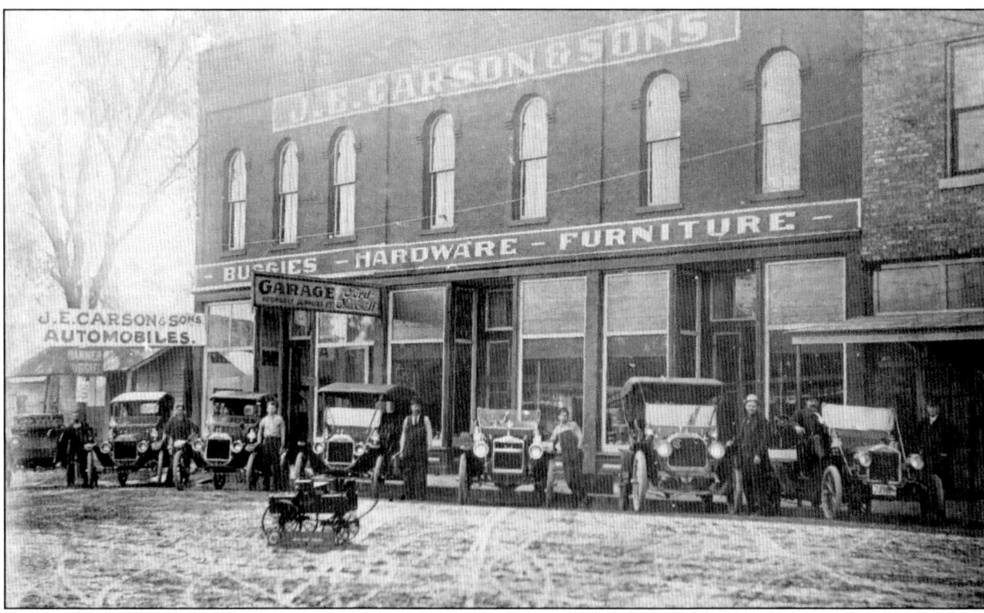

J.E. Carson had been a farm equipment dealer in Middletown before moving to Colchester, where he sold farm implements, hardware, furniture, and buggies. He became a Ford dealer in 1909, one year after Henry Ford starting mass producing the Model T. This photograph was taken in about 1912, and it shows various makes of cars in front of his dealership on Market Street. Carson is standing beside the second car from the right. He was the most successful early automobile dealer in the county.

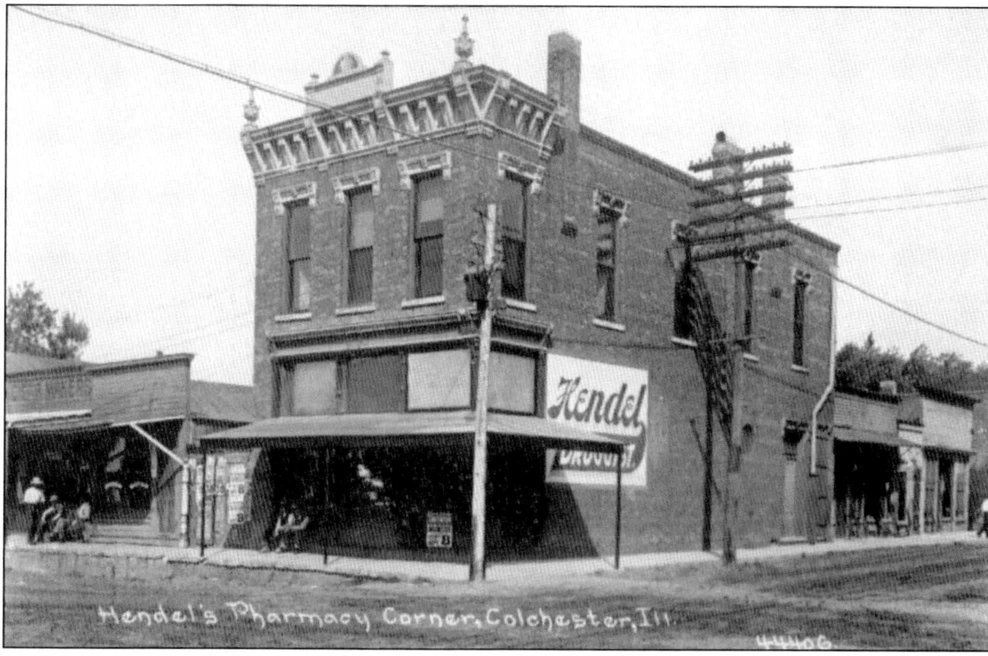

Built in the 1880s, the R.W. Hendel Drug Store is still standing at the corner of Coal and Depot streets. At this location on October 26, 1929, bootlegger Bill McGrann was shot and killed by Charles Zimmerman, who was later convicted and sent to prison. To the left of Hendel's is George P. Hotten's cigar making shop; to the right is Swan's (later Foster's) Restaurant.

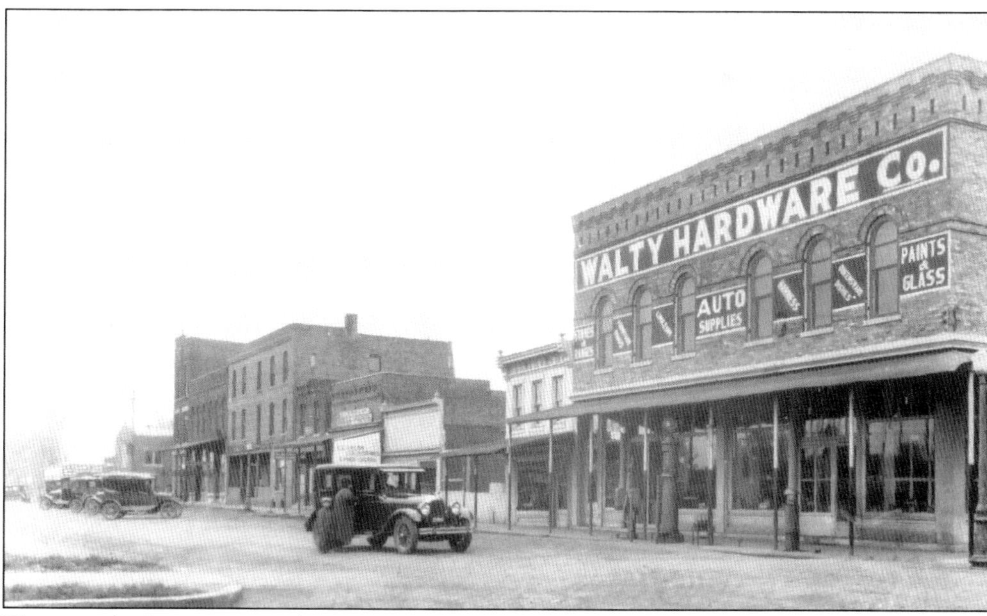

This view looks east on Market Street on the south side of the railroad tracks in early 1927. In the center of the photograph is Kelly Wagle's taxi service. The A.M. Walty Hardware Store was destroyed by fire in October of that year but was rebuilt. The large brick structure in the middle of the block is the Colchester Hotel, built in 1897, which is still standing and is now an apartment building.

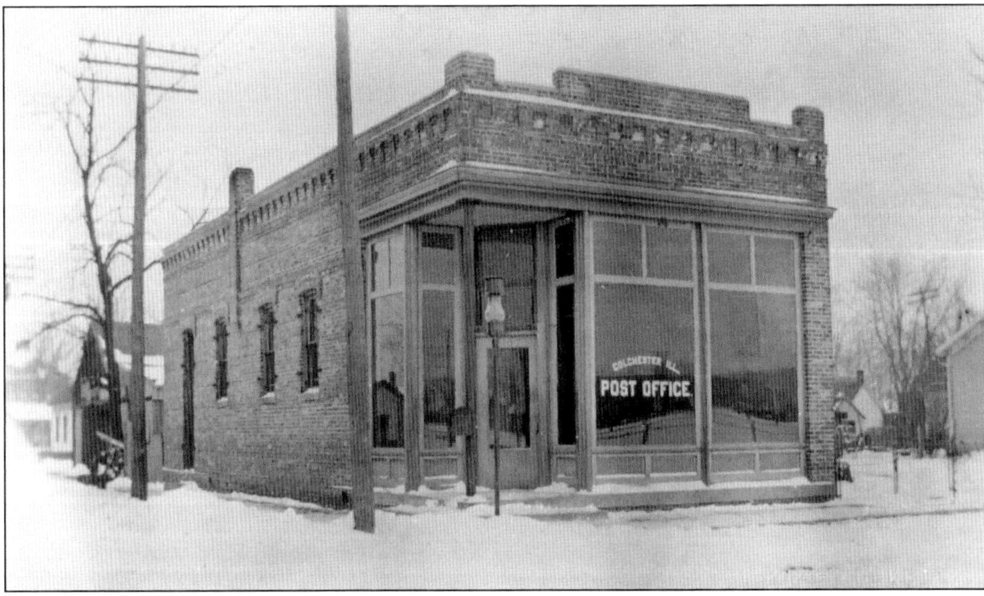

The Colchester Post Office was established in the mid-1850s. The building shown here was constructed at the turn of the century and was located just east of the present post office, at the corner of Market and Coal Streets. It was torn down and replaced by the present building in 1960.

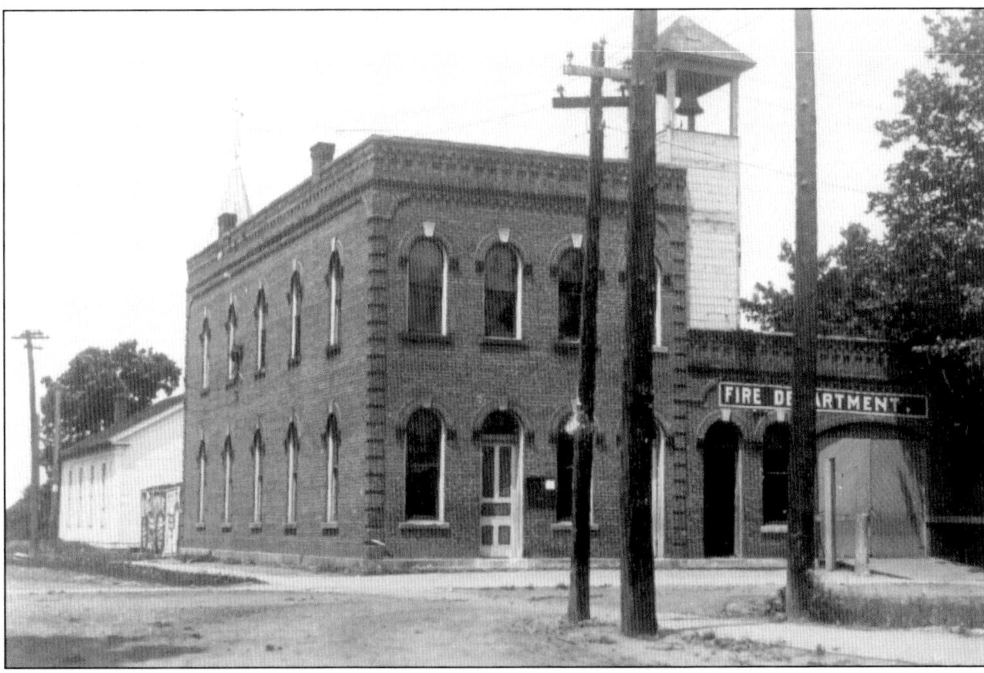

The Colchester City Building was constructed on Macomb Street in 1887. It housed the mayor's office and the marshal's office, as well as the jail. Since 1975, the main floor has been the Colchester Library. The adjacent fire station, built at the same time, was extremely busy in the early 20th century, when a series of fires in 1906, 1907, 1908, and 1910 destroyed many buildings. The fire station was later used for city offices from 1983 to 2002, and it has now become part of the library.

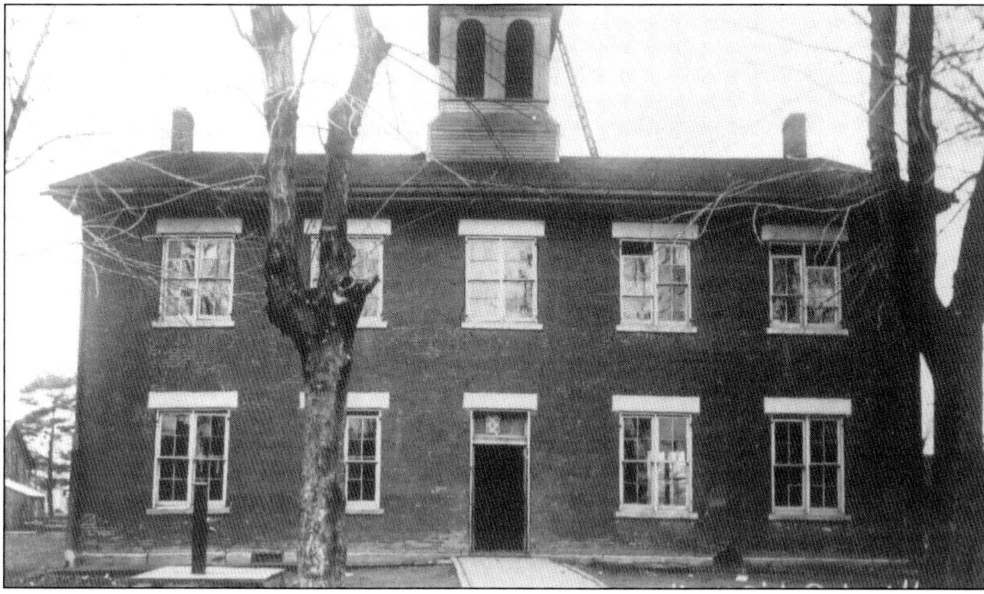

Colchester's North Side School was built in 1869 and was located on the main east-west road, now known as Route 136, just west of Coal Street. It had four classrooms. The lower-grade classes were downstairs, and the high school classes were upstairs. An addition was constructed in 1882. This turn-of-the-century photograph shows the water pump at the left in the front yard. The building was torn down in 1907.

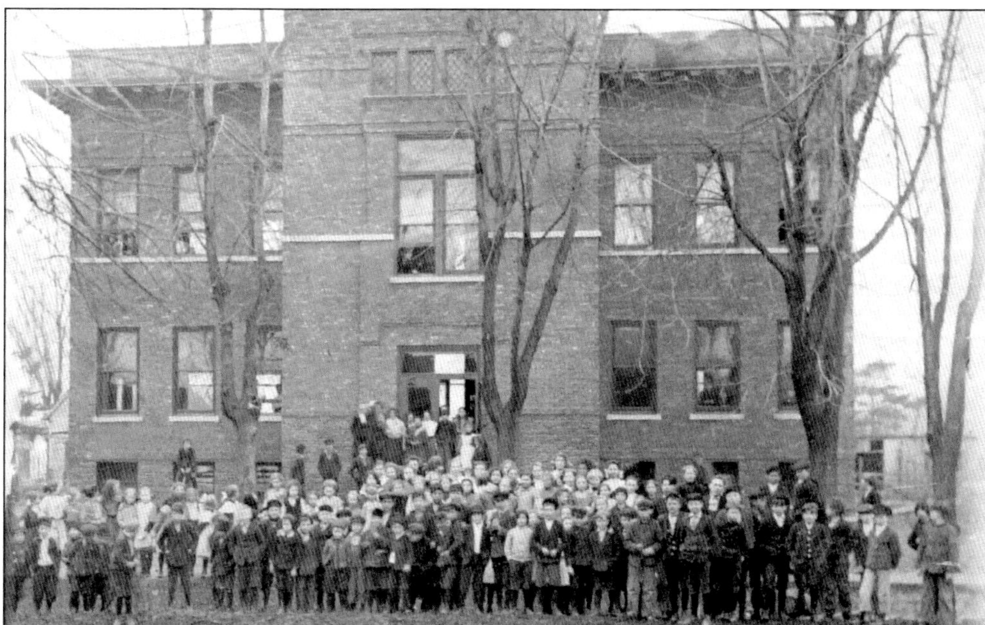

This Colchester school building was constructed in 1908 on the site that had been occupied by the 1869 school building. It had three floors, but the bottom one was below grade so stairs led down to it. This building became the high school in 1921, after a controversial vote on high school expansion. A study hall and gymnasium were added in 1932. After the current high school was built in 1969, this one was torn down.

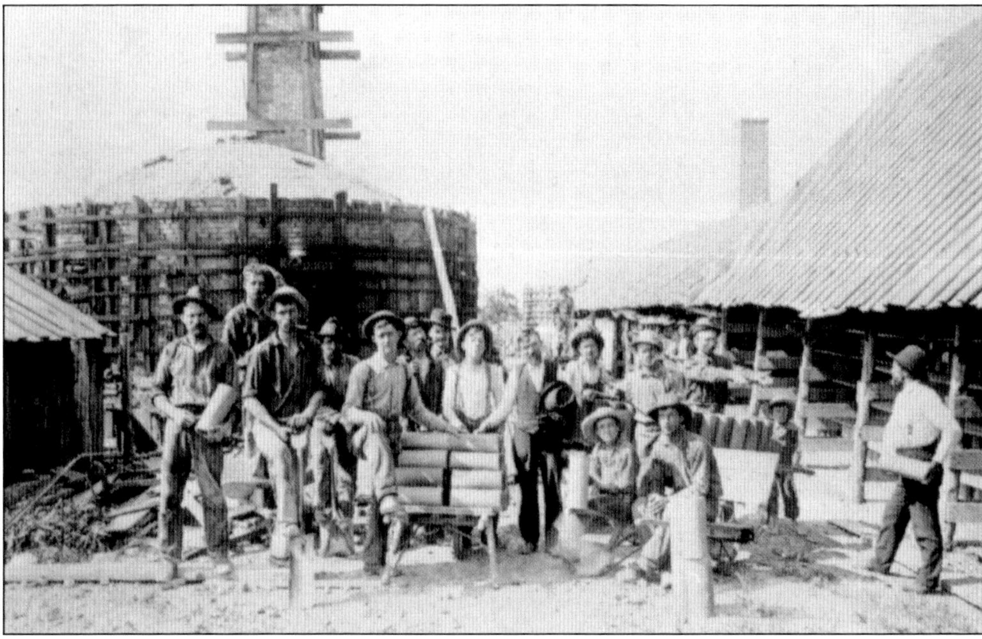

In 1867, a British immigrant named Abraham Horrocks started a brickyard a half-mile north of Colchester on Coal Street. Seven years later he sold that operation to John and Moses King, who were also from England. By the 1880s, Moses was the sole operator, and the brickyard employed 16 men. It eventually had 4 round kilns, 2 long drying sheds, and a factory building that could turn out 100,000 bricks a week. Most were shipped out by rail. In this photograph, Moses is in the middle, holding his hat.

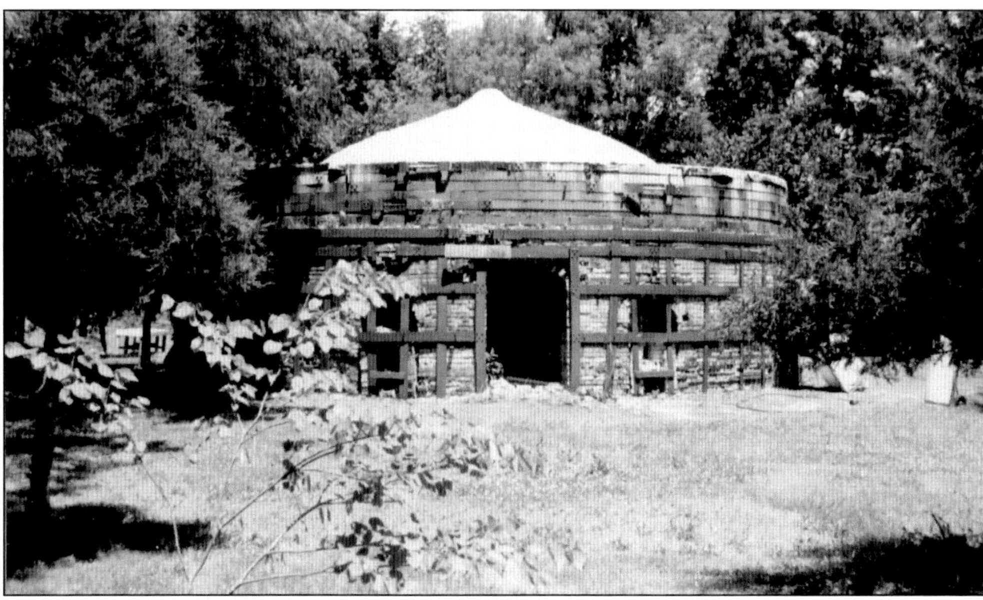

The King family operated the brickyard until 1970, when it closed. It is now being restored and landscaped by Tim Schroll and Dev Genovese to serve as an educational facility. Since 2000, the site, which includes the Moses King home on Coal Street, has been listed on the National Register of Historic Places. This contemporary photograph shows one of the four beehive kilns.

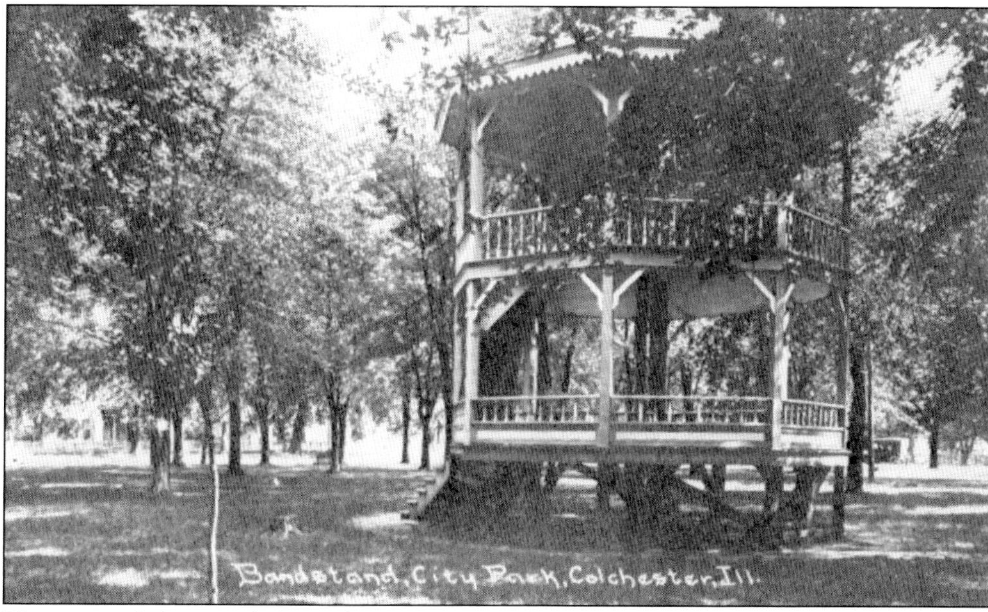

This postcard photograph shows the two-story bandstand, or "parkorium," erected in Colchester's city park during the early 1890s. In the summertime, the local band played concerts there, and the gazebo-like structure was sometimes decorated with flags and bunting for the Fourth of July. The park itself was established when the town was laid out, and trees were planted in the 1870s.

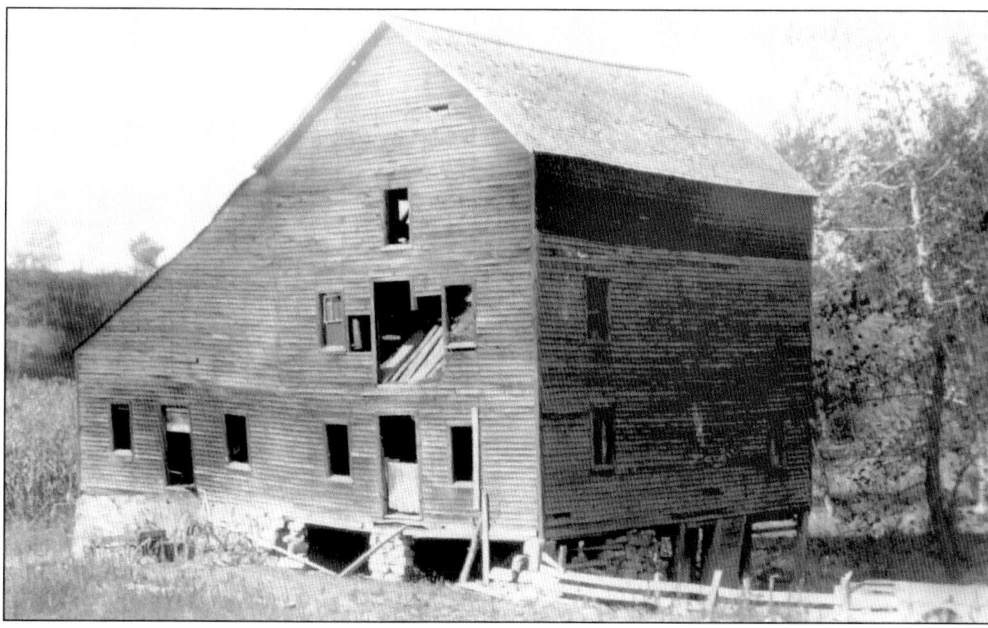

The Pleasant Valley Mill was built northwest of Colchester on the north side of the Lamoine River in 1838 by Jacob Emerick, and it was later operated by several others, most notably Joseph C.D. Carmack, then John and Newman Foster, and then John ("Jake") Myers. The mill ceased to operate by the turn of the century and was torn down in 1909, but that area was also the location of the Pleasant Valley Club, established in 1917. Members could fish, swim, boat, and picnic. Today the road leading to the old mill and park site is 500E.

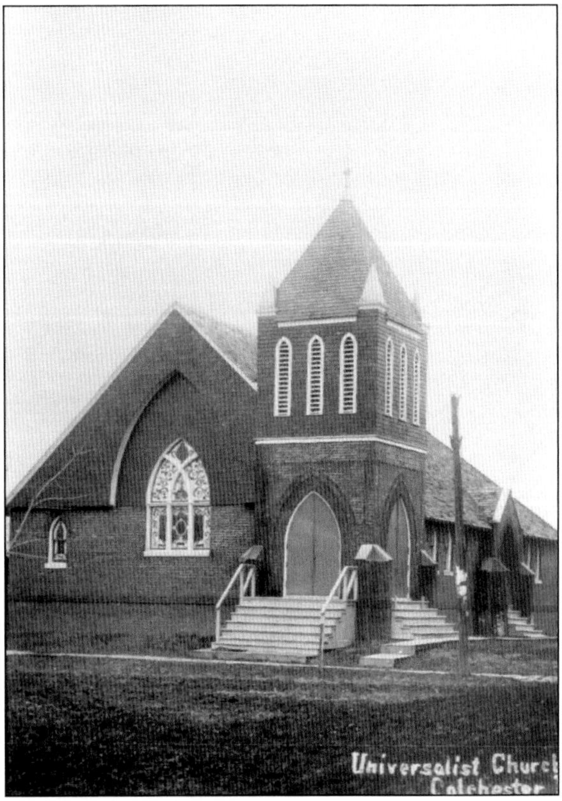

The Universalist Church was located on E. Depot Street, where the Jones Mortuary is today. The congregation was organized in 1897, and the church building shown here was constructed in 1902. The group soon disbanded, however, and in 1922, Frank Williams bought the building and converted it to a funeral home. It was destroyed by fire on February 22, 1925. The mortuary that now occupies the site has a stained-glass window that depicts the church.

The First Baptist Church of Colchester is located at 301 E. South Street. The congregation was organized in 1904, and this substantial building was constructed three years later. The structure has been remodeled, and the current entrance is where the triple stained-glass window, on the right end, is shown in this early photograph.

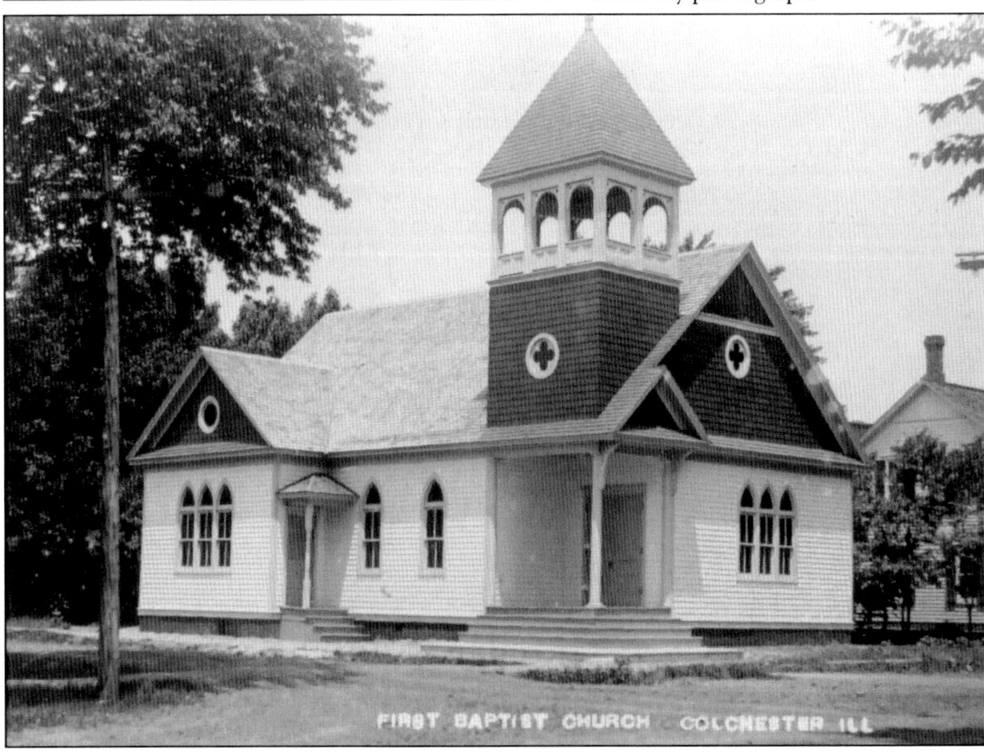

The tallest structure in Colchester was once the First Christian Church, located just west of the curve on the main road (now Route 136). The congregation was organized in 1867, and this lovely building was erected later that year. In 1907, it was destroyed in one of the blazes that was apparently set by a firebug.

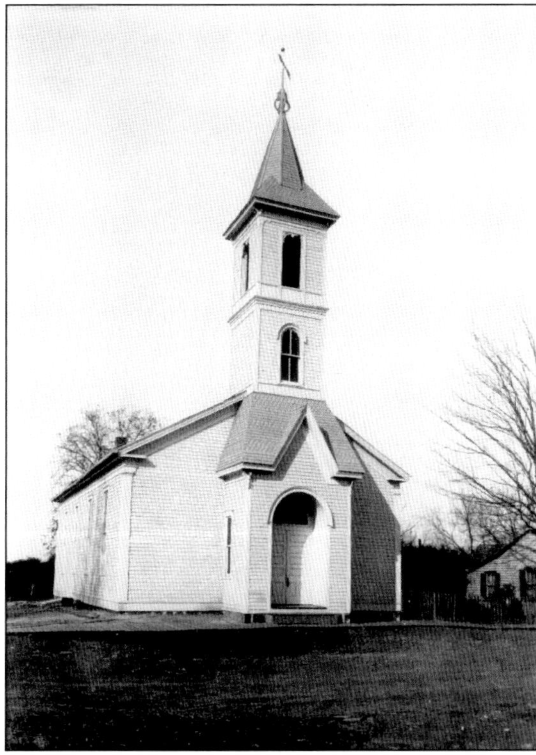

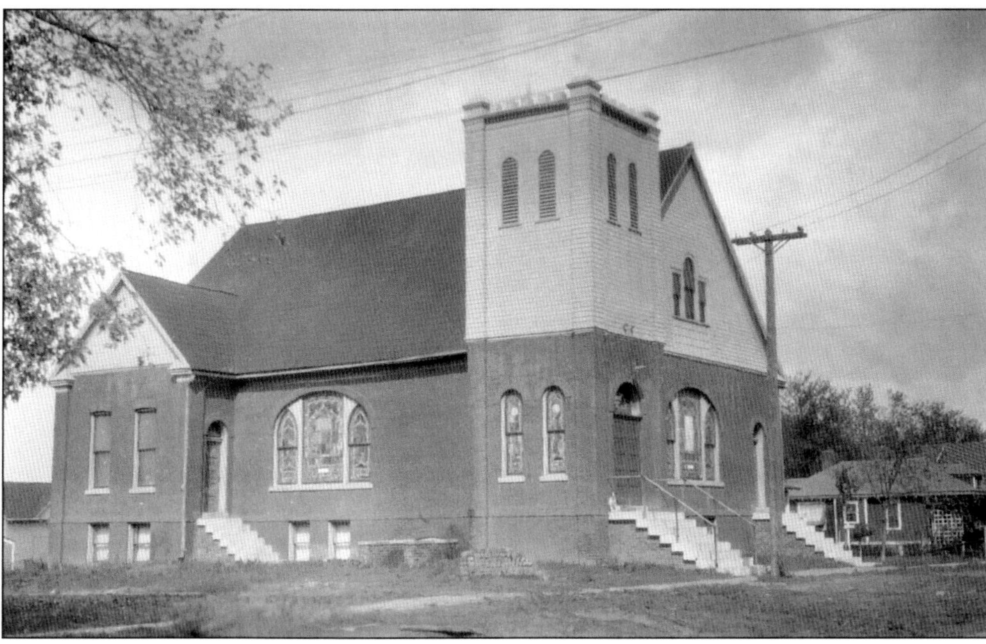

This 1930 photograph shows the second First Christian Church, which was built on the same location as the frame structure. It was dedicated in 1908, and an addition was dedicated in 1956. In 1977, the congregation erected a new building at 201 N. Hun Street, but this older one is still standing and, in recent years, has been operating as an antique shop. It features lovely stained glass windows donated by the Baird and Stevens families.

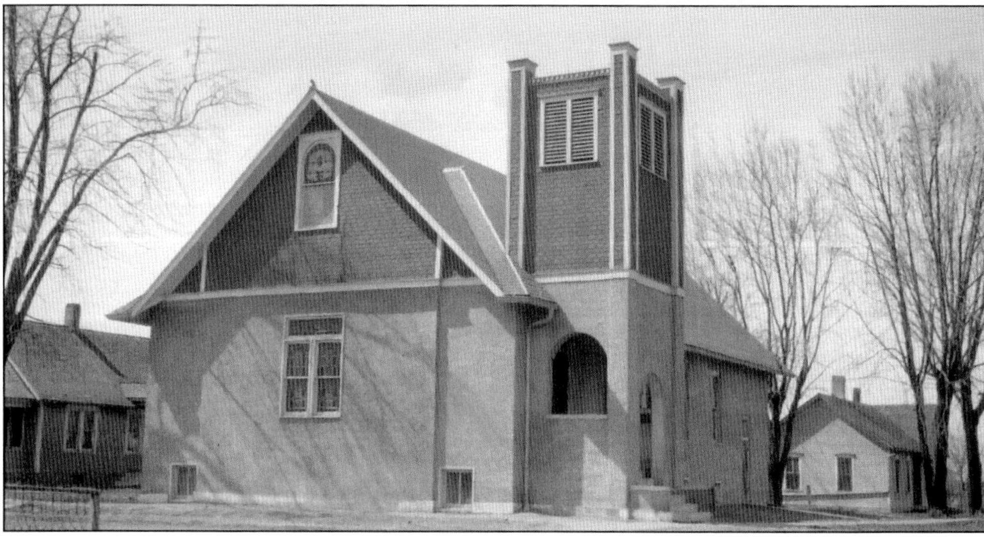

The first church in Colchester was the Methodist Episcopal (later United Methodist), which was organized in 1858. The structure shown in this 1930 photograph was erected on Elizabeth Street in 1862. An addition was built in 1886, and the church was remodeled in 1925. It was sold to the Masonic Lodge in 1966 and is now unused. The current United Methodist Church was built nearby at 218 W. McLean Street in 1964.

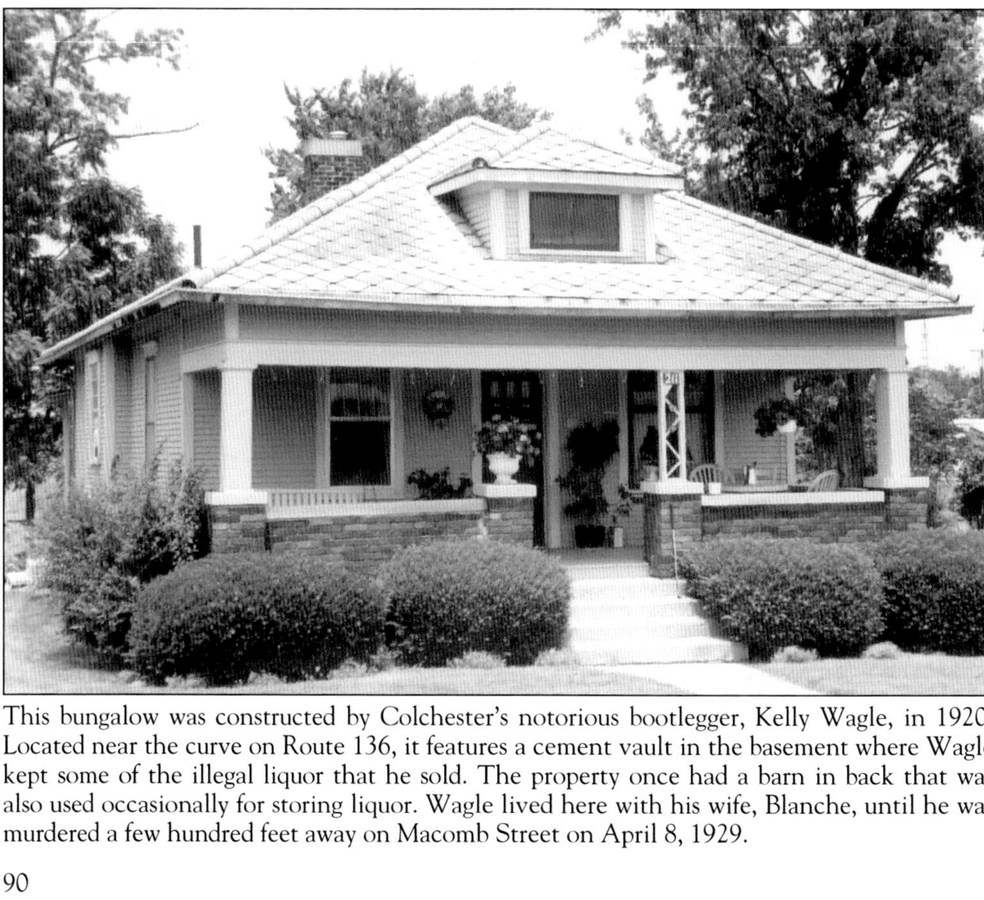

This bungalow was constructed by Colchester's notorious bootlegger, Kelly Wagle, in 1920. Located near the curve on Route 136, it features a cement vault in the basement where Wagle kept some of the illegal liquor that he sold. The property once had a barn in back that was also used occasionally for storing liquor. Wagle lived here with his wife, Blanche, until he was murdered a few hundred feet away on Macomb Street on April 8, 1929.

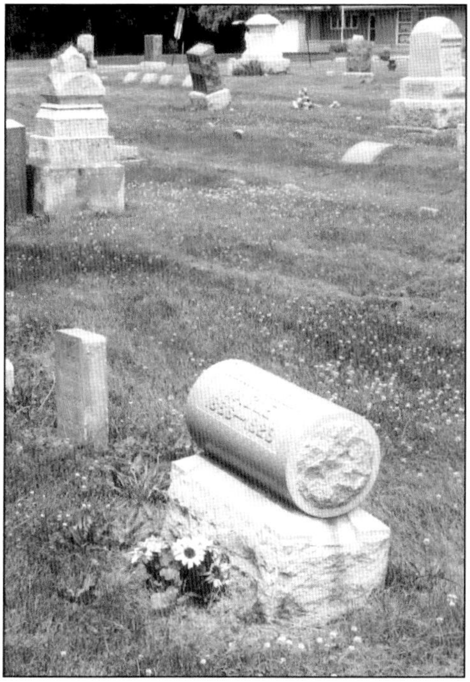

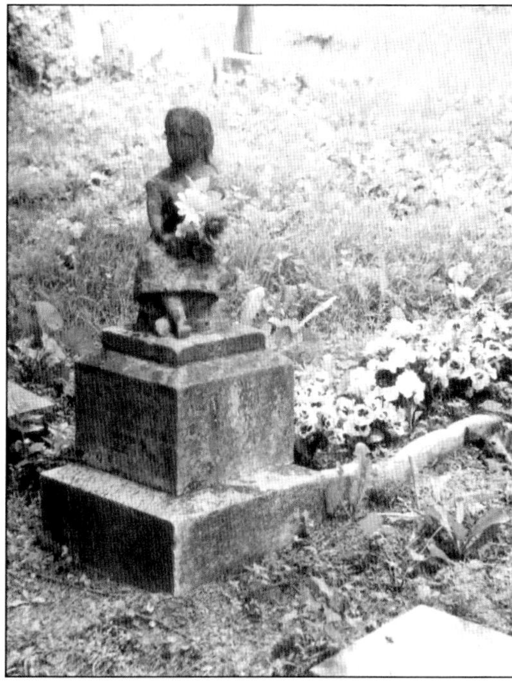

Kelly Wagle's gravestone is in Mt. Auburn Cemetery. As the recent photograph at the left reveals, someone places flowers on his grave every Memorial Day. Established in 1881 on N. Coal Street, Mt. Auburn has markers for many Colchester leaders, including James Roberts, the first and most important large-scale coal mine operator. Shown at the right is the headstone for six-year-old Gertrude Jones, who died the year Kelly Wagle was born (1886). It features the statue of a little girl.

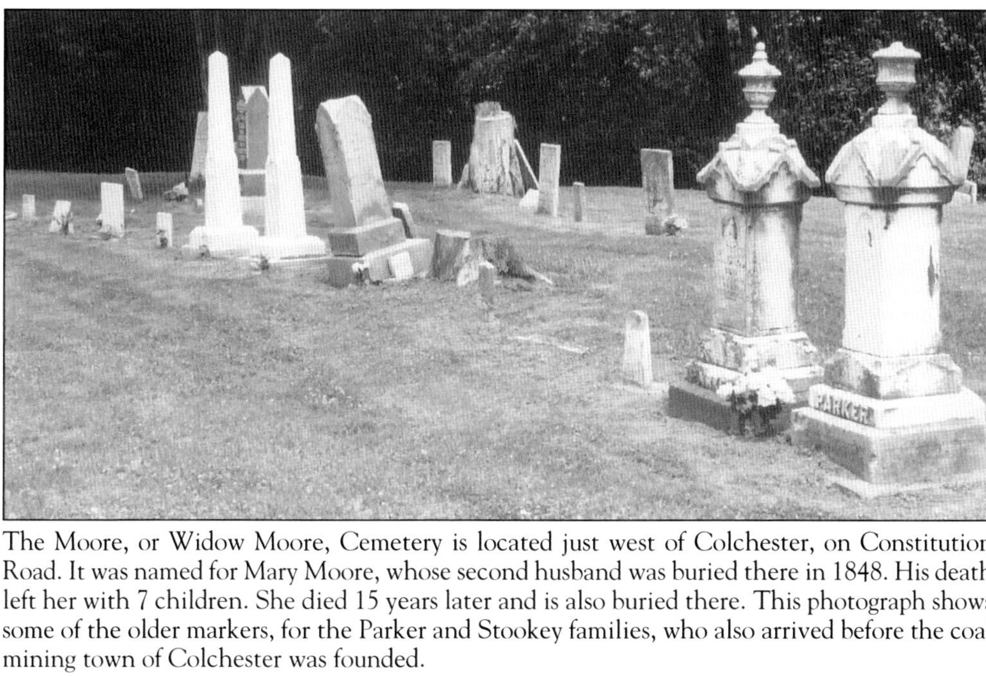

The Moore, or Widow Moore, Cemetery is located just west of Colchester, on Constitution Road. It was named for Mary Moore, whose second husband was buried there in 1848. His death left her with 7 children. She died 15 years later and is also buried there. This photograph shows some of the older markers, for the Parker and Stookey families, who also arrived before the coal mining town of Colchester was founded.

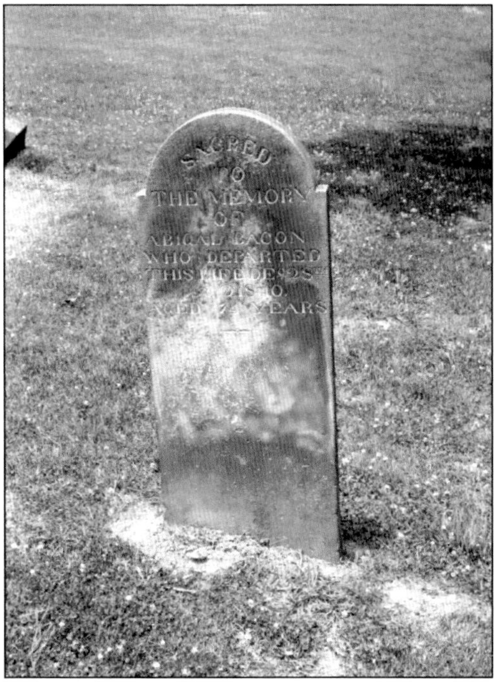
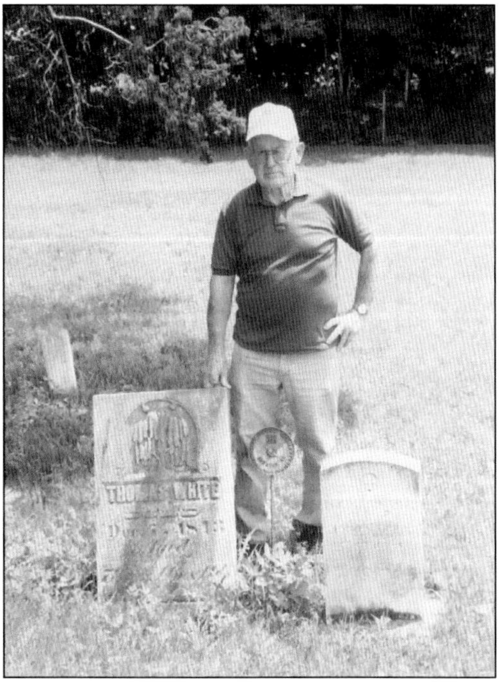

The Bean Cemetery also predates Colchester. Located east of town on road 700E, it has some very early markers for the Bacon family. The burial of Charles W. Bacon in 1838 started the burying ground. The headstone in the left photograph, for his mother, Abigail Bacon, dates from 1840. The Bacons, who operated a mill, were the earliest residents in the area where Colchester was later platted. The oldest marker in the White Cemetery, west of Colchester near road 1100N, is for Revolutionary War soldier Thomas White, who died in 1843. Standing beside it is his great-great-great-grandson, Wayne White.

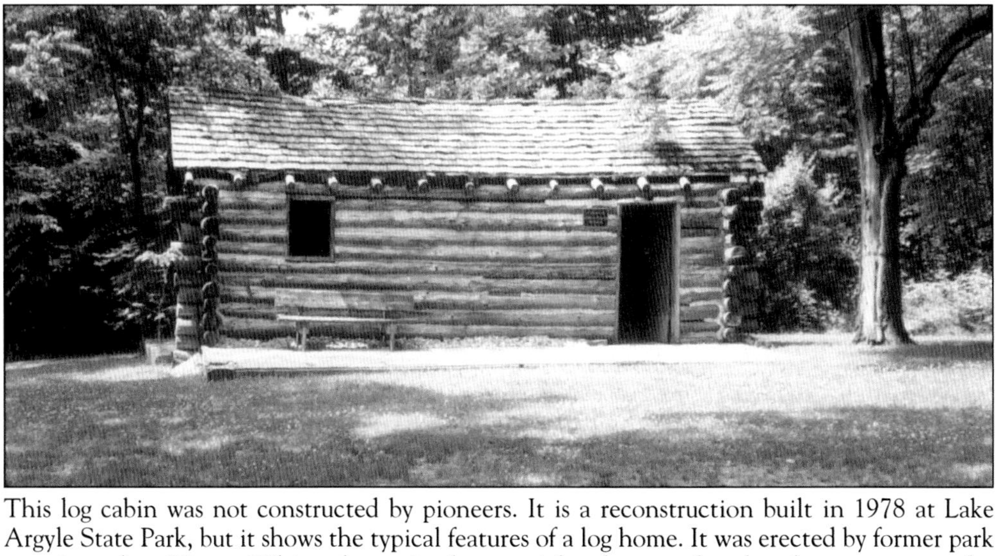

This log cabin was not constructed by pioneers. It is a reconstruction built in 1978 at Lake Argyle State Park, but it shows the typical features of a log home. It was erected by former park superintendent Wayne White, shown in the top right photograph, who also reconstructed a typical drift coal mine elsewhere in the park. The state park itself was established in 1948 in an area once known as Argyle Hollow.

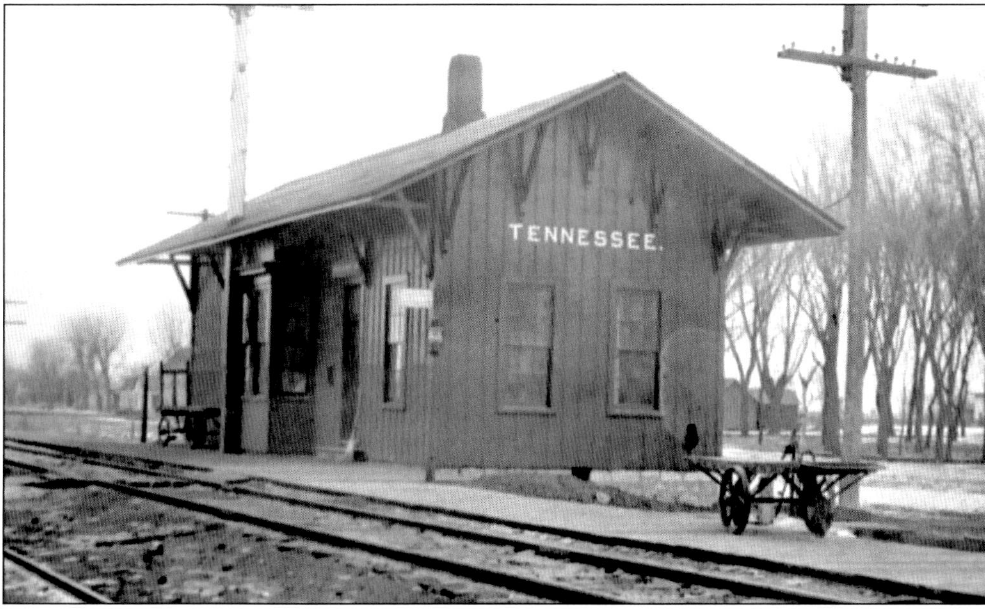

Like Colchester, Tennessee was founded because of the railroad. Platted in 1854 by Joseph B. Bacon, Steve Cockerham, and Thomas Waddle, the community was known for 20 years as "Tennessee Station." This small depot was probably erected shortly after the Northern Cross Railroad arrived in 1855, but this is an early 20th-century photograph, so the building may be a later one.

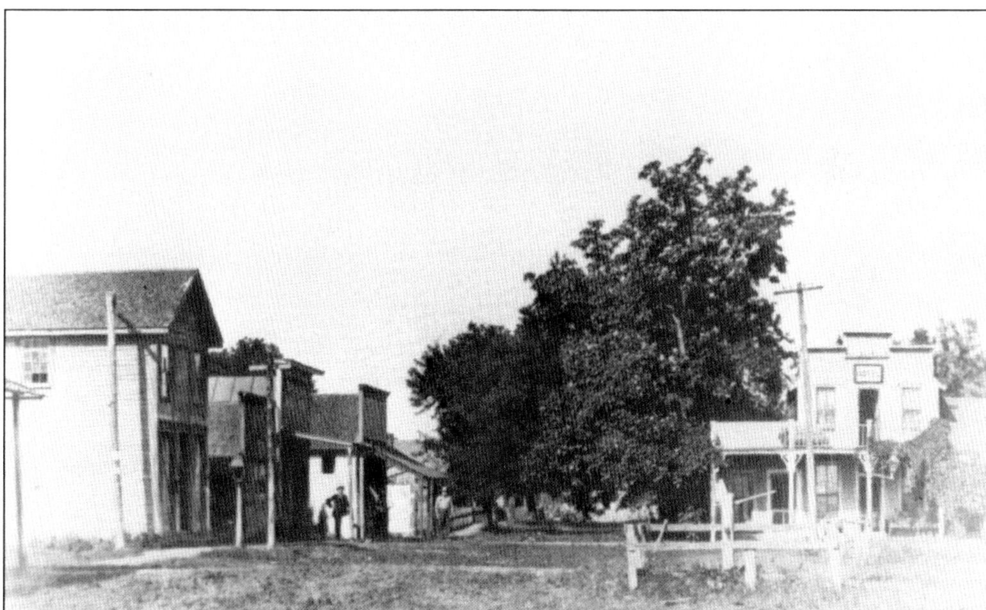

This photograph of Main Street dates from the turn of the century. The building at the far left is Douglas Glasgow's hardware store, which was built by B.F. Thompson as a general store in 1865. Glasgow, who clerked for Thompson, bought it in 1880, and Thompson built a larger store across the street. The building at the right is the Liberty House Hotel, erected by Edmund N. Driscoll in 1858. By the 1880s, Tennessee had a couple of other stores and a blacksmith shop.

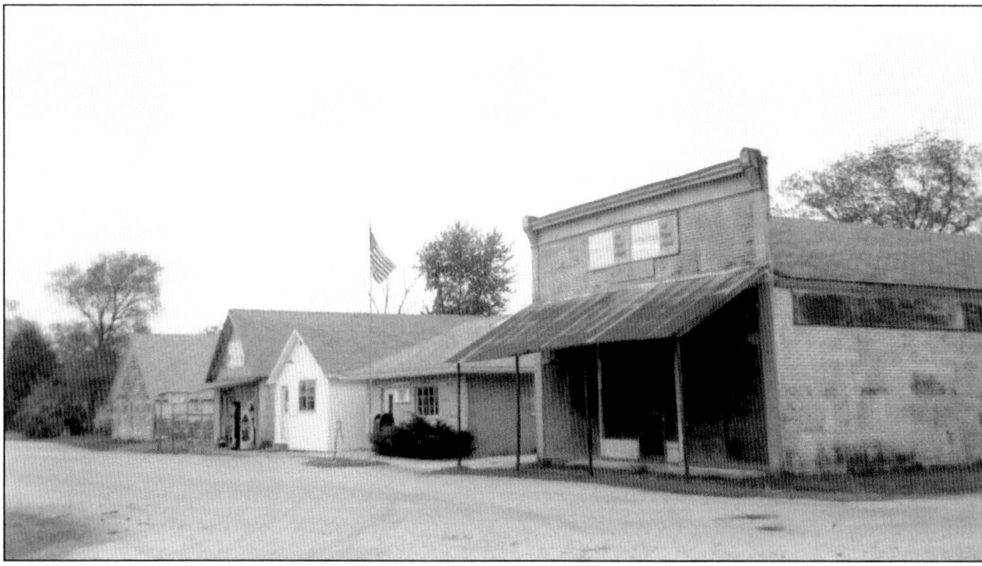

This contemporary photograph of Tennessee's Main Street shows the Keith grocery and general store, the post office, the white-sided city building, and a pool hall and barber shop, which has served as an antique store in recent years. Built at the turn of the century, the grocery store was successively operated by John Pittinger, Darrell and Lela Booz, Otis and Martha Flint, and Ted and Delores Keith. The Keiths closed the store in 1975.

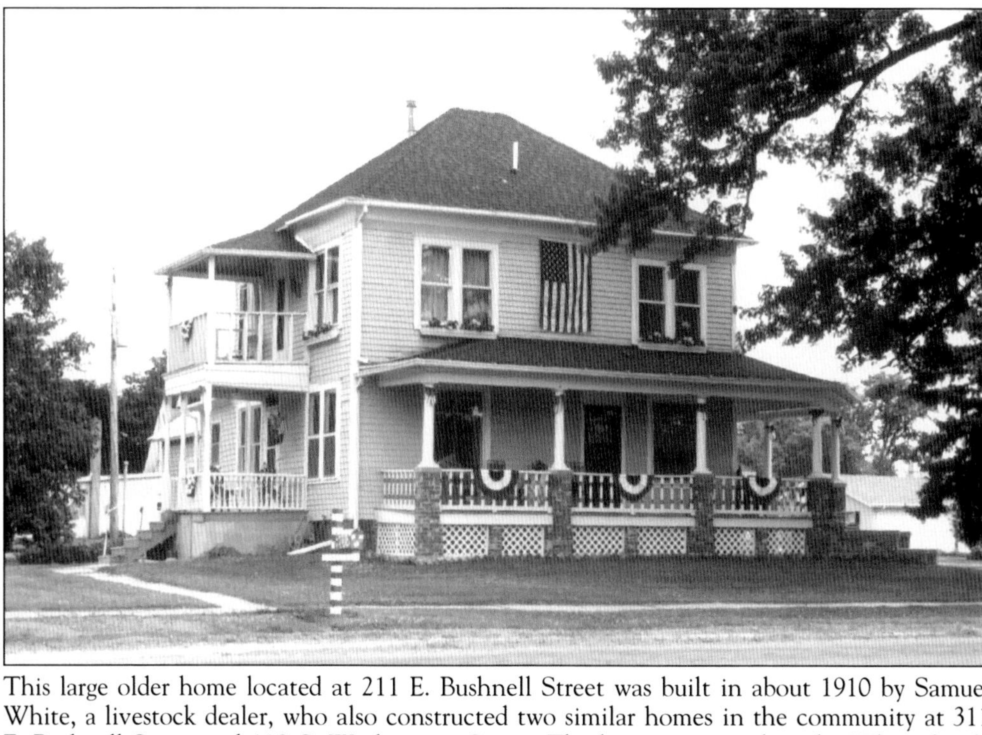

This large older home located at 211 E. Bushnell Street was built in about 1910 by Samuel White, a livestock dealer, who also constructed two similar homes in the community at 311 E. Bushnell Street and 112 S. Washington Street. The home remained in the White family for many years and is now owned by Lynn Gustafson. The small side porches lead to a well-landscaped side yard that covers half a block.

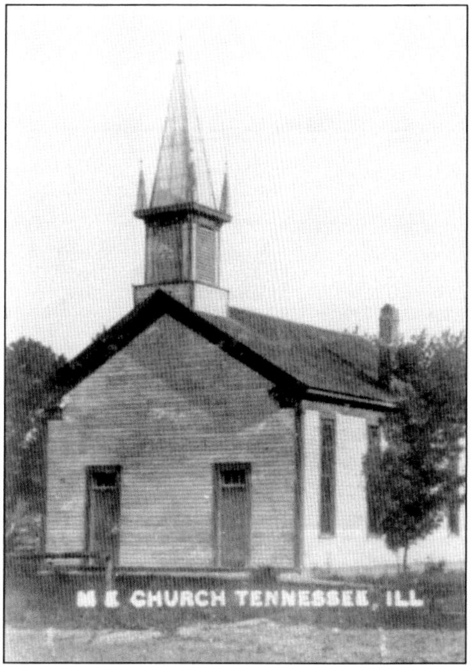

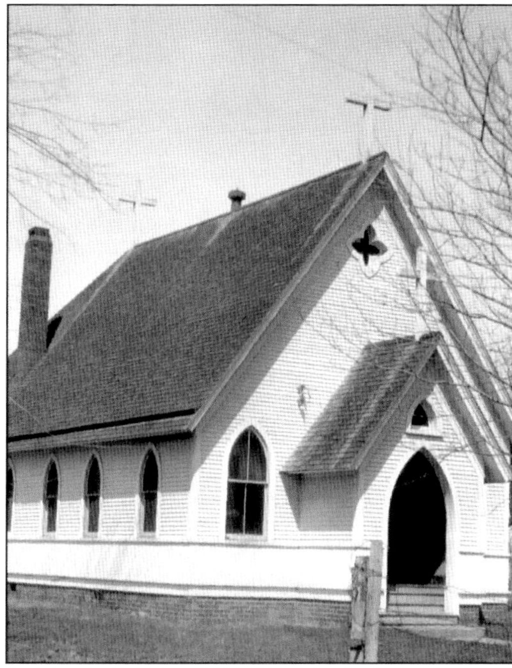

The Tennessee United Methodist Church was organized in 1861, and the church building shown at the left was erected three years later. On November 21, 1912, it burned, and the present Methodist Church was constructed on the same site at Jackson and S. Filmore Streets. Sacred Heart Catholic Church, located north of town on road 990N, was organized in 1857 as St. Mary's. A building was constructed in 1859, and the present one, shown here, was erected just west of that site in 1905. It is one of the most attractive frame churches in the county.

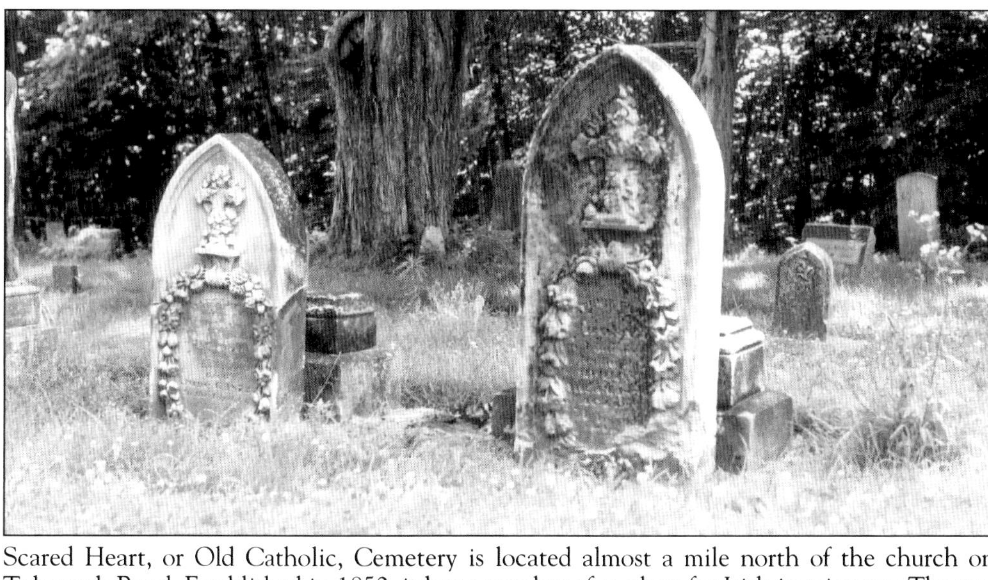

Scared Heart, or Old Catholic, Cemetery is located almost a mile north of the church on Telegraph Road. Established in 1850, it has a number of markers for Irish immigrants. The two gravestones shown here, which are now off of their pedestals, are for Patrick (on the right) and Margaret Erwin, who were from County Limerick, Ireland, and who died in the 1870s. The markers feature botonée crosses and floral wreaths.

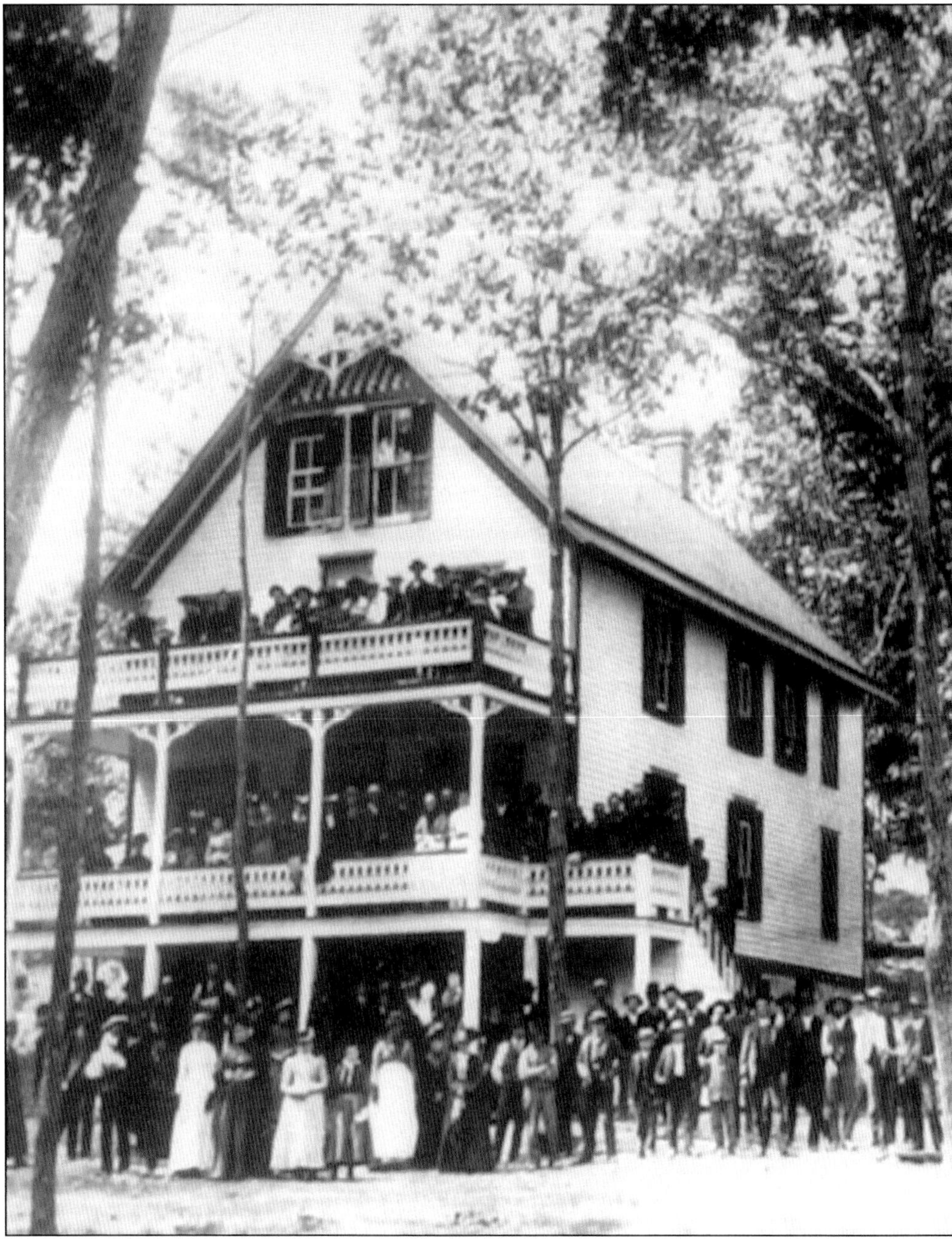

Vishnu Springs was developed by Darius Hicks on land that he had inherited from his father, Ebenezer. The town was platted in 1889 on section 7 of Tennessee Township. Claiming that the mineral waters there had health benefits, Hicks planned a kind of health resort and had the hotel shown here built that same year. The people were probably gathered for a formal opening of the hotel and springs. The town had a few stores by the early 1890s, and some people did come to picnic or drink the water. However, its location in a deep valley was too remote, and the community failed in the early 20th century. Although the dilapidated hotel building still stands, Vishnu Springs is now a ghost town located on private land south of road 1100N near the western edge of the county.

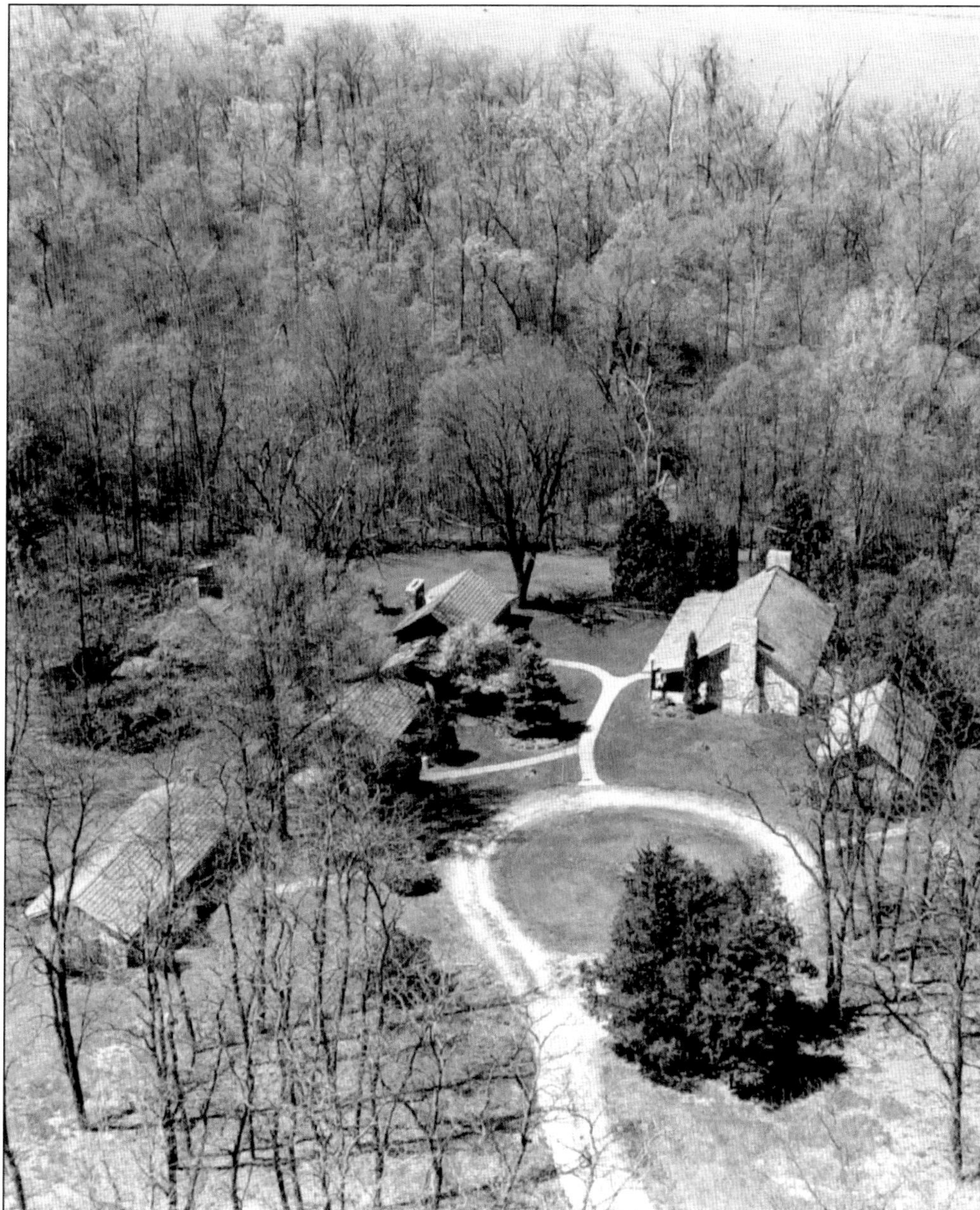

In the 1930s, William Bacon, the son of physician Joseph Bacon, built a retreat in the woods south of Macomb on what is now China Road. He constructed a brick lodge and three brick cabins. The 92-acre property was purchased in 1946 by Frank J. ("Pappy") Horn, a Macomb Coca-Cola bottler, who named it Hornlea Lodge and used it as a summer home. Western Illinois University purchased it in 1966, and since then, the Frank J. Horn Continuing Education Facility (or Horn's Lodge) has been the site of many educational programs, faculty retreats, and social functions.

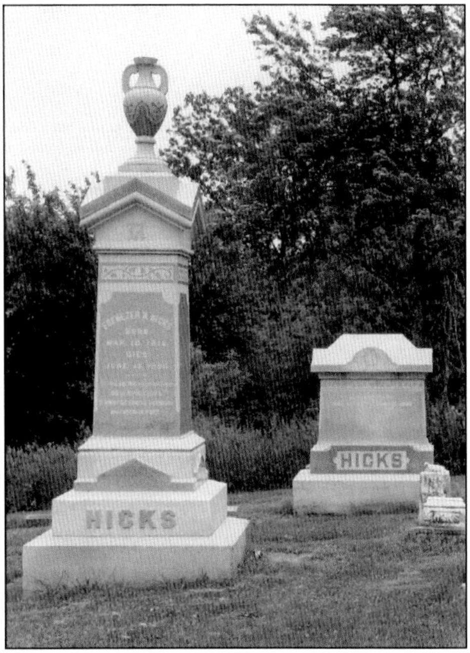

Friendship Cemetery is located a couple of miles north of Vishnu Springs on road 1200N. The burying ground was started in 1838 in connection with Friendship Methodist Church, and among the graves is that of George W. Hire, for whom Hire Township was named. This photograph shows the tall marker for Ebenezer and Jane Hicks and the nearby marker for their son Darius. Ebenezer and his wife came from Ohio in 1842 and settled in section 33 of Hire Township, where he continually bought land until he became the foremost landowner in the county, with more than 4,000 acres. He rented many farms to others, but, with his sons Darius and Frank, he raised large herds of cattle on 1,000 acres that he personally managed. He died in 1886.

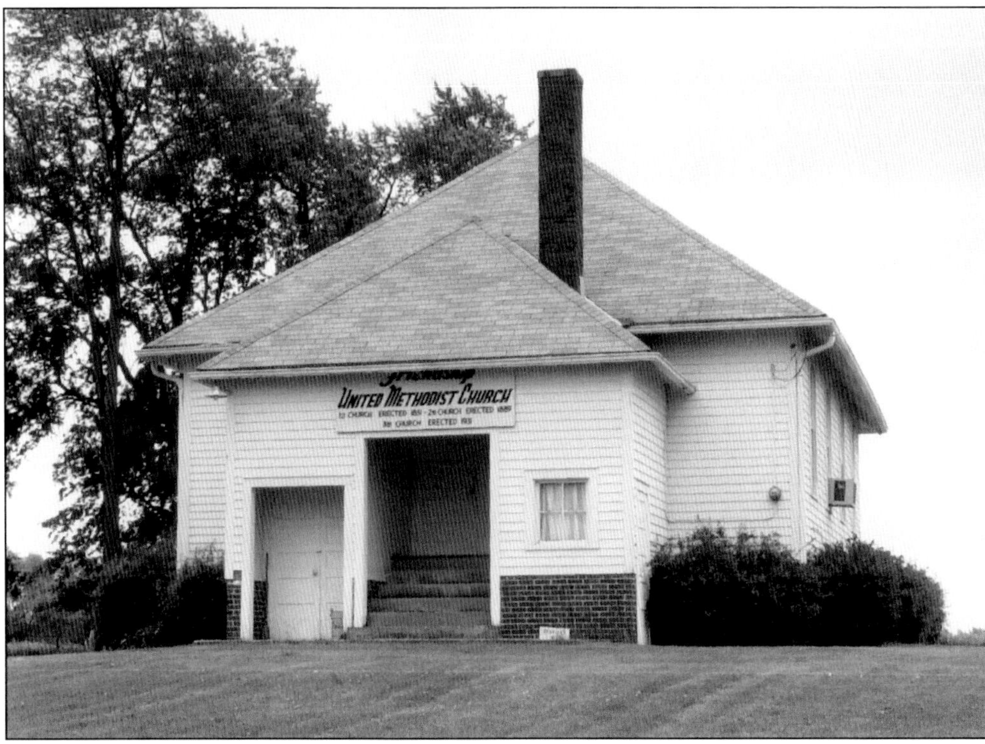

Organized in 1833, the Friendship United Methodist Church is one of the earliest religious groups in McDonough County. The first church building was not erected until 1851. A second one was constructed nearby in 1889, and the first building was then torn down. The 1889 church was destroyed by fire in 1930, and the church building shown here was erected the following year.

Another early cemetery is Hills Grove, which started in 1839 and is located west of Route 61 a half-mile south of road 750N. It relates to the now-vanished hamlet of Hills Grove, which was settled by Roswell Tyrrell (or Terrell) and two others in 1830. A community was platted in 1844 by Isaac Holton, and, by the 1880s, it had two stores, a blacksmith shop, and a post office. A graduate of the University of Vermont, Holton established Hills Grove Seminary in a log cabin, where he taught "the higher branches and classics" for 15 years. He is buried at the cemetery, as is Tyrrell, who was a War of 1812 veteran. This photograph shows the Tyrrell markers.

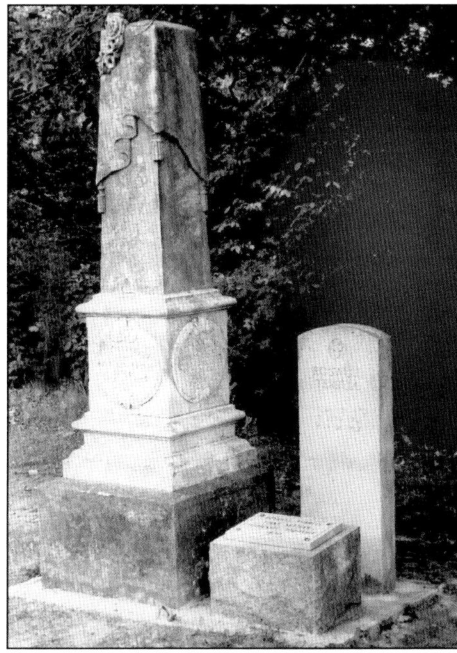

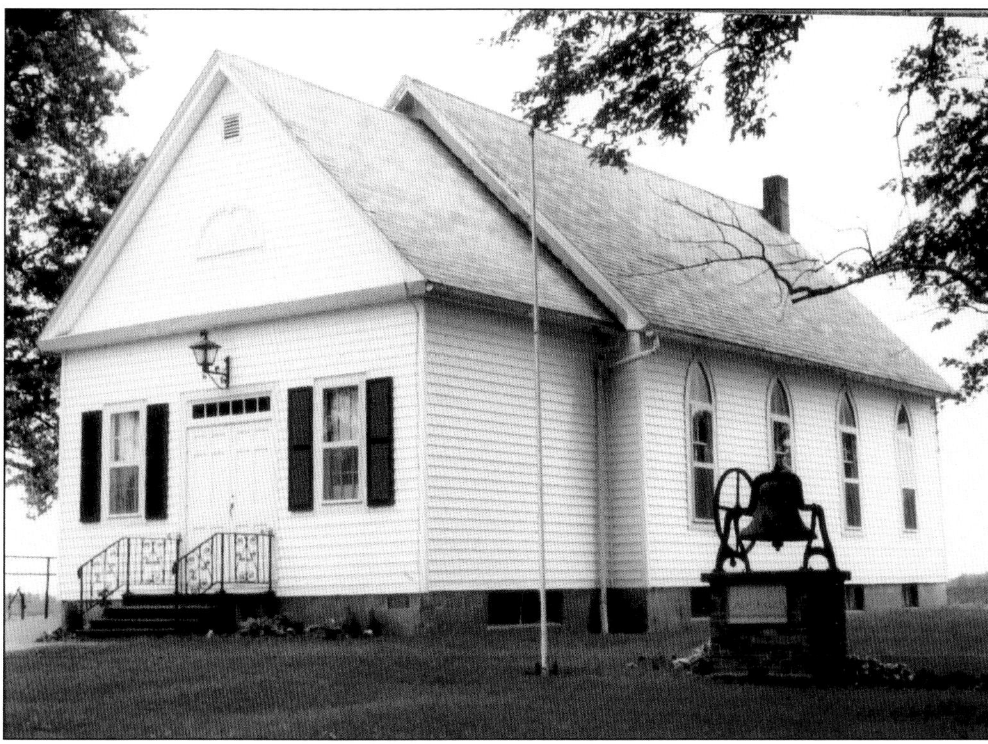

The Hills Grove Methodist Church, located east of Route 61 on Tepee Rd., was organized in 1872, although Methodists had held services at Isaac Holton's schoolhouse as early as the 1830s. The church building shown here was completed in 1891, and it was remodeled in 1953. Because of Methodist revivals in the 19th century, the Hills Grove area became known as "the old Methodist stomping ground."

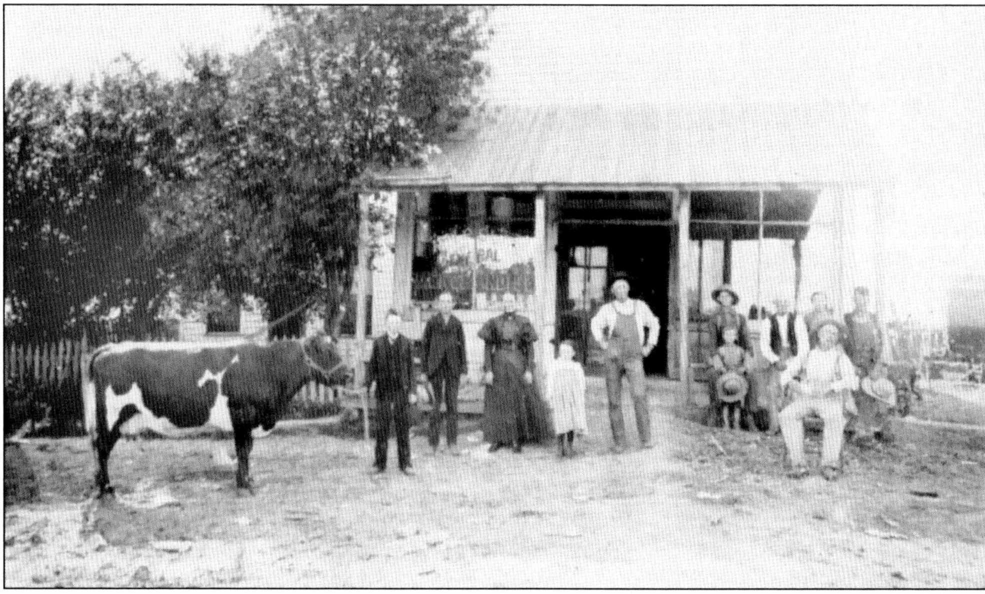

Colmar was platted along the tracks of the Northern Cross Railroad by W.M. Graves in 1858. A few stores were opened there, but by the 1880s, only the general store of John McAllister remained. A depot was erected in 1858, and by the following year it housed the post office. This photograph shows the family of Nelse Polite, who operated a general store there at the turn of the century.

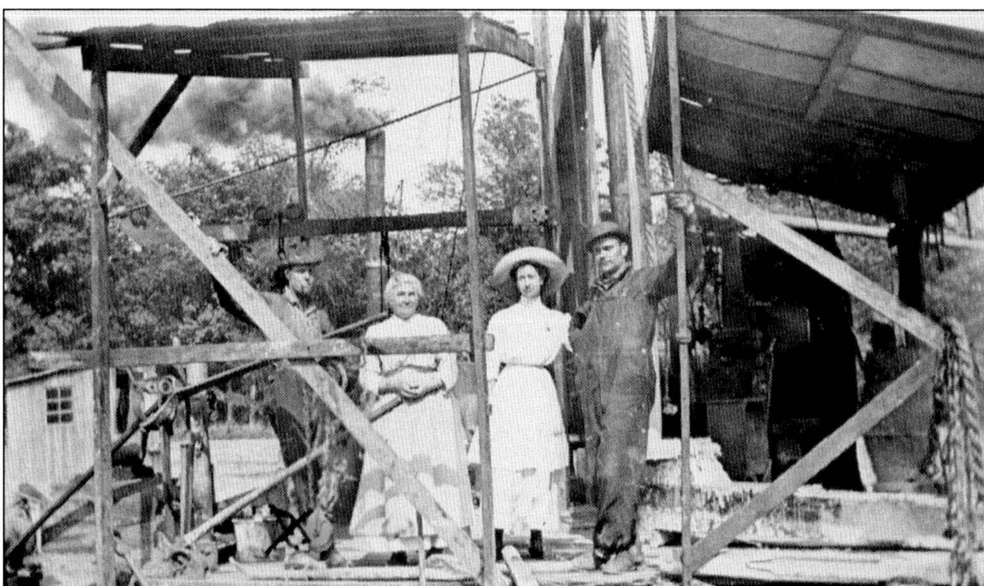

The most notable development in the Colmar area was the drilling of oil wells, which started in the second decade of the 20th century and expanded through much of the southwest corner of the county. This photograph shows the rig on the Hoing land, one mile east of Colmar, that drilled the first producing well, which came in on April 30, 1914. The women are members of the Hoing family, and the two workers are Tom Russell and Buck Cole.

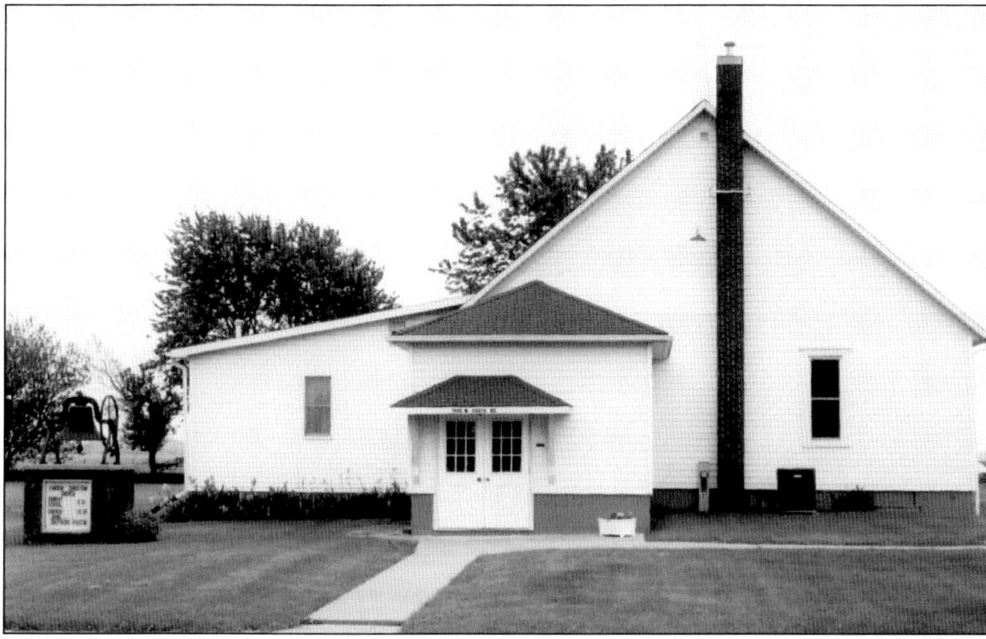

Fandon was originally named Middletown, and it was platted in 1837 by John Patrick and James Edmonston. By the 1850s, it had three stores and three taverns, and it was a lively stagecoach stop. However, when the Northern Cross Railroad did not come through, it began to decline. In the 1890s, it still had a general store, a drug store, two blacksmith shops, and a post office. The Fandon Christian Church was organized in 1890, and the building shown here was dedicated early in 1903. The stores are gone, but it remains.

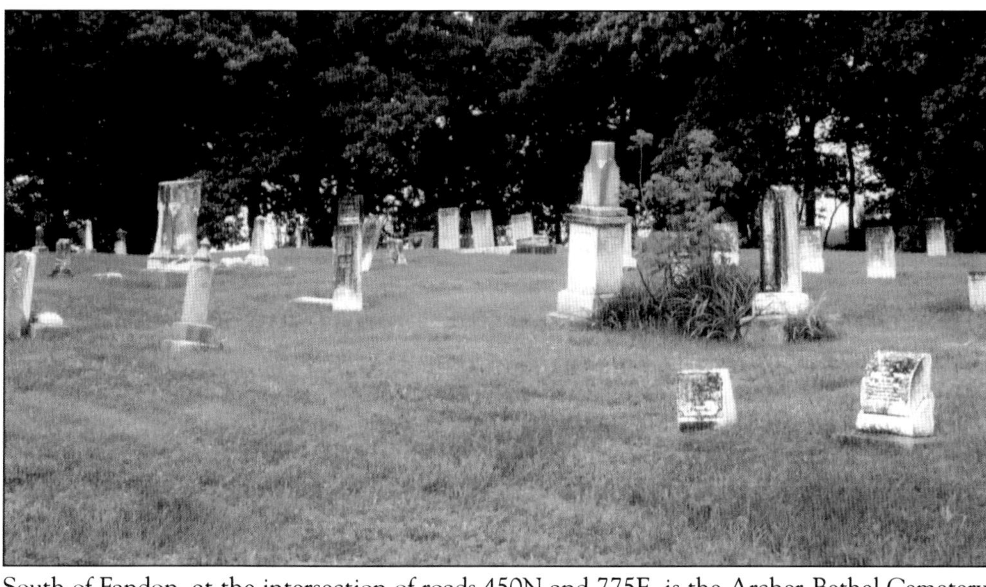

South of Fandon, at the intersection of roads 450N and 775E, is the Archer-Bethel Cemetery, which was started in 1838. It is across the road from the Bethel Baptist Church but is not associated with it. This photograph shows the older section of the cemetery. It is one of the larger and more well-kept cemeteries in Bethel Township. The smaller Gibson Cemetery, southwest of Fandon on road 700E, dates from 1840 and is also well-maintained.

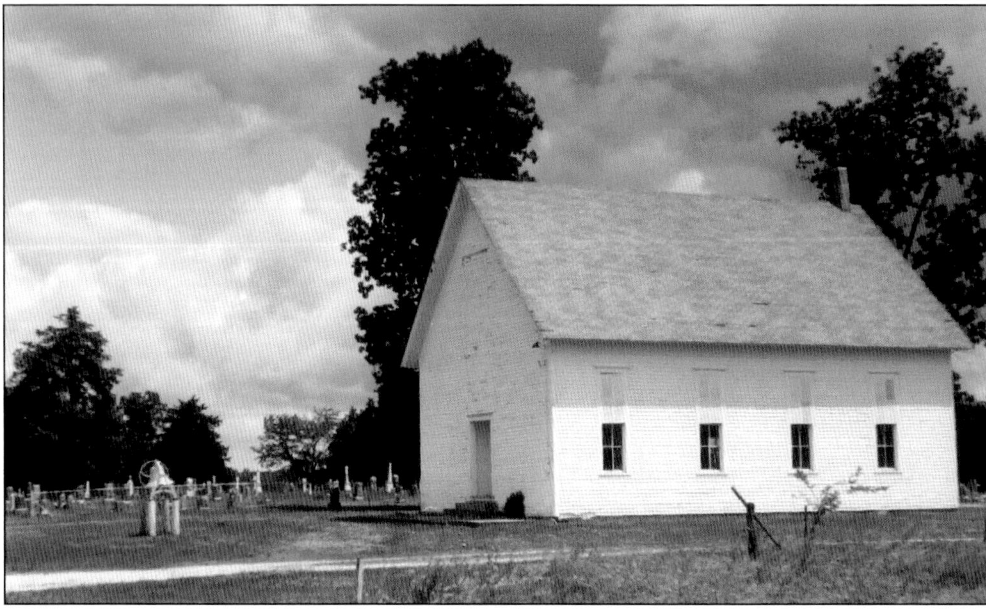

Scott's Church was organized in 1837 as a Methodist denomination, and four years later the first building was erected on road 600E in Bethel Township on a hill overlooking the rolling countryside. In 1865, a second building was constructed nearby, and in 1896, the present church was built there. The frame structure originally had a steeple, which was struck by lightning. It was then removed, and the bell was mounted on a frame in front of the church, as shown here.

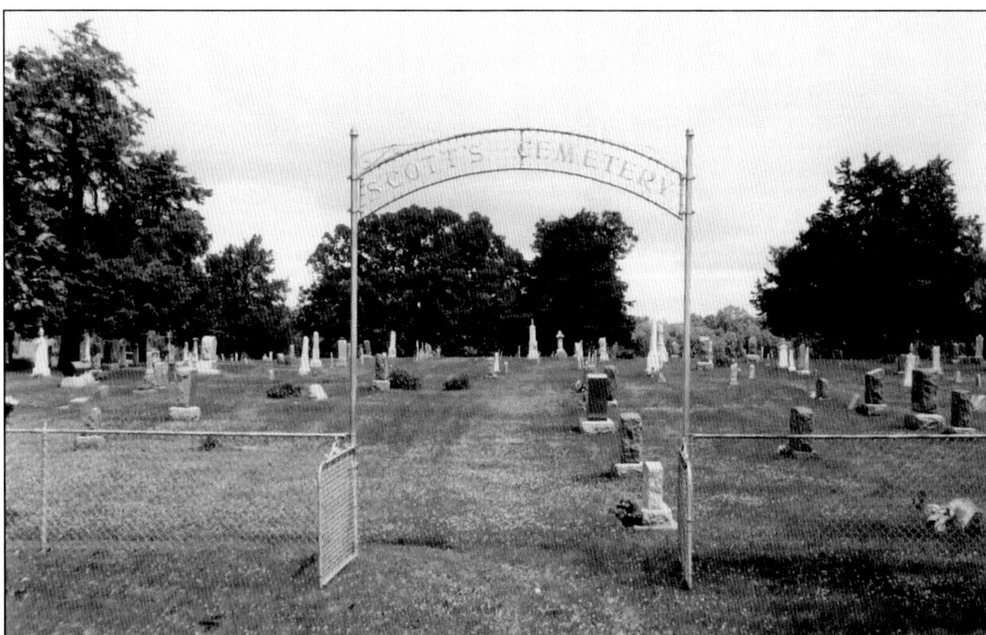

Scott's Cemetery, adjacent to the church, is one of the most attractive rural burying grounds in McDonough County. It was started around 1836, and it is still in use. This photograph looks north through the entrance gate. Scott's Church was disbanded more than half a century ago, so the old church building and the burying ground are now maintained by the Scott's Cemetery Association.

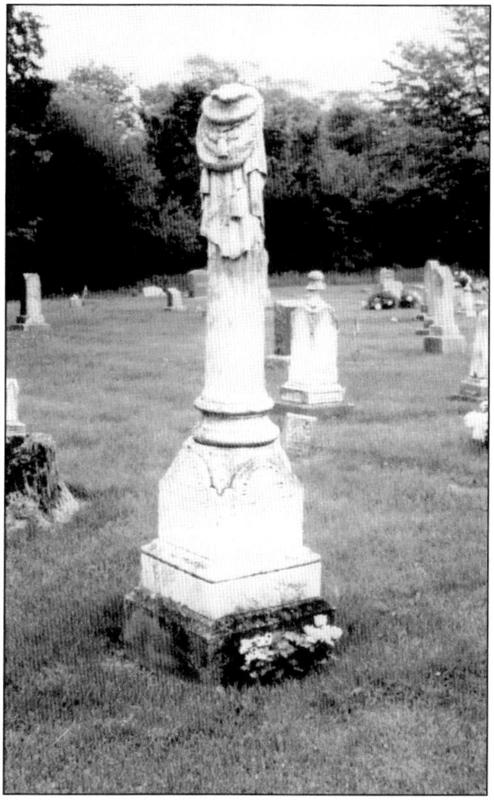
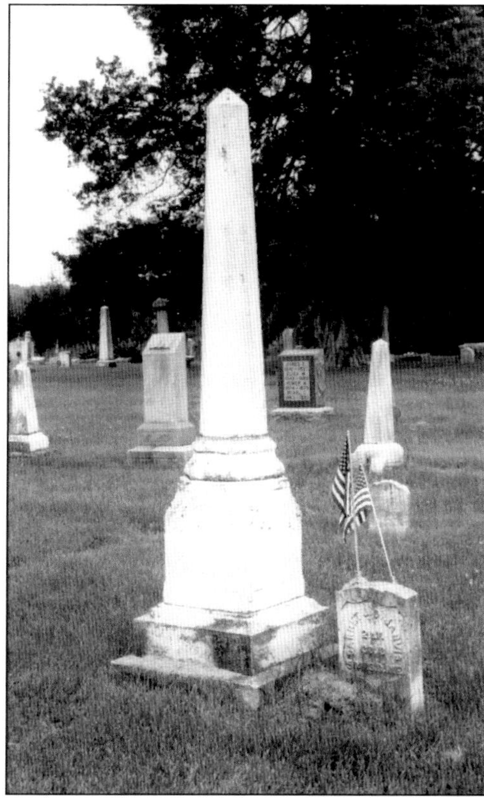

Located in Scott's Cemetery is this old shaft for Civil War soldier Richard W. Scott, who is not buried there. As his gravestone says, he was "killed and buried at the Battle of Jonesborough, Ga., Sep. 2, 1864." Scott was in the 78th Illinois Infantry and died at age 18. The shaft and small marker shown on the right are for Lt. Garret J. D. Jarvis, who was "killed at Mobile while charging the rebble [sic] works," as his marker says. He died on April 9, 1865, the very day on which Lee surrendered to Grant, ending the war. He was a white officer in the 50th U.S. Colored Infantry.

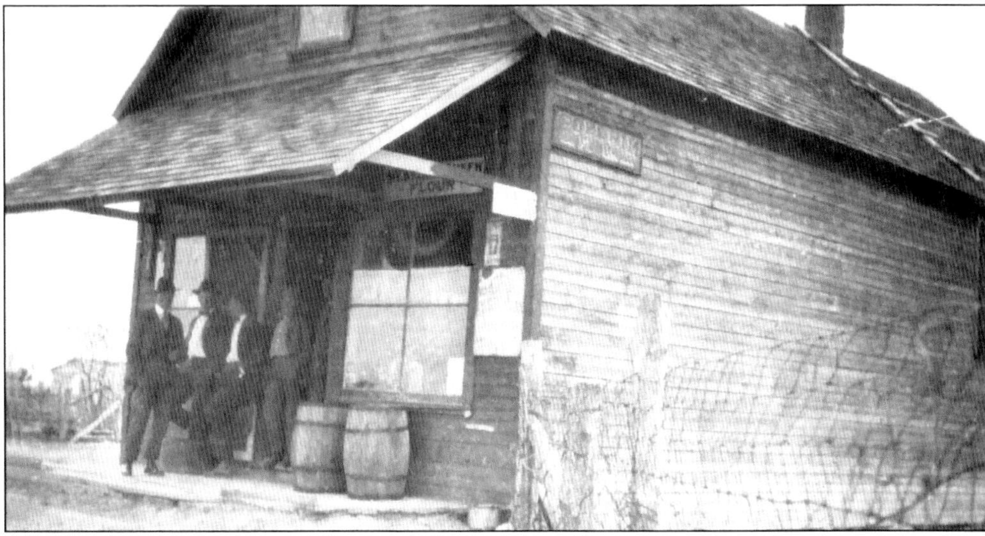

Gin Ridge, located between Grindstone Creek and the Schuyler County line, was a rural community settled by southern upland pioneers. In the 19th century, Gin Ridgers were regarded by other county residents as poor, independent, uneducated people, who were not progressive. Mt. Zion Church and Victor School were located where road 850E meets 00N, and at roads 900E and 00N, this general store once stood. The church, school, and store vanished decades ago, and strip mining has greatly altered the landscape in that area. The Willey and Stoneking cemeteries have many Gin Ridgers buried in them.

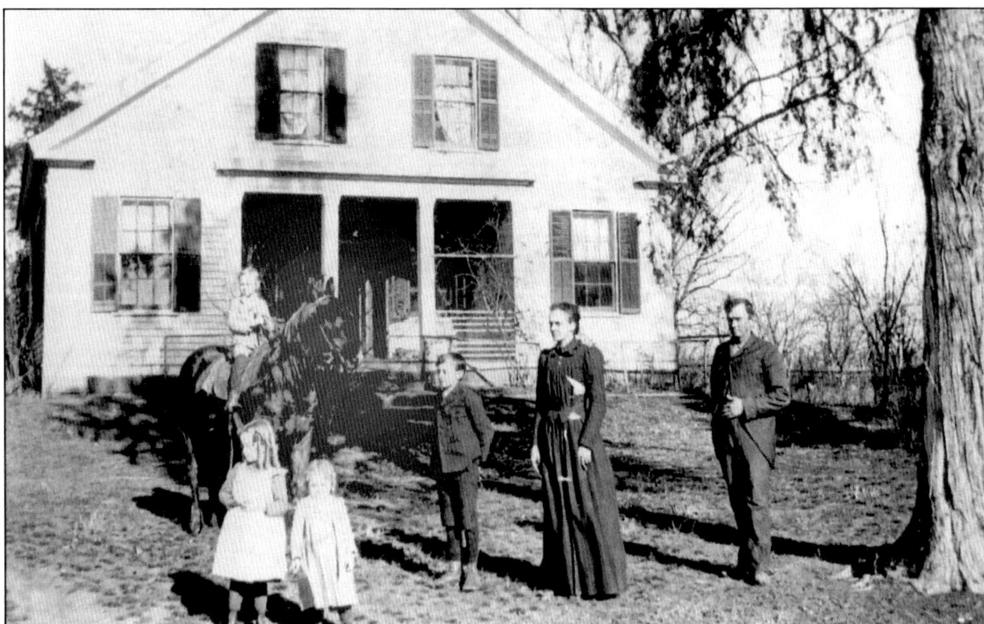

This house on road 800N, one third of a mile west of 1200E in Chalmers Township, was a stop on the Underground Railroad. It was built in 1854 by William ("Uncle Billy") and Sarah Allison. For a time, their son Harmon and his wife, Beulah—who was a member of the Brown family of Underground Railroad conductors in Quincy—also lived there. This post-Civil War photograph shows Harmon Allison II, his wife, Nannie, and their children. The house has been torn down.

Five

THE SOUTHEAST QUARTER OF THE COUNTY

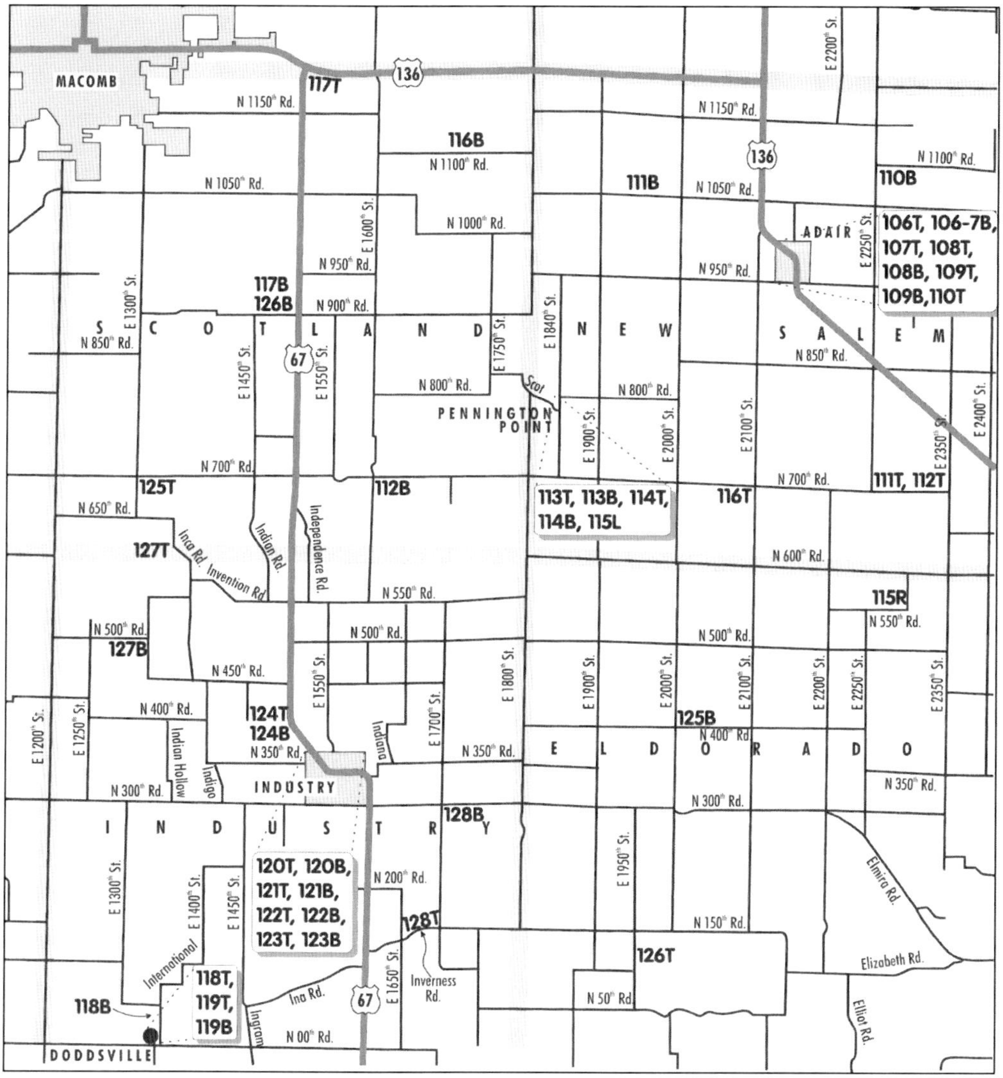

Early in 1826, the southeast quarter developed the first gathering of McDonough County pioneers, at Carter's Settlement, though that location was never platted. This area of the county has only two communities today, Adair and Industry. Like all other McDonough County towns, except Macomb, they have declined in population, and now only Industry has an active business district. The southeast part of McDonough County has been the least influenced by the railroad, yet it has had a prosperous agricultural population for generations.

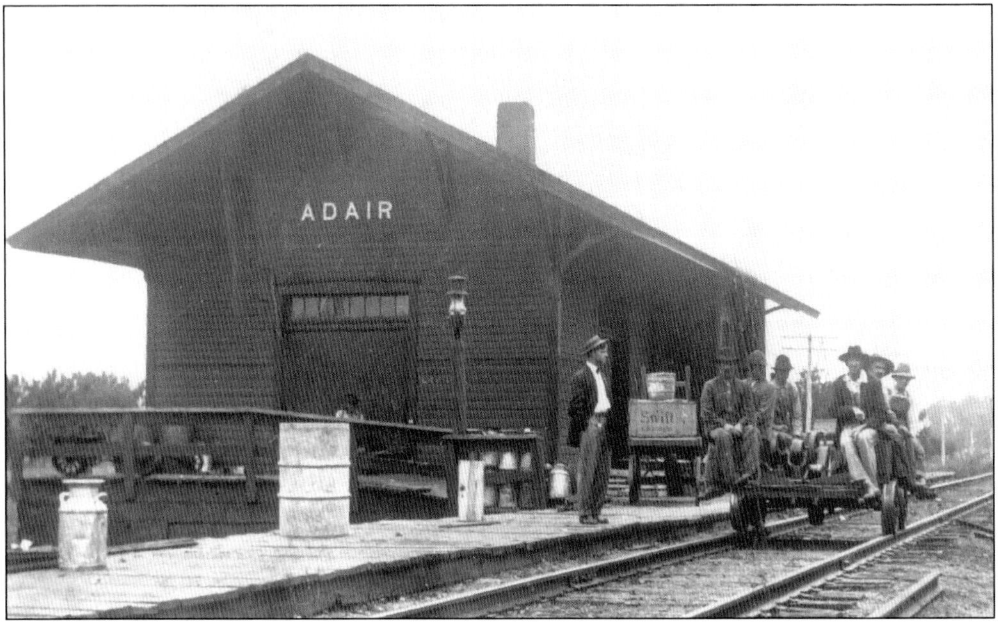

Adair was fostered by the Rockford, Rock Island, and St. Louis Railroad, which came through in 1870, but it was named Reedyville. John Reedy had donated land for the depot, and with Jacob Grimm, he had platted the town. In the 1880s, the name was changed to Adair, although it was apparently also known as Shoofly for a short time because it had a store by that name.

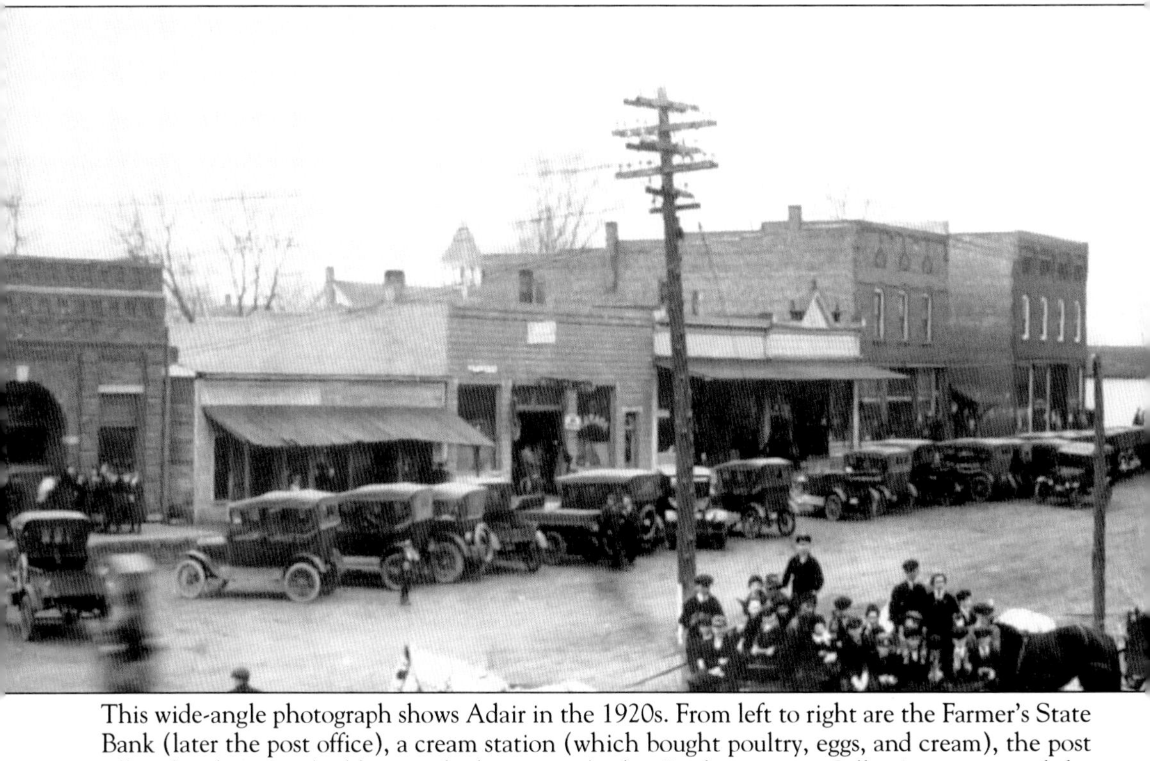

This wide-angle photograph shows Adair in the 1920s. From left to right are the Farmer's State Bank (later the post office), a cream station (which bought poultry, eggs, and cream), the post office (in the same building, with the awning), the Coplan garage, Gillam's grocery and dry

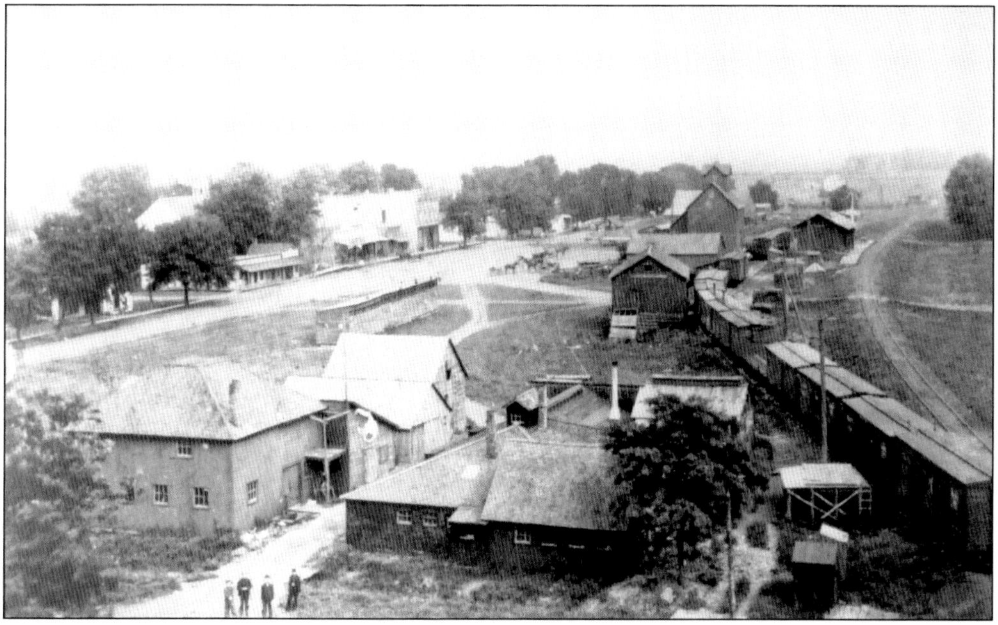

This photograph was taken early in the 20th century, before the Farmer's State Bank was built and shortly before the depot shown here was moved further north. In the foreground is a poultry business, which in the early 20th century shipped out a railroad car of dressed poultry each week. The brick building across the street is the Herndon store, built in 1895.

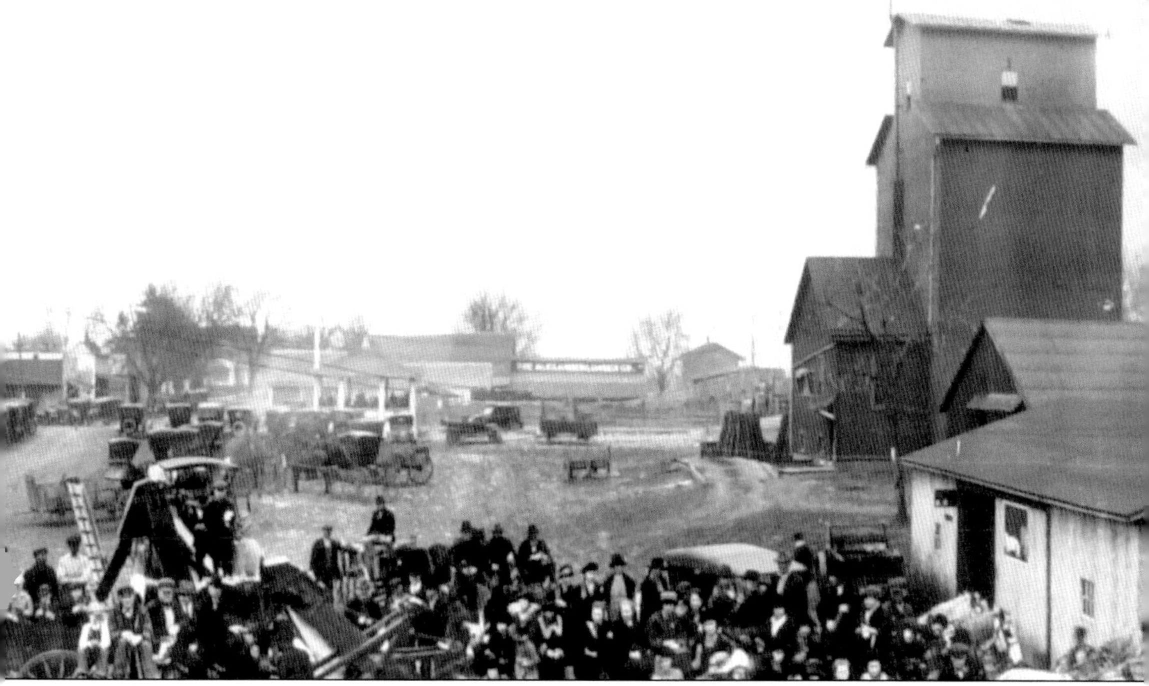

goods, H. A. Oldfield and Son's grocery and dry goods, the Herndon and Brothers hardware store, and a frame building for Herndon implement sales. The grain elevator on the right was close to the railroad tracks, and to the left of it, near the cars and buggies, is the old bandstand.

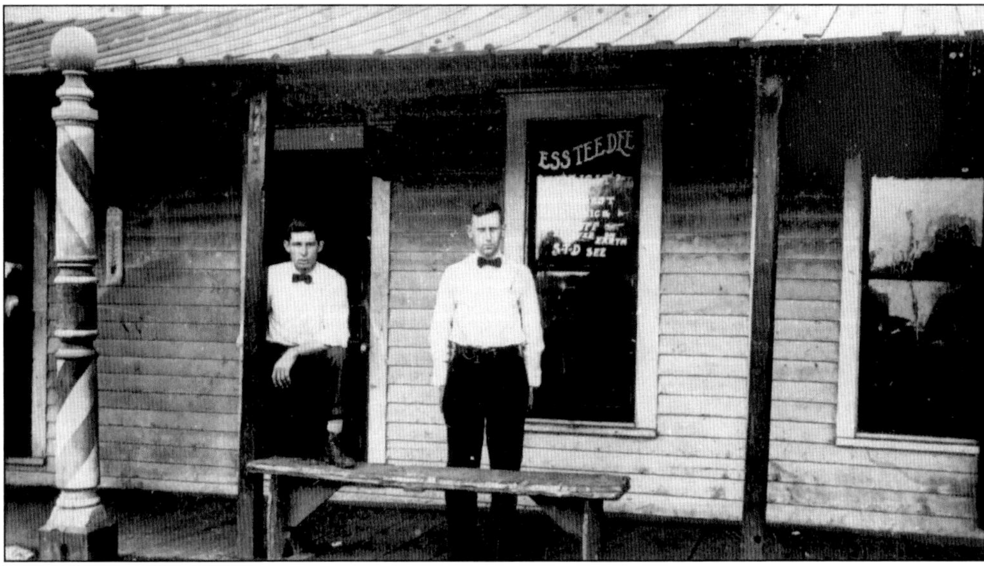

This photograph shows Fred Coats and Bert Foster, who were barbers in Adair for many years. Coats opened the barbershop in 1918, and it still stands on Main Street but has been the Adair Pool Hall since 1969. Fred's son, Arnold ("Shorty") Coats, was also a barber in Adair, and he collected old photographs of the community and hung them on the walls of his shop. Those are now on display at the town hall.

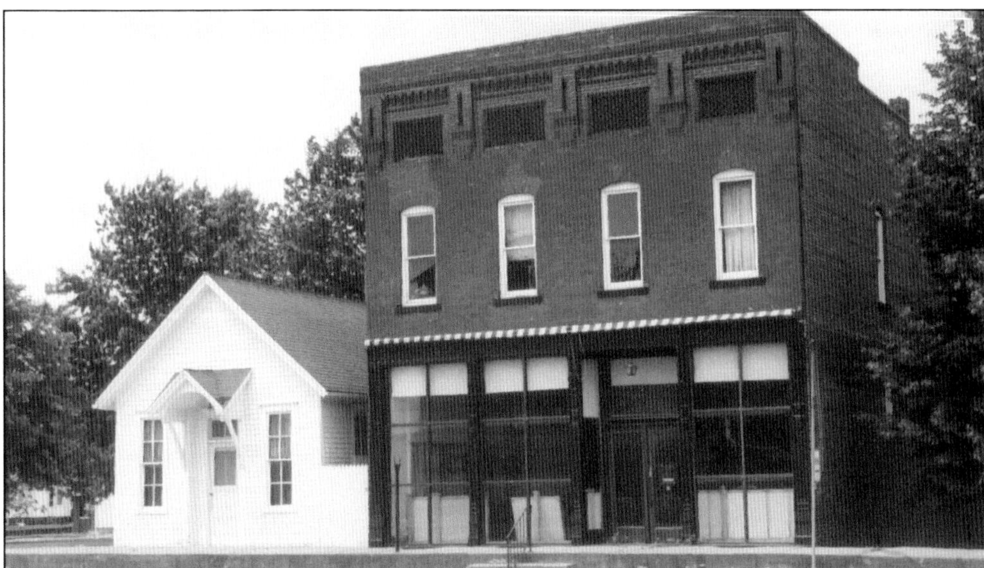

The Herndon and Brothers hardware store, which originally sold cast iron stoves, lamps, and other items for the home, was revived in the early 1970s by John Hammond, who sold antiques and gifts. It has since been closed for more than 20 years. The small frame building shown next to it in this contemporary photograph was once the Lickskillet School. (It was supposedly called by that name because it served only half a school district.) Originally located south of town at the intersection of roads 850N and 2100E, the schoolhouse was moved to Adair in the later 1920s to serve as a storage building for the Herndon store.

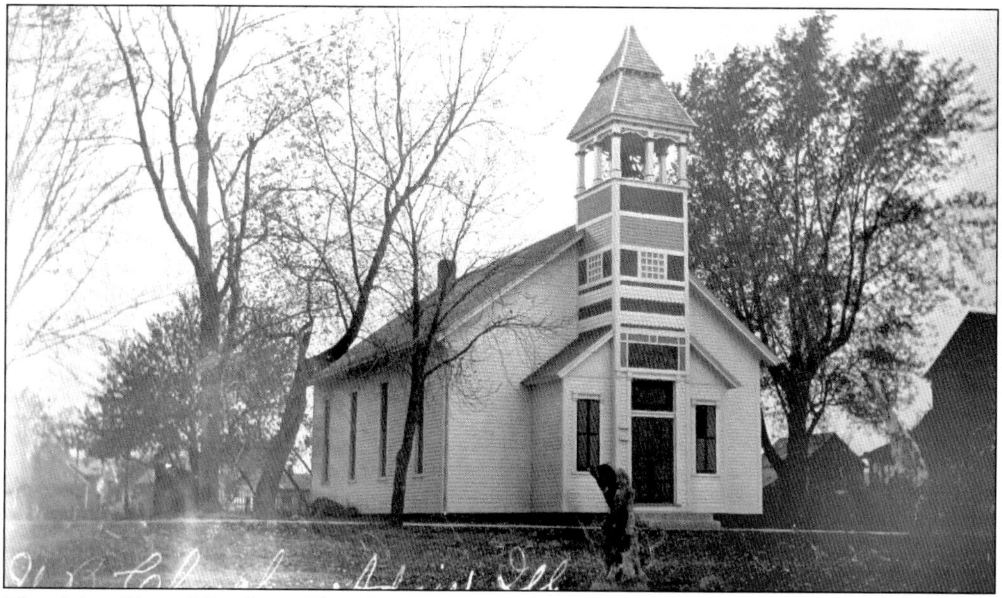

The Adair United Brethren Church was organized in 1888 by the Herndon family and others. This building, constructed the following year, was located at 319 Prairie Street. It was remodeled in 1923 and was eventually sold to the New Salem Christian Church, which then moved into Adair from the countryside. The United Brethren congregation eventually merged with the United Methodists in 1969.

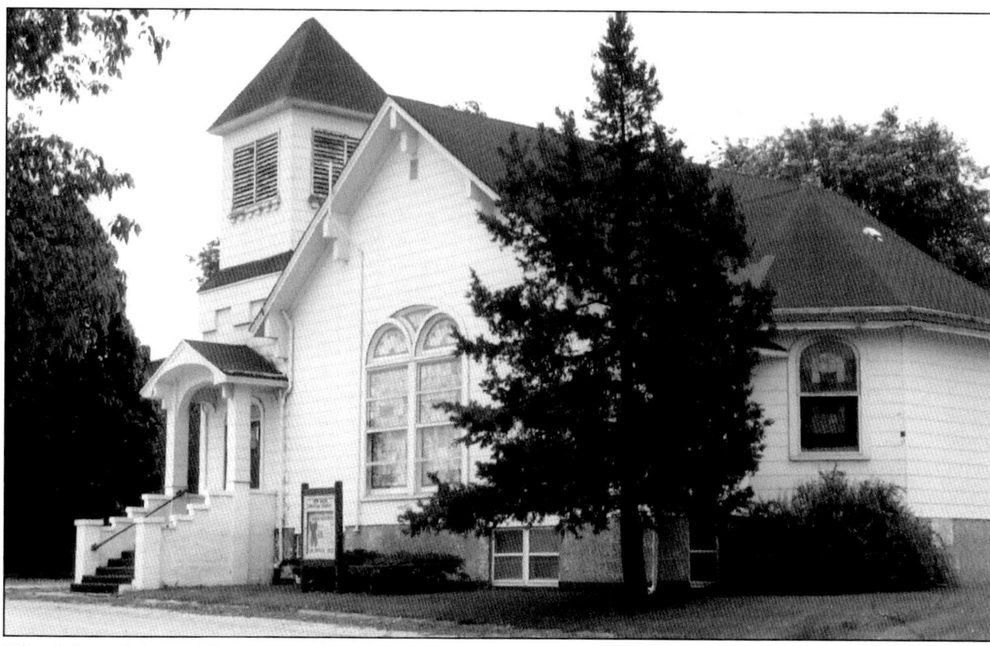

The New Salem Christian Church was organized at the Wetzel Schoolhouse in 1859. The congregation erected a building in section 34 of New Salem Township in 1867 and worshipped at that location for more than a century. In 1971, they purchased the old United Brethren Church on Prairie Street in Adair. Since being remodeled in 1923, the building has been characterized by a side steeple and a large stained-glass window.

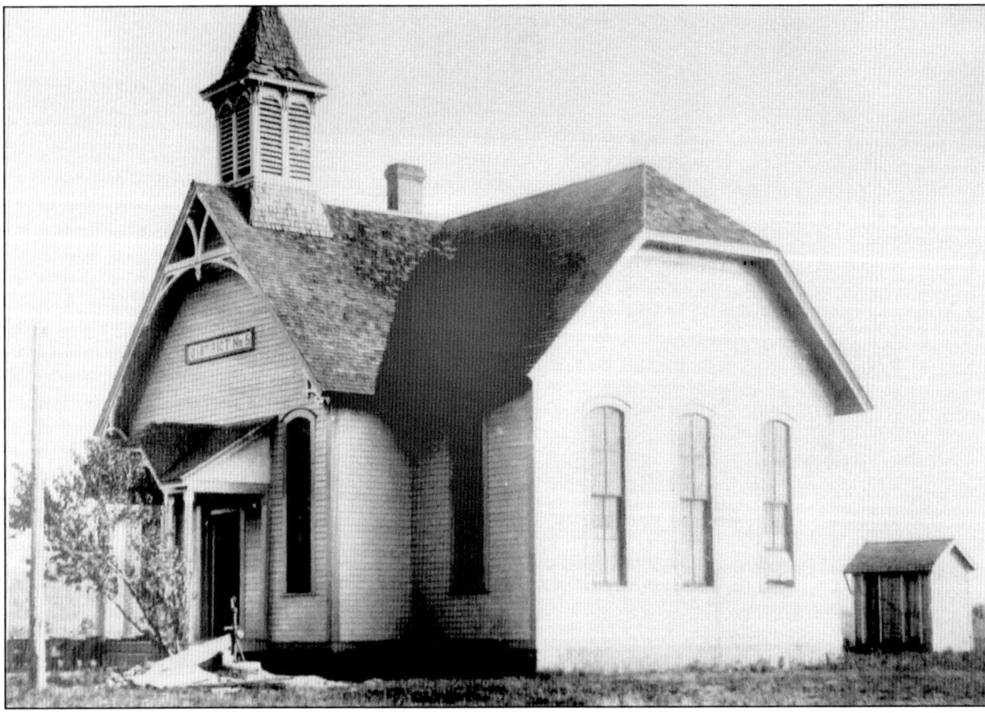

The Adair Grade School District No. 5 building was located on Oak Street where the bandstand is now. This photograph was probably taken shortly after it was built in 1882. With its louvered cupola, round-topped windows, decorated gable, and unusual portico over the front entrance, it was more attractive than most schoolhouse buildings. After it was destroyed by fire in 1924, a new brick school was built on the same site in 1926. A high school was erected nearby in 1920.

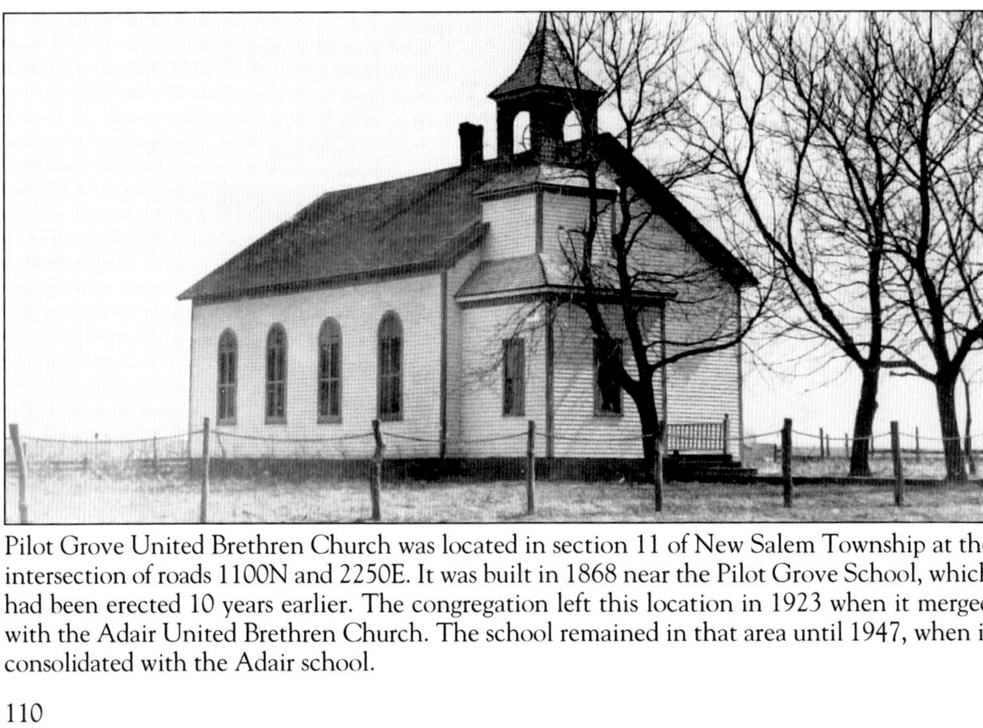

Pilot Grove United Brethren Church was located in section 11 of New Salem Township at the intersection of roads 1100N and 2250E. It was built in 1868 near the Pilot Grove School, which had been erected 10 years earlier. The congregation left this location in 1923 when it merged with the Adair United Brethren Church. The school remained in that area until 1947, when it consolidated with the Adair school.

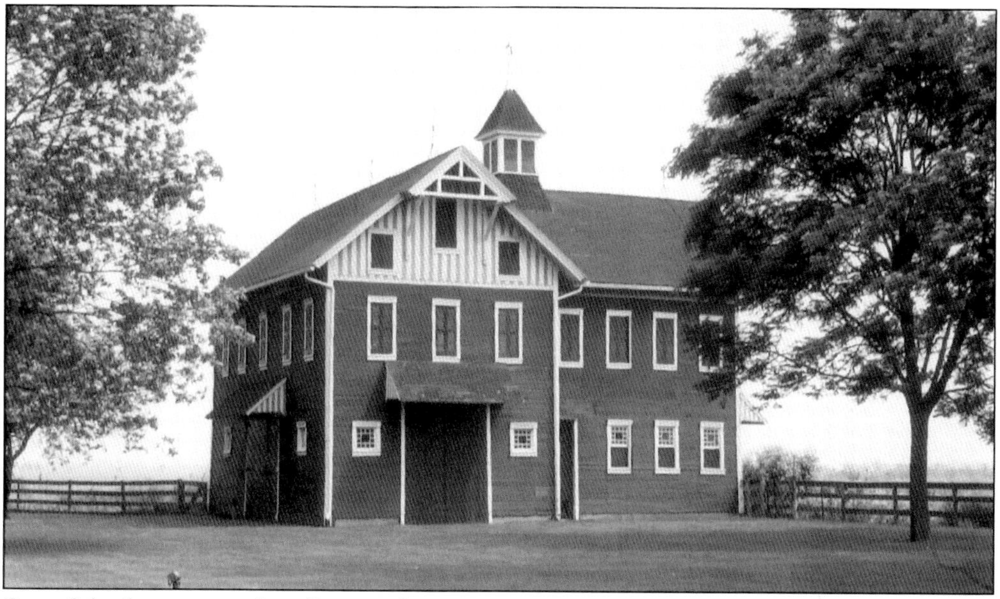

One of the finest examples of barn architecture in McDonough County is the Hammond Barn, which is located at the intersection of roads 700N and 2250E. Built in 1889 by contractor Newt Willis of Table Grove for James C. Hammond, it was destroyed by fire before it could be used and had to be rebuilt. The stick-style structure features a large number of windows in a balanced design and has an elegant cupola. The barn is now owned by Mrs. Wanda Hammond.

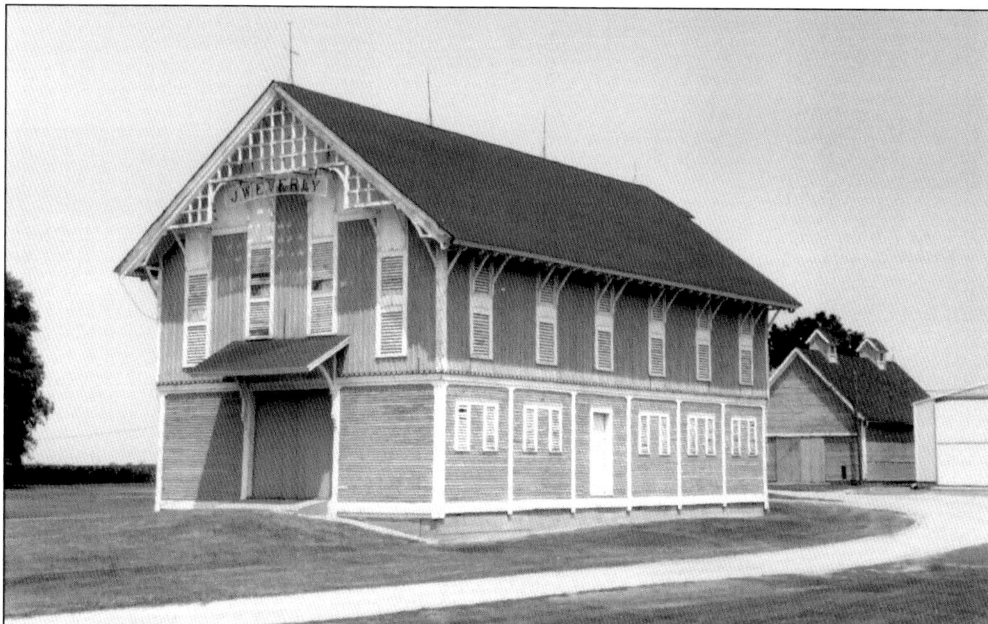

The Everly barn, located at the intersection of roads 1050N and 1950E, is another highly crafted, stick-style structure. Built in 1882 by noted barn builder Newt Willis of Table Grove, it was originally used as a show horse barn and featured a unique grain hoist. Characterized by numerous louvered windows and a highly decorated gable, the Everly barn is listed on the National Register of Historic Places. It is currently owned by the Everly Trust.

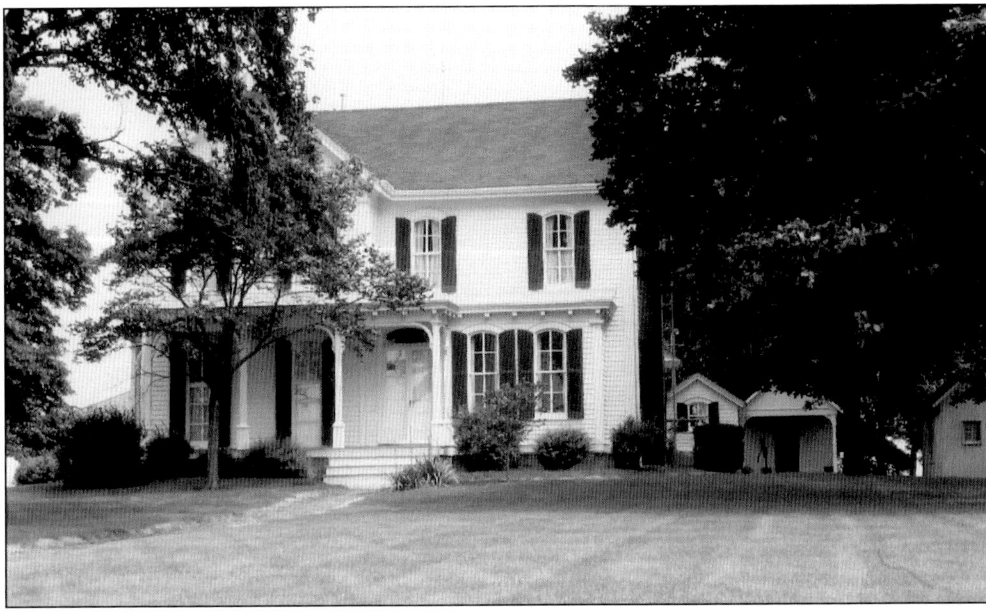

The southwest quarter of McDonough County also has some historic farmhouses. One of the most attractive is the Hammond home, which is on the same farmstead as the barn shown on the previous page. Built in 1876 for Mr. and Mrs. James C. Hammond, it features tall, curved-top windows and an elegant front porch. An addition to the home was built in 1953.

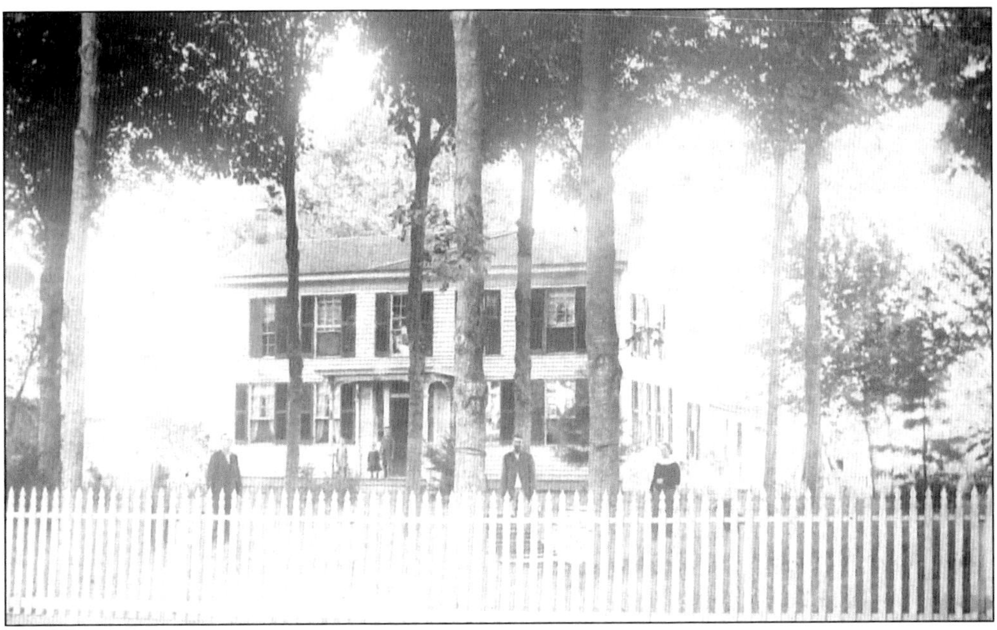

The stately Walker farmhouse, located on road 1600E just south of 700N, goes well back into the 19th century. Built in 1855 by Allen H. and Abner Walker, it replaced an 1835 log house on that site. It is probably the oldest farmhouse in the county still inhabited by a descendant of the builder. This photograph shows it in 1885. Standing on the lawn are, from left to right, Mary Ashmore Thomson, Rev. P.W. Thomson, T.G. Walker, and Emma Thomson Walker. The farmhouse is owned by Mr. and Mrs. Alan Walker.

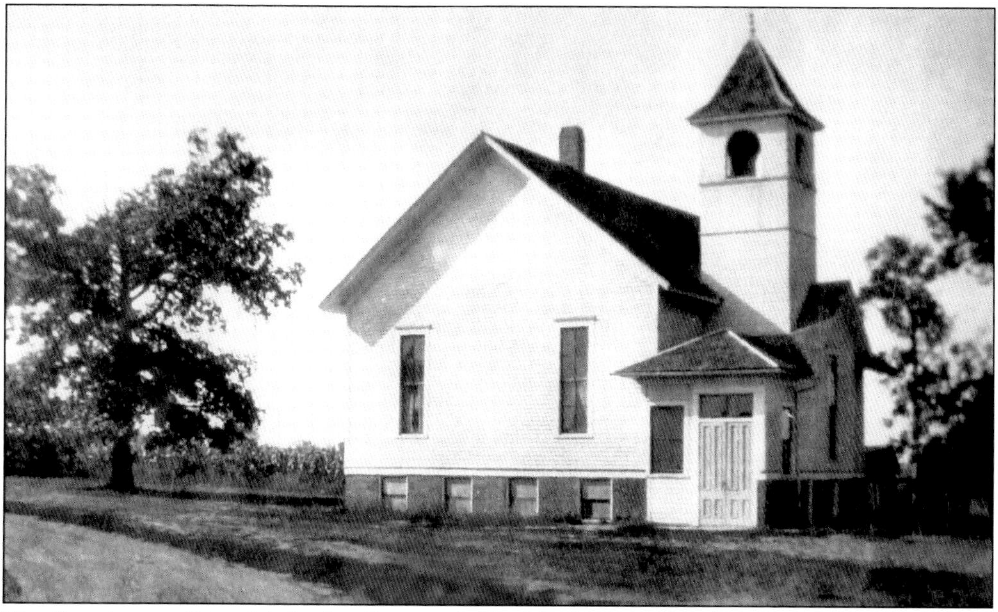

The Pennington Point Methodist Episcopal Church was established in 1835, seven years after William Pennington first settled in section 30 of New Salem Township. Stuart Pennington later provided land for a school, and his son-in-law James E. Hammer gave land for a church and cemetery. The first church building in that area was erected a half mile from the cemetery in 1856, and a new one, shown here, was constructed at that same place in 1877 and later moved to a site by the cemetery. By the 1880s, Pennington Point had a general store, a blacksmith shop, and a post office—all run by Simon Raby—as well as a doctor's office.

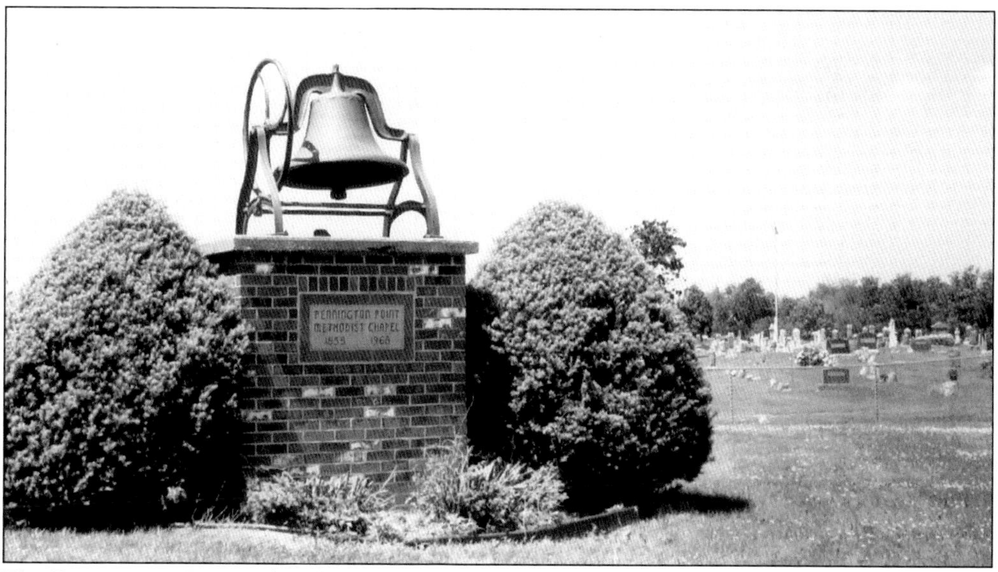

The Pennington Point Church burned in 1943 and was replaced four years later by a church building moved there from Eldorado Township. The church closed in 1968, and the building was torn down in 1972. This photograph shows the memorial to the "Pennington Point Methodist Chapel," as the church was sometimes called. It is located on the former church site beside the entrance to the cemetery.

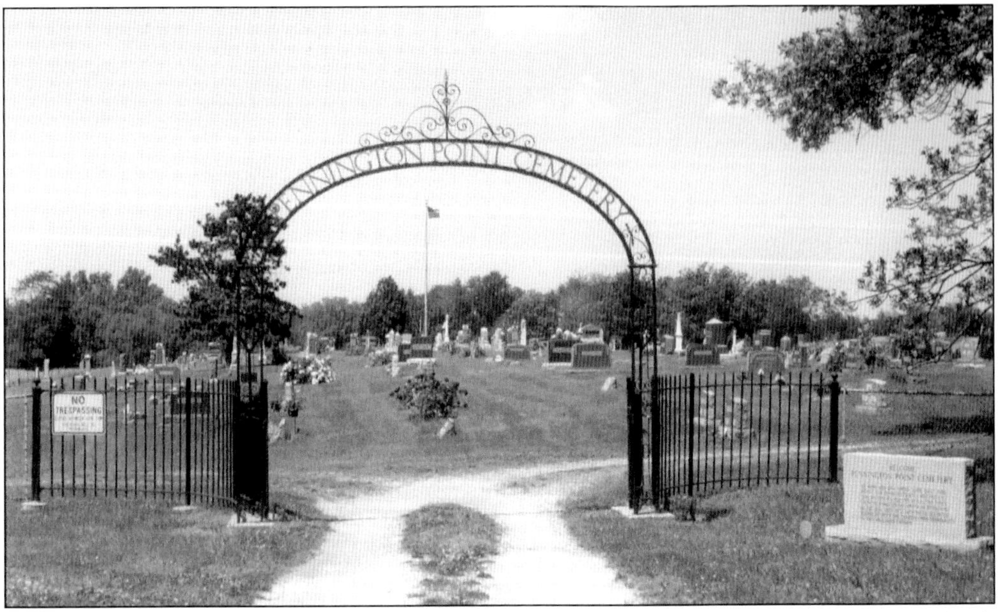

One of the most well-kept rural graveyards in the county is Pennington Point Cemetery, which has burials dating back to 1834. It became a public burying ground in 1860. Among the graves is that of John Stewart Pennington, the nephew of Daniel Boone, who was born in 1784 and came to the area in 1830. Pennington Point was named for him. He died in 1859.

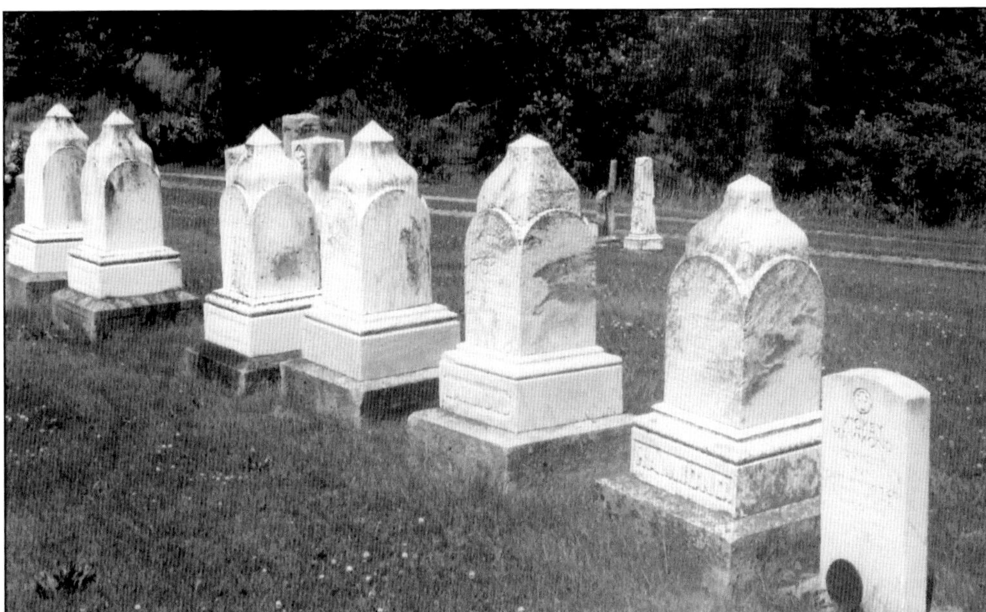

Among the interesting markers in the Pennington Point Cemetery are these six identical but strangely shaped headstones for the Hammond family. The sixth one, on the right, is for Mickey Hammond, who fought in the War of 1812. As his second, smaller headstone states, he served in "Capt. W. King's Co. / E. Tenn. Militia," and died in 1880. Civil War soldiers are buried in that cemetery as well. The marker for Eli Elwell says that he was "killed at the Battle of Stone River, Tenn., Dec. 31, 1862, while defending the flag of his country."

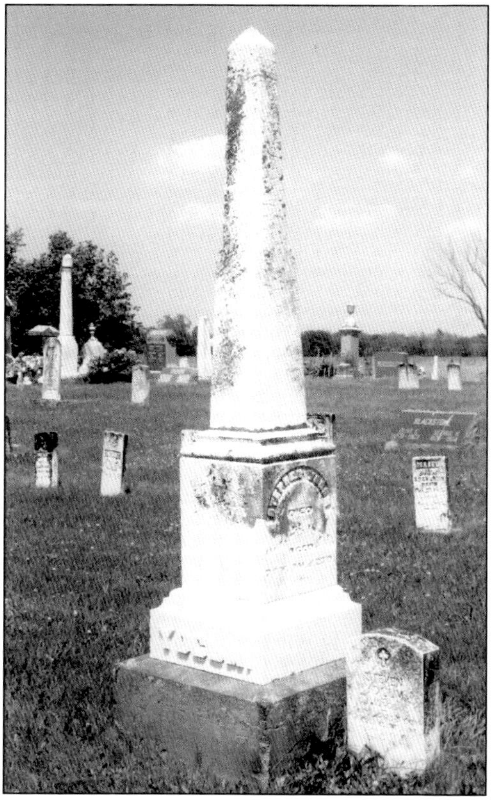

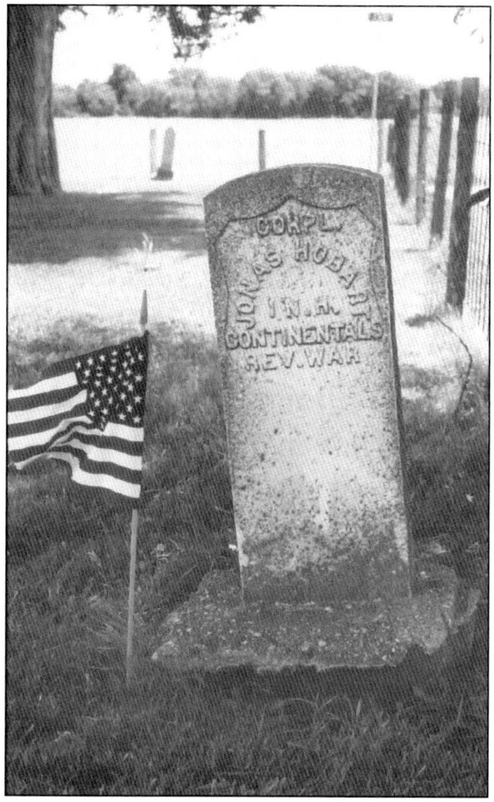

Two Black Hawk War soldiers are also buried in Pennington Point Cemetery. One is Stephen Yocum, whose two markers are shown at the left. The smaller one says that he served in "Lt. Dobbins Co. / 1 Brig. Ill. Mtd. Inf. / Black Hawk War." Nearby is the marker of Thomas Dorns, who served in the Illinois Mounted Rangers in the same frontier conflict, which occurred in 1832. The photograph at the right shows the Jonas Hobart headstone in the Foster Point Cemetery, which is located at the intersection of roads 550N and 2300E. One of three Revolutionary War soldiers buried in the county, he was a corporal in the First New Hampshire Continentals and was wounded at the Battle of Ticonderoga. He died in 1833.

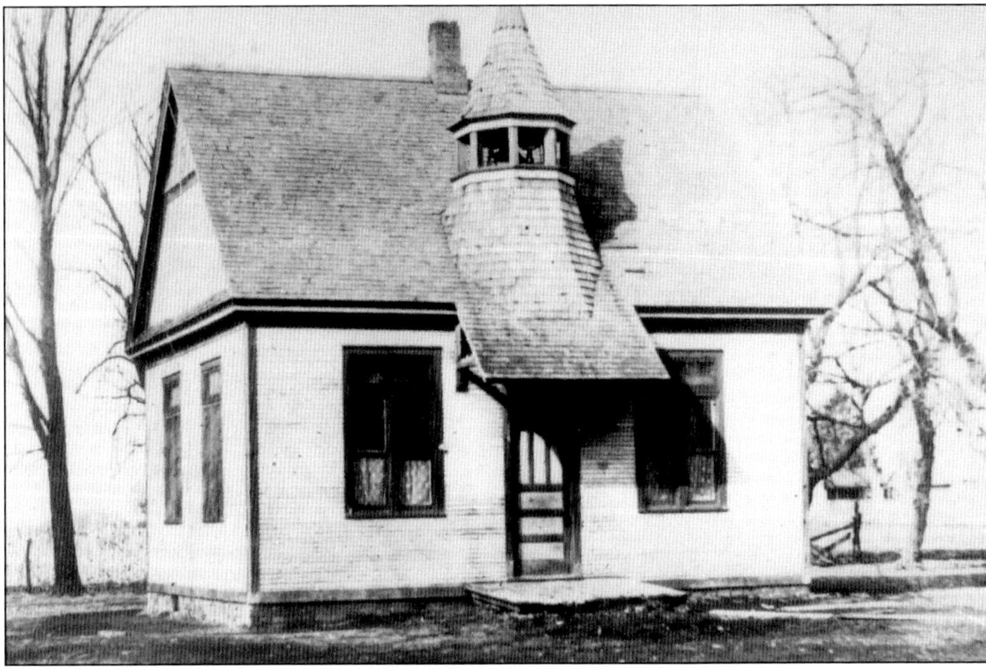

The southeast quarter of the county had many rural schools. Some were named after features of the landscape, such as Corn Hill, Frog Pond, and Maple Grove. Others were named after individuals or families. Wetzel School was named for New Salem Christian Church Sunday School Superintendent John Wetzel. It was located at the intersection of roads 700N and 2100E. Built in 1858, it was remodeled in 1883, when the unusual belfry was added.

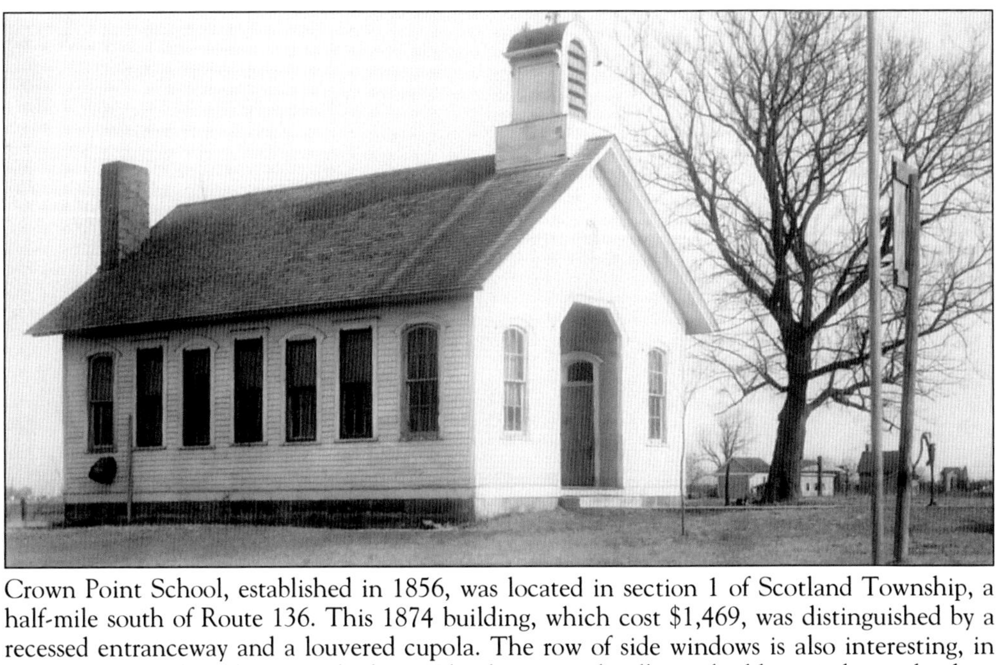

Crown Point School, established in 1856, was located in section 1 of Scotland Township, a half-mile south of Route 136. This 1874 building, which cost $1,469, was distinguished by a recessed entranceway and a louvered cupola. The row of side windows is also interesting, in that every second one has an arched top. Clearly, some schoolhouse builders tried to make their structures distinctive.

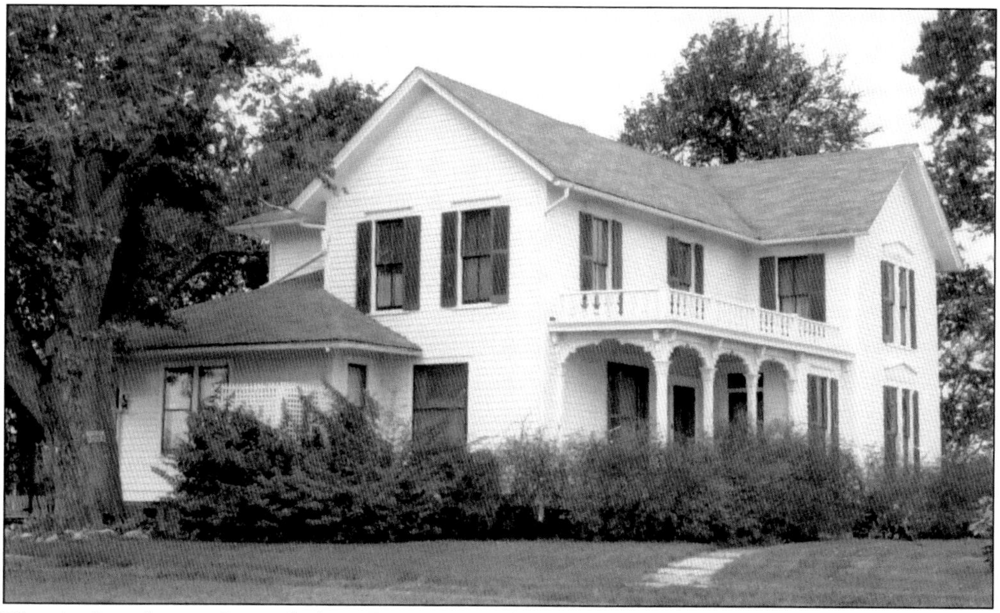

The Ausbury home, located along Route 136 a few miles east of Macomb, is one of the oldest farmhouses in the county. It was constructed in 1850 and was the family home of Robert Ausbury, who chaired the McDonough County Board from 1970 to 1982. Also located on that farmstead is a notable barn that was constructed by Wilbur Wetzel in 1918. The windows in it resemble those of a church.

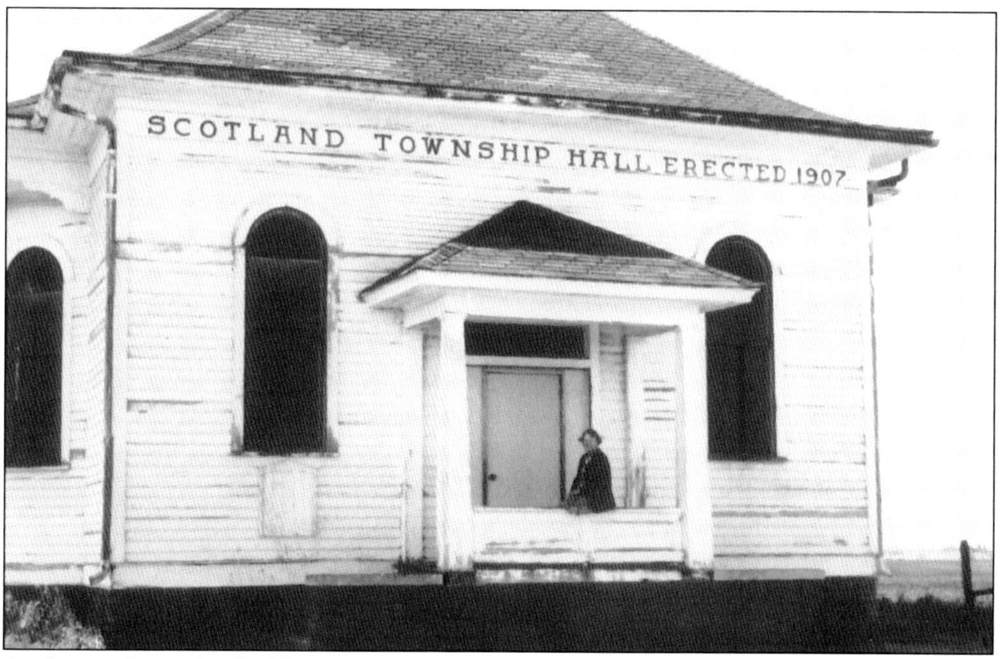

As the words on this building indicate, the Scotland Township Hall was erected in 1907. It was located at the intersection of roads 900N and 1500E, in the exact center of the completely rural township. The Center Point School and the Camp Creek Church were also located at that easy-to-reach intersection. The township building was razed in 1987.

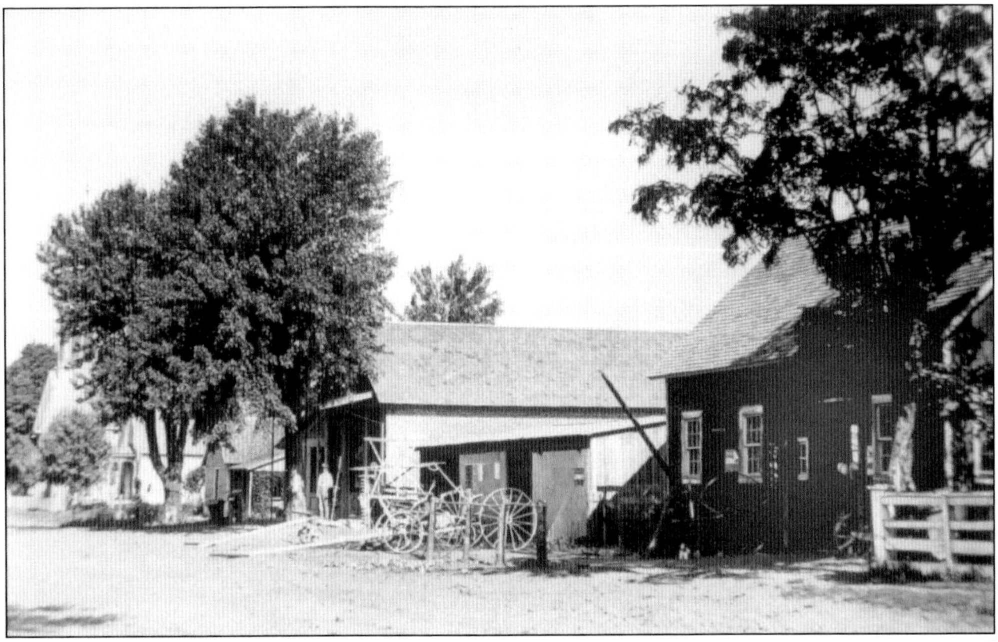

Doddsville was platted by Samuel Dodds, Charles Bacon, and Paris Wheeler in 1836. Located along the road from Vermont to Quincy, it was partly in Industry Township and partly in Schuyler County. Although it was never more than a hamlet, it did have a post office and a few businesses. This turn-of-the-century photograph shows the north side of Main Street.

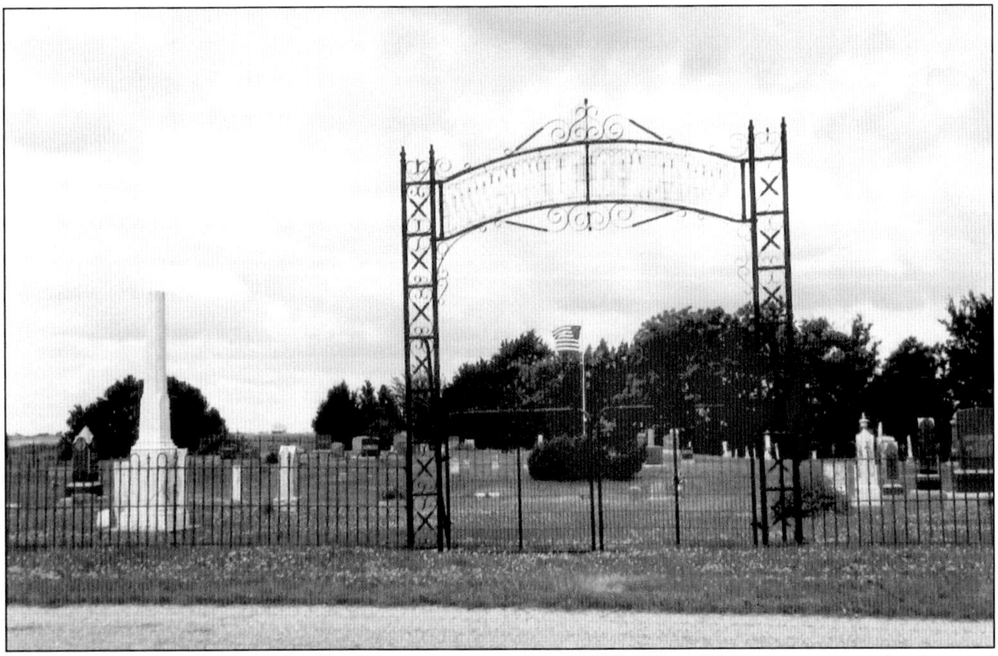

The first burial at the Doddsville Cemetery dates from 1839. The old burying ground is located just north of the town site, on road 1350E. The land was donated by town founder Samuel Dodds, who died in 1874 and is buried there. His grave marker is the tall shaft at the left of the entrance.

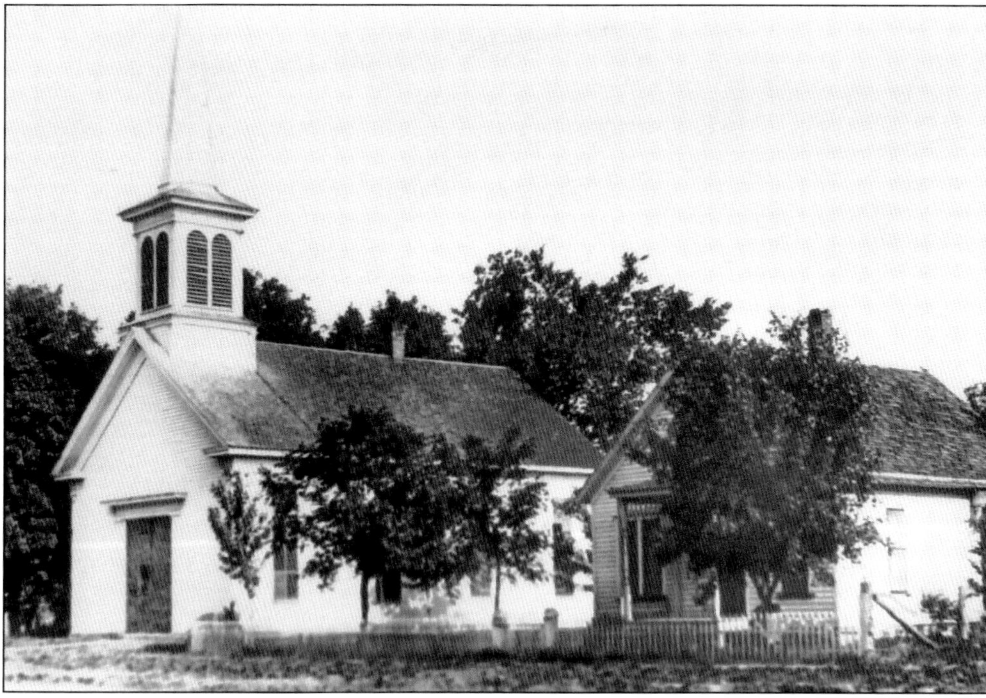

This photograph shows the Doddsville Presbyterian Church and parsonage. The congregation was organized in 1843, and they erected a church building in 1855. That one was replaced by the structure shown here in the late 1870s. Located at the intersection of roads 00N and 1350 E, it burned down in 1917.

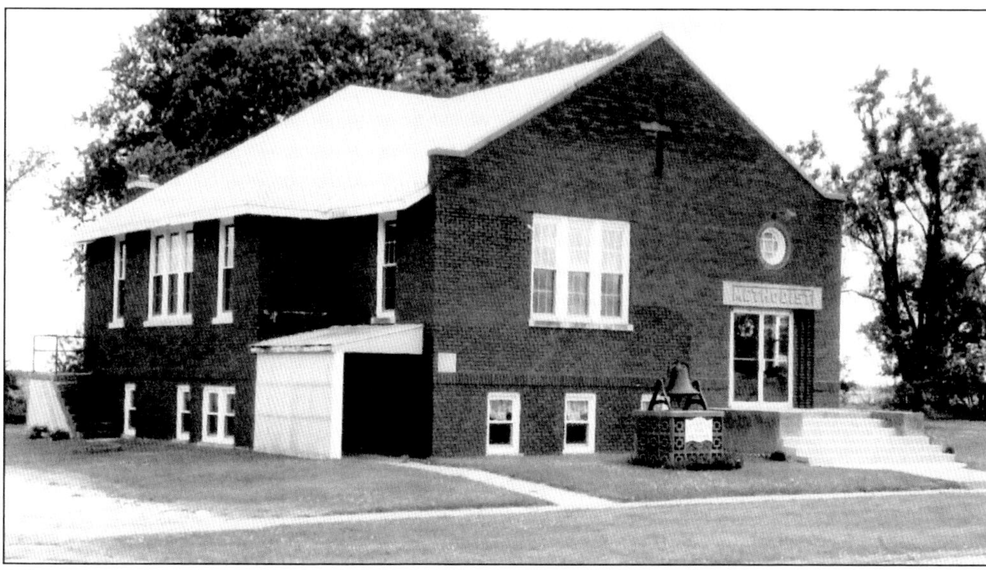

After the Doddsville Methodist Church was organized in 1851, the congregation used a church building that was just over the border of Schuyler County. When the Presbyterian Church burned in 1917, that congregation joined the Methodists to form the Doddsville Community Methodist Church. The building in this contemporary photograph was eventually constructed on the former Presbyterian Church site in 1925. It was gutted by fire in 1949 but was rebuilt.

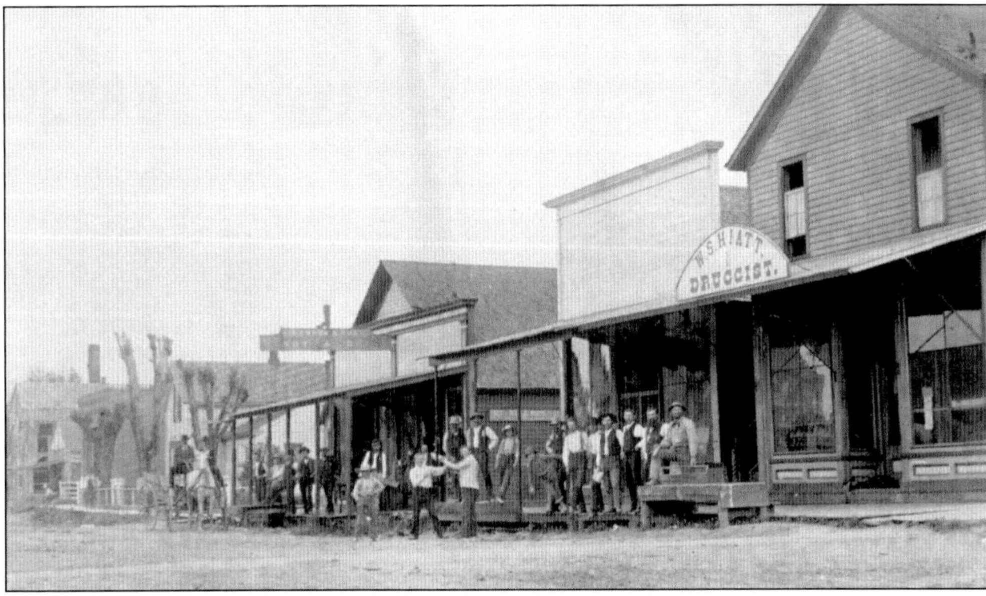

Industry was not established near a railroad, and thus its formation occurred slowly. The town began in 1846 when blacksmith John M. Price was enticed to move there by settlers who gave him land and erected a shop for him. Nine years later the village was platted, and it was not until 1860 that the first store opened. At that time, local shops manufactured corn cultivators, seed sowers, and sorghum evaporators, which apparently resulted in the town's name of "Industry." By the 1880s, the town had more than a dozen stores, plus a hotel and restaurant. This photograph of Main Street looking east is from the 1890s.

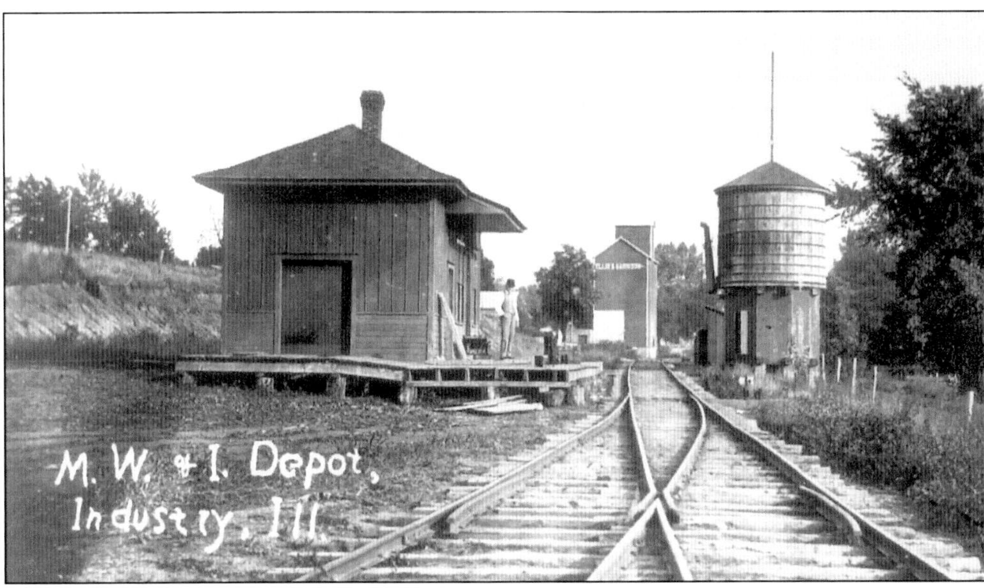

Industry was on a railroad for less than 30 years. By 1904, it was served by the Macomb and Western Illinois Railway, which was developed largely for shipping purposes, although it did carry passengers as well. That company soon failed and was reorganized as the Macomb, Industry and Littleton Railroad, but that failed also by 1932. This 1911 photograph shows the depot and water tank, which were located west of town. A grain elevator is in the distance.

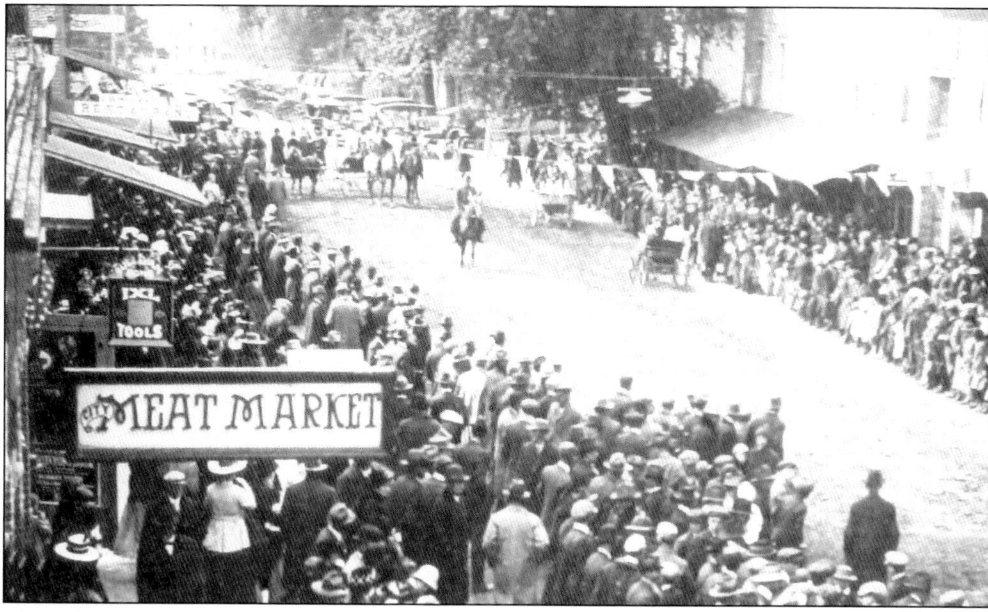

This photograph of a parade on Main Street was taken during the Industry Horse Show, an annual event that drew sizable crowds to the community. It looks west from a location by the City Meat Market. By the turn of the century, Industry had about 800 people, and it was known for its thoroughbred horse stables.

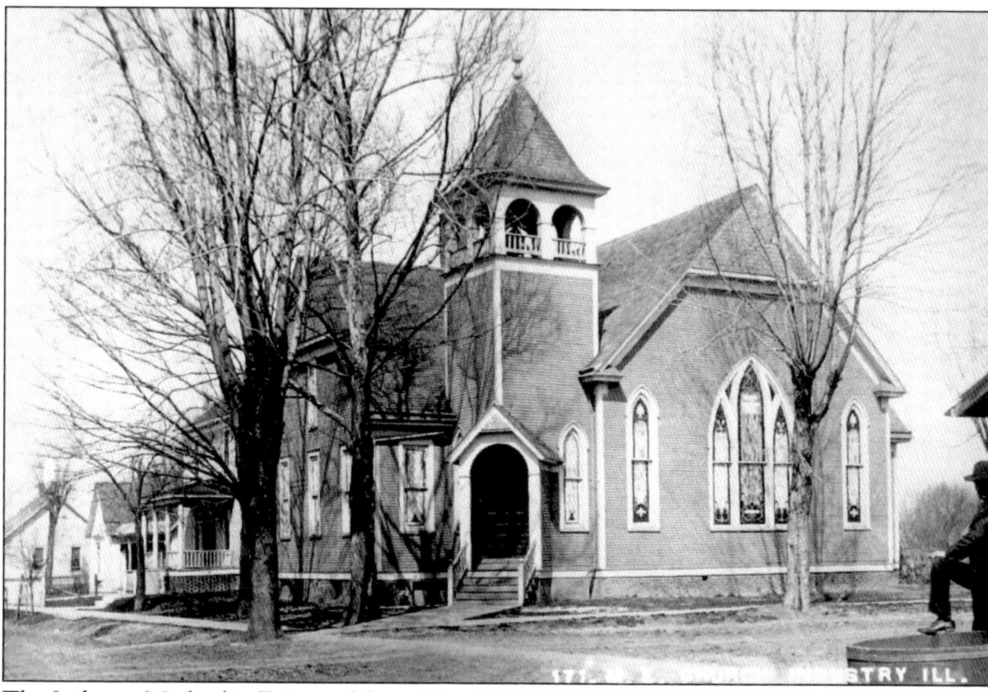

The Industry Methodist Episcopal (now United Methodist) Church was organized in 1855, and in 1866, this building was erected at the northeast corner of Main and Sullivan Streets. The structure was later torn down, and the present church building was constructed on that site in 1902. The stained-glass windows shown here were incorporated into the later building.

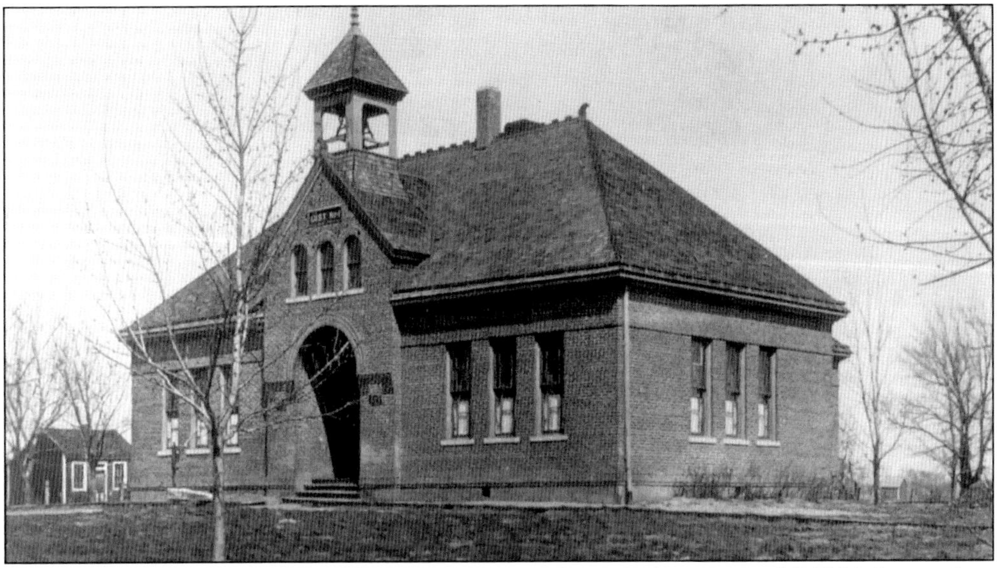

This handsome brick school building was constructed in 1895 at a cost of $4,350. Located on Price Street, it was the pride of the community for many years. At the turn of the century, it had about 150 students and was divided into primary and intermediate classes. The principal was Charles Lawyer.

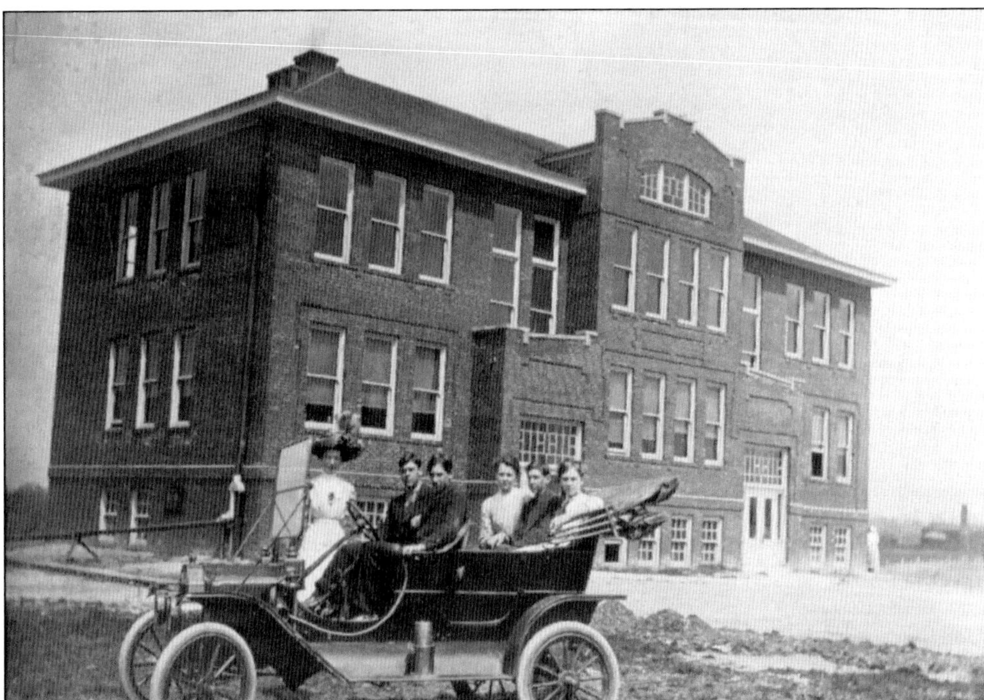

This photograph shows Industry Township High School in 1934. The building was constructed in 1910 and was located on North Avenue. The sophomore class is sitting in the car, and standing nearby is their teacher, Miss Foster. The building was closed in the mid-1950s, when the current high school was erected, and it was demolished in 1983.

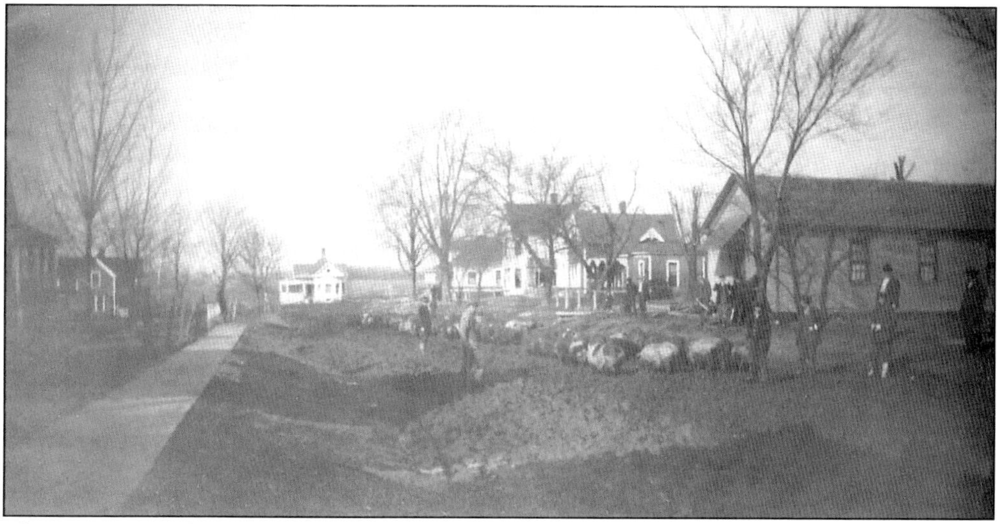

The controversial Pilgrim Band originated in about 1884, when Methodist minister W.H. Rayburn was forced to leave that church. He was soon joined by former Methodist minister Caleb Obenshain. Inspired by the Holiness Movement, they claimed to be sinless faith healers, and were influential in the small communities of Williamsville, Erwin, and Industry. Rayburn, the bishop of the Pilgrims, amassed considerable wealth and lived northwest of town. This early 1900s photograph shows Pilgrim Hall on the north side of W. Main Street. It was taken when someone's hogs were being driven through town.

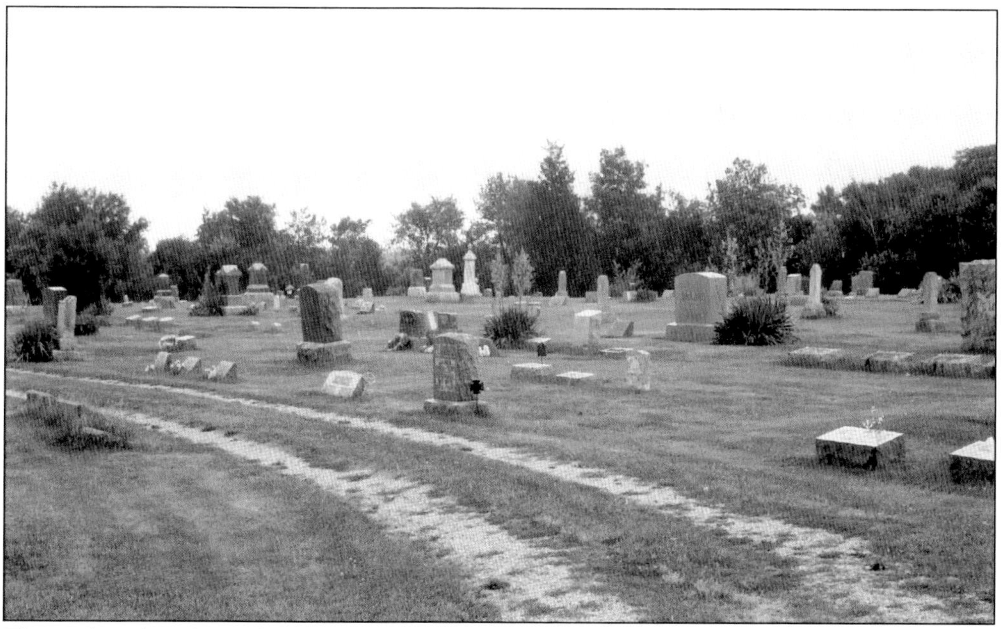

The earliest burials in the Industry Cemetery date from 1845 and 1851, but most came after 1880. This photograph shows the older section of that burying ground, which is at the north edge of town on Pierce Street. Included among the burials are various Civil War veterans, including a former Confederate soldier, Joseph Cockron. Two War of 1812 veterans, Richard Craig and Sam Vail, are also buried there. Perhaps the most controversial person interred there is Rev. Caleb Obenshain of the Pilgrim Band. He died in 1924.

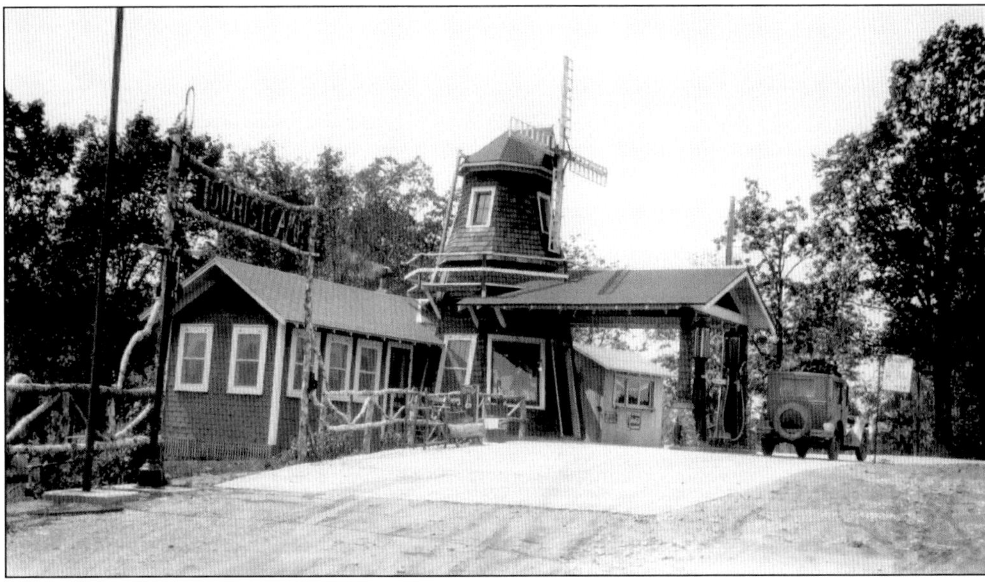

One of the landmarks near Industry today is a small windmill that stands on the curve west of town. That contemporary reconstruction reflects this enterprise, launched in 1927. The Old Dutch Mill Tourist Camp was established to provide gas, oil, and automobile service for the increasing numbers of people who were driving cars. The windmill at first stood alone, but the wing at the left was soon added to provide a restaurant.

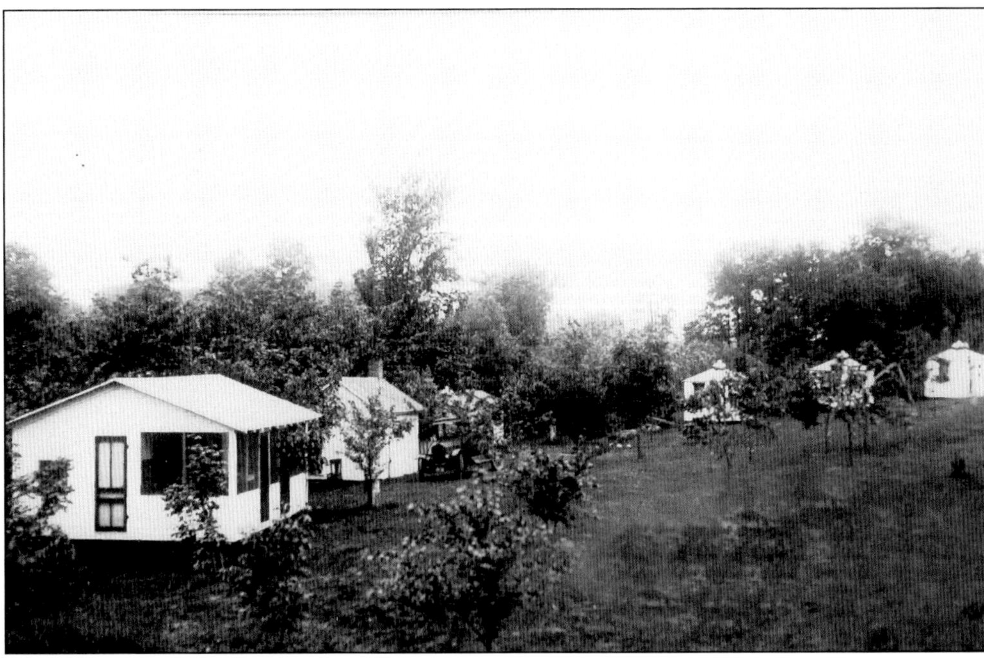

As this photograph shows, behind the gas station and restaurant on what is now Route 67 were cottages that could be rented. That part of the operation, the "Tourist Camp," was the equivalent of a motel. The unique business enterprise, built and owned by Ralph Swearingen, did not last very long, perhaps because few people traveled very far, and the Great Depression soon arrived.

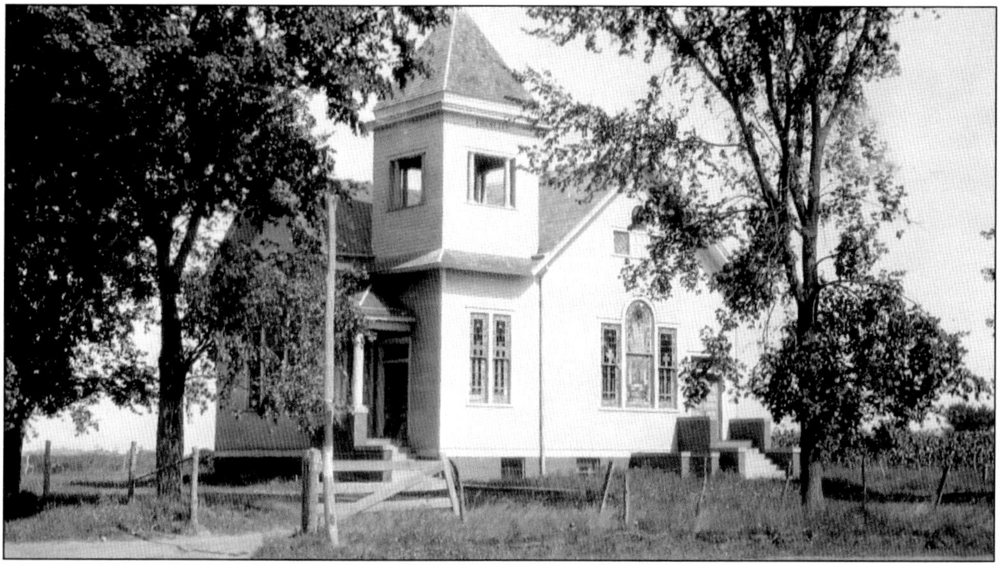

The southeast quarter of the county has had a number of long-lived rural churches. Ebenezer Presbyterian Church was located at the intersection of roads 1300E and 700N. In 1861, the congregation organized and erected its first church. That Greek-Revival-style structure was replaced by this one, dedicated in 1912. The church closed in 1992 and has been torn down. However, a monument now stands on the site, and the manse is nearby. The congregation joined with the Camp Creek and Bardolph Presbyterian churches in 1993 to form Scotland Trinity Presbyterian Church.

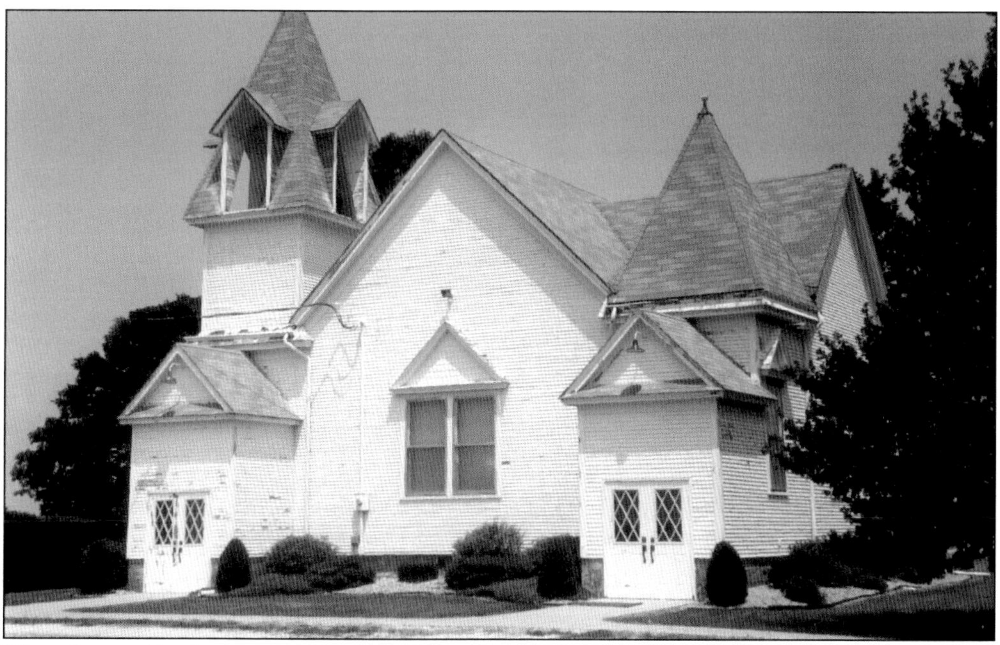

West Prairie Presbyterian Church is located at the intersection of roads 400N and 2000E. Organized in 1852 as a Cumberland Presbyterian group, the congregation built a plain frame church building in 1867. The original structure was replaced by the one shown here in 1905. It features twin entrances and an outstanding steeple, which still has the old bell in it.

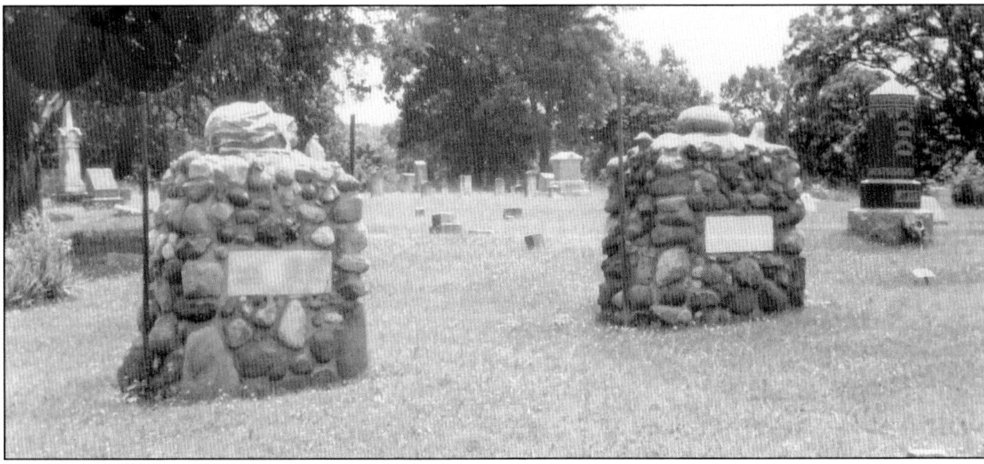

A congregation called the Salem Meeting House of the Brethren in Christ was organized in 1857 in Eldorado Township, and it soon constructed a church near the intersection of roads 150N and 1950E on land provided by members of the Chockley family. The church is no longer there, but the adjacent Chockley Cemetery remains. It has graves dating from as early as the 1840s, and notable also are the two fieldstone monuments shown here. Erected in 1921 and 1926 by Albert L. Adams, they memorialize American soldiers who died in World War I (right) and "President Wilson, the Unknown Soldier, and the Red Cross Nurse" (left).

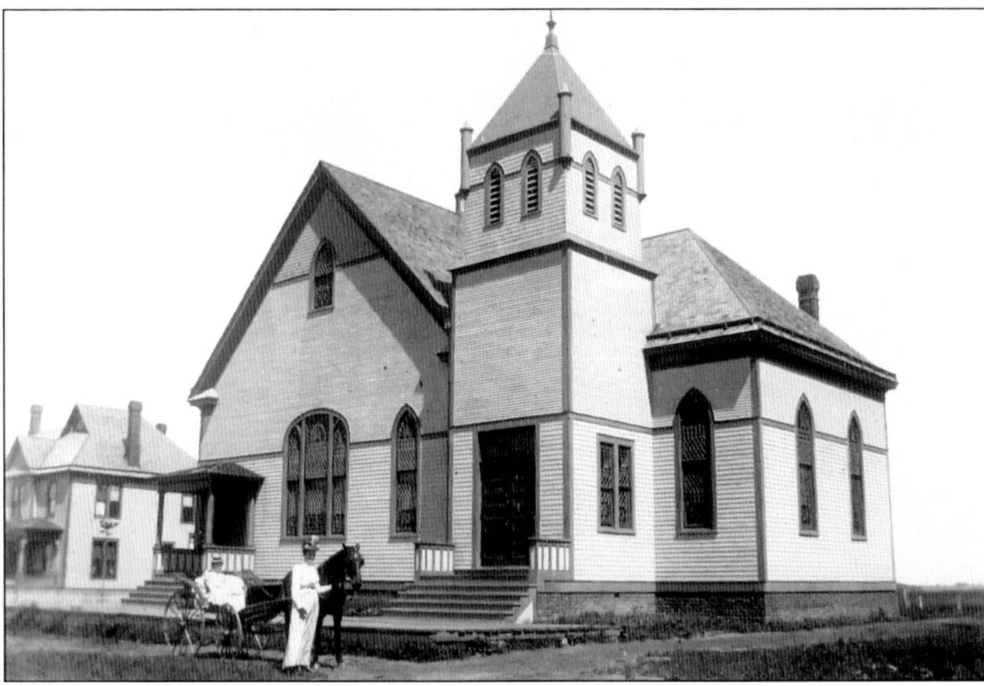

Camp Creek Presbyterian Church was organized in 1839, and the members erected a building four years later, in section 33 of Scotland Township. A second church was constructed in 1861 in section 27 of that township, and the one shown here was built a couple of miles north, at the intersection of Route 67 and county road 900N in 1898. In the background is the parsonage. The church burned down on October 31, 1991. Scotland Trinity Presbyterian Church was erected on that site in 1994.

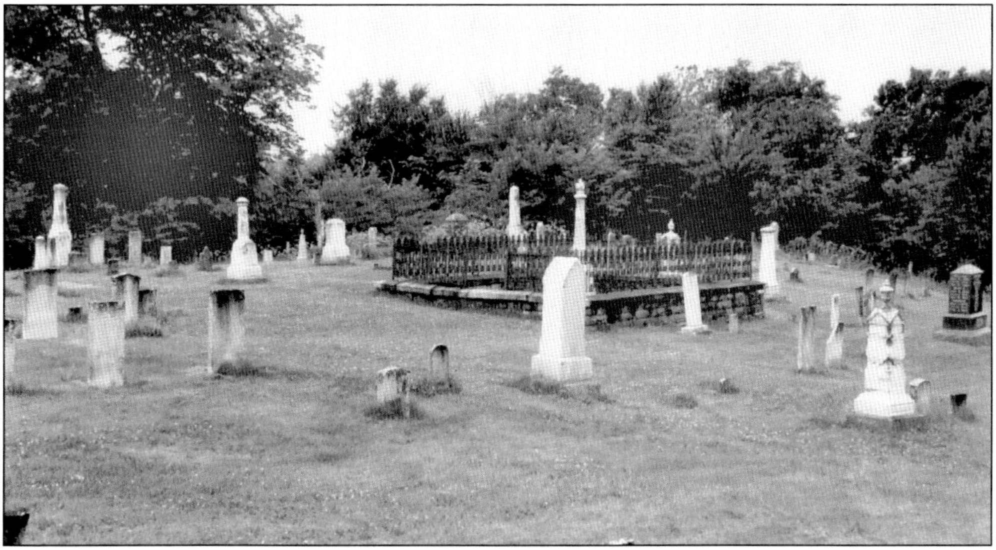

Camp Creek Cemetery, located between roads 650N and 550N in Industry Township, is the oldest McDonough County cemetery that is still in use. This photograph shows part of the older section, which has burials dating back to 1831 or 1832. The fenced enclosure surrounds a Walker family plot dominated by a shaft marking the graves of Joseph and Mariah Walker, who died in 1846 and 1840 respectively. Nearby is the marker for lawyer and politician Cyrus Walker, the county's most famous early resident, and his wife, Flora. They both died on December 5—she in 1862 and he in 1875.

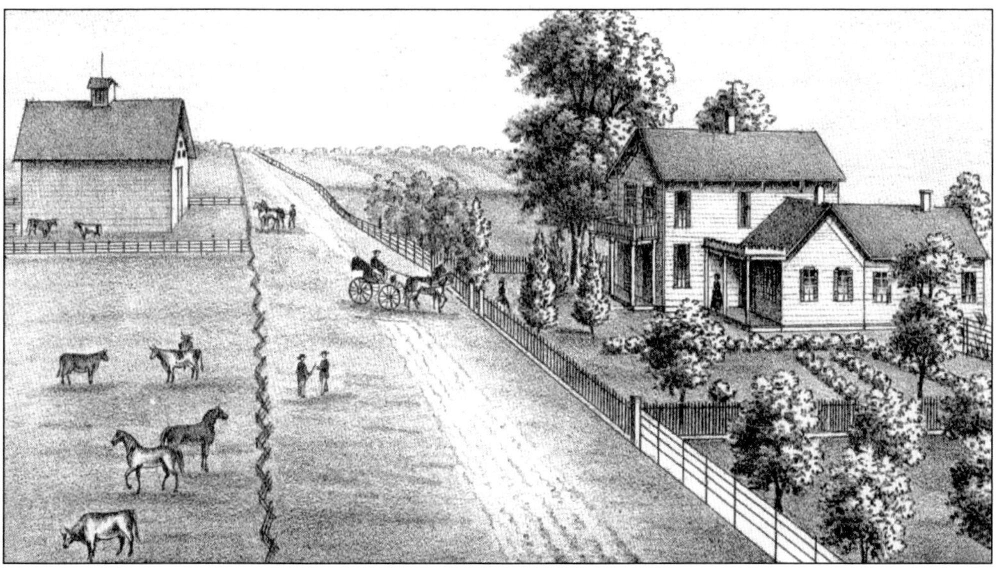

Also buried in the Camp Creek Cemetery are John Blazer and his two successive wives, Mary and Mary Ann. Mary died in 1854, Mary Ann died in 1898, and John died in 1903. The Blazer home in section 8 of Industry Township was a stop on the Underground Railroad, which ran from the Burton home in Plymouth to the Allison and Blazer homes in McDonough County, and then on to Fulton County. This 1871 lithograph shows the Blazer home, which was located at the intersection of roads 500N and 1325E. Supposedly, Blazer helped to transport more than 200 slaves during the 1850s.

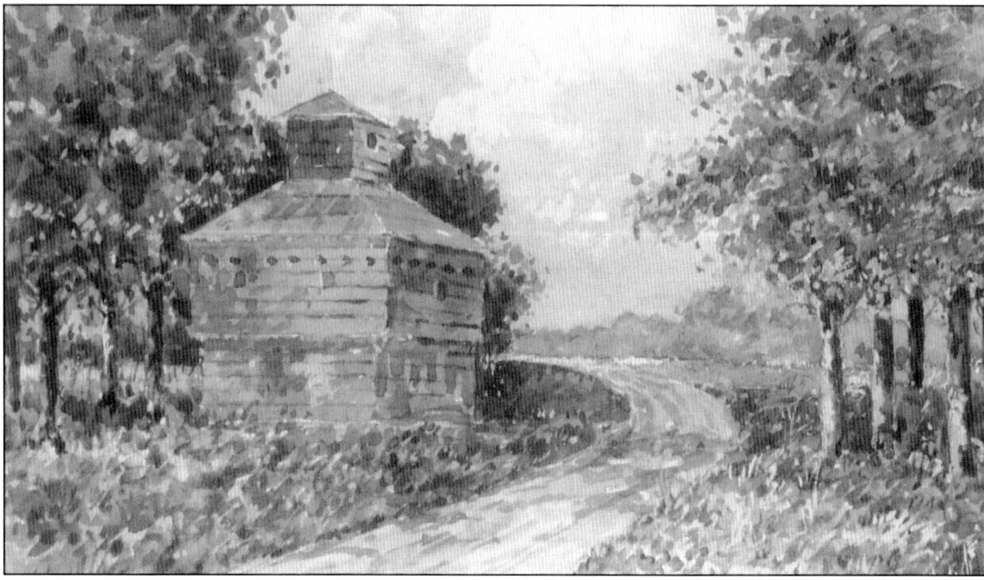

The earliest settlement in McDonough County was located in and around section 26 of Industry Township. Known as Carter's Settlement, it was named for William Carter, who came there with Riggs Pennington in 1826. Concerned about Indians, Carter and others built a two-story log fort, with an upper story that projected over the lower one and with many holes through which guns could be fired. Constructed in 1827 and located at the intersection of roads 140N (Inverness Road) and 1650E, it was never used, except to house settlers like Rev. John Logan, who lived there in 1828. This watercolor painting by George Hodgkinson was owned by Martha (Champion) Thompson, who once lived near the old fort.

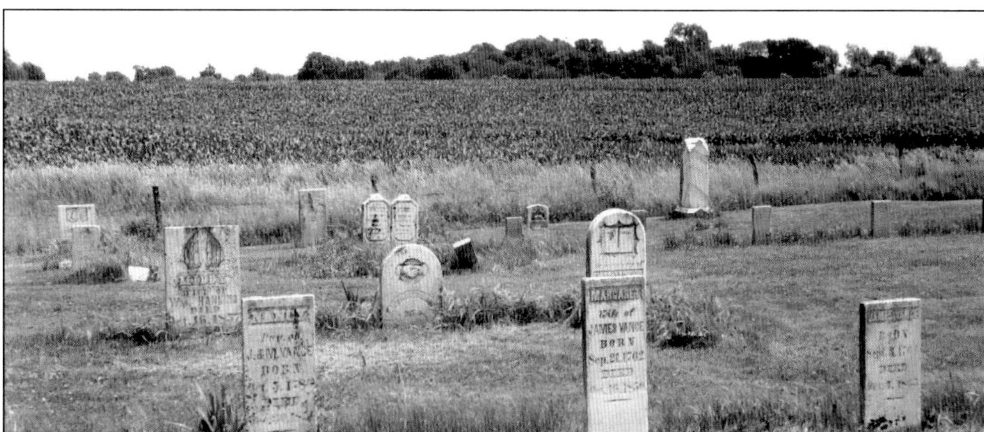

Located east of Industry at the intersection of roads 300N and 1700E, the Vance Cemetery is also a very early burying ground. The first burial there was James Vance, who also came to Carter's Settlement with his family in 1826. His 1835 gravestone is at the right in this photograph, and to the left are those of his wife, Margaret, and daughter Nancy. Vance was an early county commissioner and justice of the peace. Born in 1864 and 1862, James and Margaret Vance lived through the Revolutionary War and raised a family while moving west, finally settling where their lives had a lasting impact. Their gravesites in this well-kept cemetery symbolize the many family and cultural links that connect the McDonough County experience with the history of the nation.